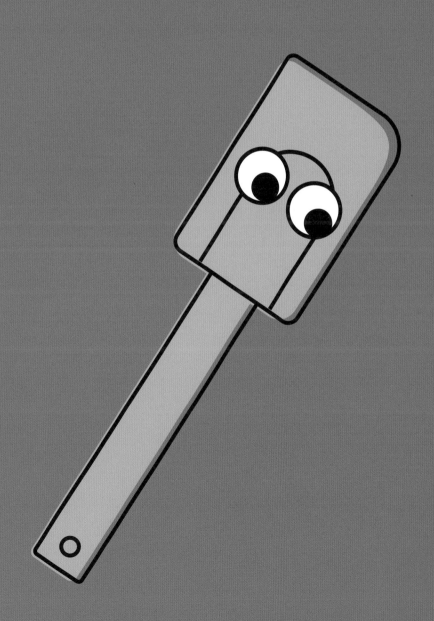

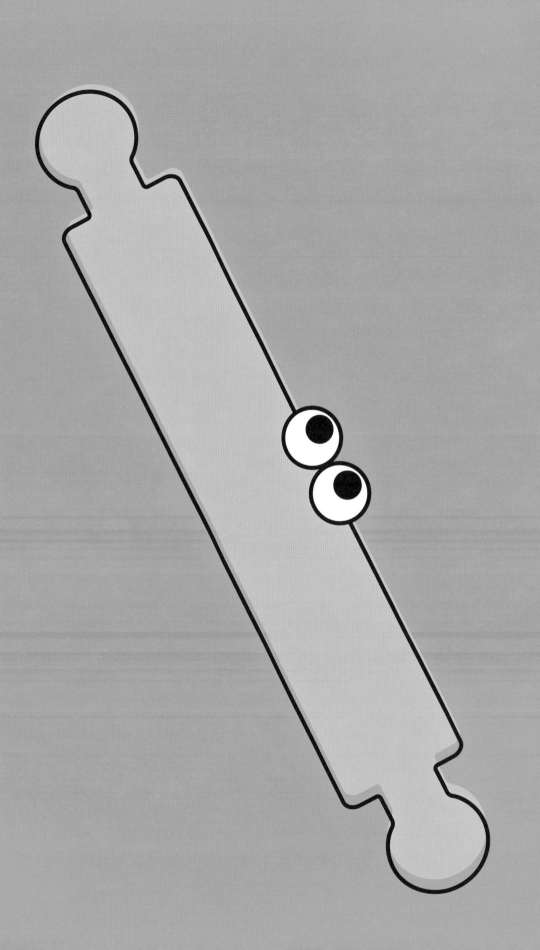

THE

VEGAN

BAKER

The ultimate guide to plant-based breads,
pastries, donuts, cookies, cakes & more

THE
VEGAN
BAKER

Zacchary Bird

Smith
Street
Books

Contents

Introduction

Are you ready to fall in love with baking again? Vegans have spent years outside bakeries peering at treats seemingly so far out of reach – but you can consider that glass window now shattered. We've come to understand exactly how animal products work in baking applications, and realised that they're far from the only ingredients that can enrich, bind, raise and taste damn delicious.

Welcome to your choose-your-own-adventure vegan baking education. This book is over-proofed and bubbling over with just about every rad technique you never got taught, and nifty substitutes you'll kick yourself for not thinking of first. You could travel the world via garlic bread alone! Start in India with garlic naan (page 97), then head to Korea for cream cheese buns (page 292), try Ukraine's pampushky (page 301), Hungarian langos (page 272) and, finally, compare the French fougasse (page 74) to Italy's focaccia (page 76)!

For dessert, race through the airport to catch your flight to another global adventure across the donut landscape. Into cookies? We're rotating through French, Italian, Greek, South American and Japanese on the specials board at the moment. on the specials board at the moment. Not of this mortal realm? There's a sourdough inspired by a descent into hell that you may enjoy.

As we bake and snack our way to a kinder future, it's high time to rediscover the joy of turning flour into the miracle of dough in all its wondrous forms, and brush up on the crispy, crusty curriculum of skills that the bakes of this book aim to equip you with.

While baking certainly is a science, it's also an art that gives you infinite results once you realise how to use dough as a template for your dreams. The recipes in this book are put together so that no matter what is in season or abundant near you, there'll be a dish ready to celebrate that fresh ingredient or flavour with a technique to add to your repertoire. Exquisite vegan versions of your favourite desserts might seem complex – but as you're about to learn, they're just a piece of cake.

May this book serve as my personal middle finger to every time I've been offered a gluten-free menu when I've asked whether anything on the menu is actually vegan. It's time to raise awareness that vegan baked goods can be full-flavoured, full-textured and are charging full speed into the future. And the future is now – because everything you need is in these pages and possibly in your very own kitchen already.

Grinding grains and making dough is a process that has evolved alongside most of civilisation, but the advent of humanity's hunger to substitute animal products didn't start with the coining of the word 'vegan'. Last-century wartime rations and Depression-era scarcity forced creativity out of home bakers, who began producing treats without butter, dairy and eggs.

Long before that, religious traditions normalised the art of recreating traditional foods with a vegan bent – such as Jewish water challah or Greek Orthodox *nistisima* (fasting food made without animal products). Pizza marinara, the 'patient zero' of tomato-topped pizzas, has been traditionally completely vegan the moment it hit menus.

The phrase 'accidentally vegan' is banned from this cookbook, as I'm far too proud of how far vegan professionals and ingenious home cooks alike have come in creating one-for-one versions of just about every baked good on the planet. *The Vegan Baker* is here to remind you that anything can be made vegan – and then teach you exactly how to veganise just about every single thing.

Now that's all out of the way, clear your mind, belly and benchtop, because here's exactly what you 'knead' to know.

Equipment

For those being inducted into the baking lifestyle, carefully selecting a few key additions to your equipment inventory can grow your home repertoire as though it's been left to rest and double in size. When you're ready to commit fully, expanding that collection can help take bread making from an occasional workout to a daily practice. Here are a few of my favourite tools I use to pull off the wheaty feats in this book, and how they're used.

Measuring scales & measuring spoons

Using scales and making baking perfection are conjoined twins, and I'm so sorry to inform you that there will be catastrophic consequences if they were to ever be separated. This is because while a gram is a gram, a cup cannot be trusted to be a cup. Each country has a slightly different idea of how many millilitres constitutes one cup, which is why there's few cup measurements in this book. In a precise art such as baking, using scales is the only way to be certain that you're recreating the recipe as written by the author. If you consider the drastic difference in the weight of a cup of flour and a sifted, aerated cup of flour, then it quickly becomes clear that measuring by weight is the best way to consistently get accurate measurements and better baking outcomes.

Even some of the tablespoons of the world bicker among themselves about a unified milligramage, so until they find a compromise, be sure to check that yours match the 15 ml (½ fl oz) tablespoons called for in these recipes. Teaspoons are a standard 5 ml (¼ fl oz).

Stand mixers

While I understand that real estate on a kitchen benchtop is hotly contested, hear out my pitch for you to consider developing a little space to add an electric stand mixer. They can range from high-end to fairly cheap, but the good news is that every recipe in this book has been made using the cheapest stand mixer available to brilliant results. A stand mixer will halve your prep time for most of the recipes here, and is essential for the other portion to produce commercial-quality enriched doughs with enough kneading.

Many food processors these days also have an additional dough hook attachment available, which will do the trick as well, without compromising on bench space.

Silicone mats

For the environmentally conscious, using baking-friendly silicone baking mats is a low-waste alternative to lining baking trays with baking paper. Silicone mats serve many kitchen purposes: they can be baked on, so can be used in lieu of baking paper; some are printed with measuring charts, so you can roll your doughs to the exact dimensions atop them; and they can be used for rising doughs on a surface to transfer easily from the fridge, freezer, benchtop and all the way into the oven, without disrupting the gluten tension.

Baking tins

There are three main tins that will suffice for most basic bakes: cake tins, loaf (bar) tins and brownie tins. Classic round cake tins (for sponges, bread rolls and pies) are about 20–23 cm (8–9 in) in diameter; the springform variety (the kind with a removable side) isn't essential, but will make your life easier. A classic loaf or bar tin for breads typically measures about 11 cm × 22 cm (4½ × 8¾ in), and is about 6 cm (2½ in) deep. Brownie tins (also called lamington tins) are shallow and rectangular, measure about 23 cm × 33 cm (9 × 13 in), and can be used for baking goodies such as brownies, sponges, focaccias and bread rolls.

This book also uses six-hole jumbo muffin tins and 12-hole cupcake tins. Sheet pans (large and flat with a shallow rim) and baking trays (that come with a deeper rim) can generally be used interchangeably.

Note that, like cars sitting in the sun, the darker your tins, the more heat they will absorb – and vice versa with light-coloured tins. This may mean your bakes need a minute less or more thanks to the difference this can make.

You can also use silicone baking tins, with the added advantage of being able to microwave cakes in them. The disadvantage is that some silicone can be floppy, which makes sagging while transferring the silicone full of batter a slight occupational hazard.

Specialist baking tins

Bread comes in all shapes and sizes, so it's fitting that their baking tins showcase the same diversity. Specialist tins can help you make unique breads and bakes you wouldn't be able to achieve normally. They can also be used to elevate simple bakes with intricate details – such as the sticky date pudding on page 259, which uses an artisanal bundt tin for extra texture. In the interest of decluttering, if you're not intending to use a bundt tin semi-regularly, then it won't be worth the space it takes up in your cupboard.

A lot of the specialist tins in this book are given multiple outings, so that you get the most value out of them. In this book we use long baguette-baking tins, classic bundt tins, six-ring donut baking trays, pullman loaf tins (with a sealable lid), and round perforated pizza trays.

Bannetons

These are special proving baskets that you'll definitely want if you're making sourdough. The materials used vary, but they all allow the dough to breathe as it rises, without sticking to the sides. You can find rounded ones for boules, or long ones for loaves. Either variety is fine – pick one to begin your sourdough journey and add more to your collection once you get the hang of the process. If you can't find one, line a colander with a thin tea towel, coat well in rice flour and pray for the best.

Bannetons can sometimes come with a special cloth/cap to cover the dough when proving, but a plastic shower cap, tightly tied plastic bag or even plastic wrap will do, too.

Baker's couche

A baker's couche is a special baker's linen cloth, to be thought of as a sort of pliable banneton. The fabric lets the dough breathe, while not sticking to it (don't forget a dusting of non-gluten flour to help discourage separation anxiety). The fabric is quite stiff, so that it can be creased like a starched handkerchief into sections, to separate different doughs as they rise. Thanks to that fact and the length of the couche, it's especially ideal for rising many long baguettes on at once while preserving the traditional shape.

Baker's lame

This simple tool is a handle that holds a double-sided razor, used to slash loaves just before they hit the oven. It provides a sturdy grip so that you can confidently score the loaf without putting your fingers near the blade.

Cast-iron cookware

Cookware with a cult following must mean it has a little extra panache. Cast iron's party trick is its ability to retain heat. This means a cast-iron vessel such as a lidded casserole dish (also called a Dutch oven) takes longer to preheat, but rewards a sourdough baker with an extra-hot, perfectly shaped oven-within-an-oven environment that produces rounded loaves full of oven-spring. By baking with the lid on, the moisture inside the bread is kept in as steam within the dish, which helps with both rising and a crispy crust.

Kitchen thermometer

When working at high heat ranges, such as during deep-frying or candy making, it's important to be precise with temperatures, as going even slightly over or under can ruin your results. A hybrid candy/oil thermometer is an inexpensive way to instantly master fried goods and make your own syrups and caramels at home. This is an essential piece of equipment for many recipes in this book.

Ovens & oven thermometers

The temperature inside an oven can vary drastically from the temperature purported by the dial. The different areas inside an oven, from rack to rack and front to back, will also hold temperature variations. An inexpensive oven thermometer sits inside the oven and tells you exactly what temperature it is at the precise location you'd place the food, so it's the most efficient way to cut through uncertainty.

Another factor in the true heat your food bakes at is your oven setting: whether or not you're using a convection (fan-forced) or conventional (heated from top and bottom) oven setting. Unless specified otherwise, this book calls for fan-forced temperature settings.

If your oven will not begrudge you a fan to force, and you're stuck with a conventional oven setting, increase the temperature given in the recipe by 20°C (25°F).

Your oven should let you know when it's come to temperature, but for normal preheating, you should allow about 15–20 minutes. But when high temperatures (above 220°C/430°F) are called for, or when pizza trays, Yorkshire pudding trays or cast-iron dishes are required to preheat as well, you should allow up to an hour.

Microwaves

Some doughs and batters can be cooked in a microwave. As microwaves target the water content inside your food, it steams and rises, but doesn't brown – making it appropriate for light bakes such as sponge cakes, or some breads that will be baked later on.

When it comes to baking, there's no extra points for extra effort – only for great results. Don't be afraid to use your microwave as a modern tool in your baking arsenal to expedite processes such as warming milk, melting chocolate, softening butter and so on.

Not all microwaves are built the same, so there's a chance you'll need to adjust microwave directions in recipes to suit your own oven. This just means checking a bit more frequently the first time you try a recipe to see when your goods are ready.

Ingredients

A few good eggs

APPLESAUCE

Here we have binding and sweetening all in one: thanks to its pectin content, a jar of applesauce in the fridge means you'll never have to nip to the shops for a stray egg in a baking recipe again. For baked goods that call for one egg, substitute 60 ml (2 fl oz) of applesauce to approximate the same results.

You can also use mashed banana in the same proportions, but with a stronger flavour that's best hidden by even stronger flavours like chocolate.

AQUAFABA

This is simply the liquid from a tin of beans (commonly chickpeas/garbanzo beans), or from cooked dried beans. In its pure form, aquafaba (which literally translates to something like 'bean water' or 'water of beans') works like a substitute for egg whites, uniquely able to foam, be whipped into peaks, and to emulsify other ingredients. In this book it's the key to making an Italian meringue (in the mini lemon meringue pies on page 184) and macarons (page 238).

When crumbing ingredients for frying, or brushing egg wash on baked goods before baking, aquafaba will achieve aquafabulous results. Dose it out in 45 ml (1½ fl oz) portions to substitute one egg in recipes.

BUTTERMILK

While introducing moisture, buttermilk also helps bind other ingredients. It also reacts with baking soda in a batter, producing bubbles and assisting the leavening process. To make a vegan buttermilk that's almost as thick as someone arguing that plants have feelings, simply add a tablespoon of vinegar to 250 ml (8½ fl oz) of soy milk.

EGG WASH

Substitute with your choice of plant-based milk for savoury baked goods. Whisk a splash of maple syrup into the milk ahead of brushing onto sweet baked goods to add a hint of sweetness, or for savoury applications, whisk a splash of oil into the milk to encourage crispier crusts.

FLAXSEED MEAL & CHIA SEEDS

Adding water to chia seeds or flaxseeds (also called linseeds) in a 3:1 ratio makes a gel that works as a binding agent. When combined with leavening ingredients, this gelatinous goo does the job of an egg. Weird flax, but okay.

PSYLLIUM HUSK

It's so super absorbent that you only need a teaspoon of ground psyllium husk in baked recipes to provide a structural boost without introducing unnecessary flavour. You can use it in a straight dough (mixed all at once, without adding water to the husk first) if you allow for plenty of moisture in the dough.

STARCHY ROOT VEGETABLES

Precooked root vegetables are a game-changer for those wanting lighter crumbs and longer storage time by upping the starch and lowering the gluten content. Potato adds moisture to dough with a fairly neutral flavour profile, and results in fluffier and lighter baked goods.

Pumpkin (winter squash) and sweet potato each have their own flavours to play with, and both also help mimic enriched doughs normally made with eggs and dairy. Pureed, approximately 60 g (2 oz) of each will perform the same tricks that eggs can.

Milking the magic

ALMOND MILK

Recipes calling for almond milk have been around since medieval times. Back then, no dairy conglomerates were purporting that the word 'milk' misled consumers, but that's partly because back then you'd get lanced for stupidity. Almond milk has low nutritional value, but many brands fortify it with calcium, giving it a comparable amount to dairy. While almond milk uses more water to produce than other plant-based milks, it is still dramatically more environmentally friendly than the dairy products it specifically exists to replace. Almond milk is slightly sweet, with a distinct nutty taste, and can be used as an egg wash or milk replacement in pastries or dough.

CASHEW MILK

The queen of creaminess! Cashews in recent years have become the sweetheart of vegan creams and cakes, due to their natural lack of overpowering flavour and slight sweetness. For one of the creamiest homemade milks, soak 1 part cashews with 4 parts water overnight, then blend the next day. Use your homemade cashew milk as the base for the custard and cream recipes in this book.

COCONUT CREAM

Coconut cream is prepared in a similar way to coconut milk, but with a higher concentration of coconut meat. This thicker cream is a popular dairy-free whipped cream substitute, as it only needs to be chilled in the fridge before it can imitate whipping cream. Scoop out only the hardened, thick portion into a mixing bowl or stand mixer. Use a hand mixer or the whisk attachment to beat the cream into soft peaks, and add icing (confectioners') sugar to taste.

COCONUT MILK

Loaded with natural fats, coconut milk is a top choice in recipes that rely on cream and high-fat dairy products such as yoghurt and ice cream. This milk has a distinct flavour, which can be used to your advantage by pairing it with complementary flavours such as banana, pineapple, mango, caramel, chocolate and more.

HEMP MILK

A relative newcomer that naturally contains more calcium than dairy, and is nut- and grain-free. Made from the seeds of the hemp plant, this milk contains no THC/CBD, but it does come loaded with nutrition. Hemp seeds are a great way to supplement your diet with a complete plant-based protein that contains both omega-3 and omega-6 fatty acids. Flavour-wise, hemp milk tends to be neutral, if not slightly nutty – so if you're not a fan of soy flavour, then hemp milk is the mellow alternative you wanna hang with. In most baking recipes, hemp milk can be used 1:1 where dairy milk is called for.

OAT MILK

Oat can gloat about being G.O.A.T. in coffee shops thanks to the creamy, thick body the oats provide to the liquid. Oat milk can contain higher levels of sugar than many other milks. When frothing, oat milk performs well, and creates a foam similar to dairy milk, albeit with larger bubbles. Due to its neutral flavour, oat milk is a popular option to pair with delicate flavours, such as vanilla, that other plant-based milks would be too strong for. Oat milk can be used 1:1 where dairy milk is called for.

RICE MILK

Milk made from rice has existed in various forms, such as horchata, for hundreds of years (as has tigernut milk, another dairy alternative). It can be made from either white or brown rice, and is fairly calorie-sparse. As the texture of plant-based milk relies on protein and fat, rice milk has the thinnest viscosity – meaning that it's great in smoothies and on cereal, but won't do a thing if you try to foam it for coffee. It is naturally sweet and the least allergenic of all milks, making it a safe bet when catering to a variety of dietary requirements. I rarely use this milk outside of an egg wash.

SOY MILK

The original alternative, soy milk has been a key ingredient in many Asian cuisines for thousands of years. It has a similar protein content to traditional dairy, so it makes for a no-fuss 1:1 substitution in most recipes as it behaves similarly. Soy can have a distinct bean flavour that isn't usually noticeable for most people when used as an ingredient in baking and cooking. When in doubt, soy is your safe bet for reliable dairy replacements. You can buy store-bought soy creams with added ingredients that make them suitable for beating into whipped cream.

Vegan butter

When called for in this book, vegan butter can interchangeably mean either the recipe on page 28 or store-bought vegan butter or margarine.

Block butter, wrapped in foil – as distinct from tub margarine – is specified in recipes where fat is laminated into the dough, as margarine will not create separate layers.

Coconut oil can be used to replace vegan butter when greasing tins or in doughs. It is important to always choose refined, deodorised coconut oil, which has had the coconut flavour and scent removed, to preserve the flavour of your baking. Raw and virgin coconut oil will impart coconut flavour into whatever you make, so avoid the vegan pitfall of making everything taste like coconut and go for the refined stuff.

Salts

Salts can be purchased in all sorts of particle sizes for different purposes. Iodised salt, or table salt, is very fine and doesn't clump, and it's the one normally used in a dough. Kosher, or coarse salt, and flaky salt are better choices for topping cooked dishes. Smoked or herb-infused salts can add a hint of flavour. Black salt (kala namak) is often chosen in vegan recipes as the sulphuric flavour is very similar to cooked eggs.

Basics

Eggs

In a vegan cookbook, we don't need to wax lyrical about how wonderful eggs are when it comes to the job of binding, leavening, tenderising, emulsifying and/or flavouring dough. Well, they were, but now they have been made redundant by the wide world of plants that can do the exact same jobs without involving a cloaca.

The pioneering vegan baker may have noticed through trial and error that quite often in basic bakes, leaving out an egg in a recipe doesn't lead to drastic consequences. But now, through the creative collective research of keen home cooks, every nuance that eggs could add to dough has an easily sourced equivalent, with no need to go without.

The modern vegan home baker's egg carton is so diverse that it isn't hard to crack the case of which ingredient is appropriate for each baking application.

Meringue

(EASY)   **MAKES ABOUT 500 G (1 LB 2 OZ)**

The vegan rosetta stone to egg-less macarons, meringues, breaded goods and more was finally cracked by online vegan home-baking communities that stumbled upon something that had been under our noses and in our pantries all along: the miracle of aquafaba. It just so happens that the liquid from cooked beans (tinned, or cooked at home) has all the right properties to replace eggs in many recipes, particularly egg-white heavy dishes that rely on the ability to whip air into a mixture. Chickpeas are the sexy poster boy of the movement, but any neutral-flavoured 'bean water' (butter/lima beans or cannellini) will turn out aquafabulous results.

See how meringuenificent it truly is by baking this simple, light French-style meringue mixture into mini-nests, then heaping whipped cream (page 29), mango curd (page 24) and fresh fruit into each.

vinegar, for dabbing
250 ml (8½ fl oz) chilled aquafaba
½ teaspoon cream of tartar
240 g (8½ oz) caster (superfine) sugar
½ teaspoon xanthan gum

Use a paper towel dabbed with vinegar to wipe out a large metal bowl or the bowl of a stand mixer and the attachments on your electric beaters. Pour the aquafaba into the bowl and add the cream of tartar. Beat on high speed for 5 minutes. It will bubble, froth and foam, and then turn into soft peaks much like meringue.

Turn the beaters to medium and add the sugar 1 tablespoon at a time, incorporating each tablespoon into the meringue before adding the next. At the end the meringue should have formed stiff peaks. Mix in the xanthan gum and beat on high for another minute. The meringue is ready when it doesn't budge when you flip the bowl upside down. If you don't have a very large bowl, you might like to do this process in two batches.

Use the meringue in recipes that call for it in this book or read on to make mini pavlovas.

Preheat the oven to 110°C (230°F). If you and your oven have an untrustworthy relationship, it doesn't cost much to invest in an oven thermometer, especially when working at fiddly low temperatures such as for this recipe.

Line two large baking trays with baking paper. Use a marker to trace about ten 8 cm (3¼ in) circles (about the width of a mug). Flip the paper over once done. Fit a piping (icing) bag with a thick nozzle and spoon the meringue into the bag, but don't overfill it so that you can twist it tightly shut. Pipe the meringue in a spiral to fill each of the circles, making the edges higher than the centres.

Place the baking trays on the middle and top shelves of the oven and dry the meringues (we're not trying to bake them) for 2 hours or until the tops feel crisp. Switch off the oven, leave the door closed and forget about them until they're completely cool.

Top with whipped cream, mango curd and fresh fruit seconds before serving.

Custard

This recipe makes a regular, pourable custard – compared to the thicker custard in the Vanilla slice recipe on (page 150), which uses coconut cream to hold up better as a filling. Add a splash of brandy or rum for a custard that could get you taken into custardy.

—

165 g (6 oz) caster
   (superfine) sugar
65 g (2¼ oz) vegan-
   friendly custard
   powder
1 litre (34 fl oz) soy, oat
   or coconut milk
1½ teaspoons natural
   vanilla extract, or
   1 teaspoon vanilla
   bean paste

In a saucepan, thoroughly whisk the sugar, custard powder and one-quarter of the milk together. Place over medium heat and stir for 3–4 minutes, until it begins to thicken. Gradually whisk in the remaining milk, continuing until the mixture is bubbling and thick throughout.

Switch off the heat and stir in the vanilla. Cool for 15 minutes, then transfer to an airtight container and lay plastic wrap directly over the surface of the custard to prevent a skin forming.

The custard will keep in the fridge for up to 5 days.

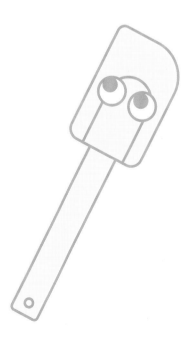

Lemon curd

So tangy and so sweet, we're kicking eggs to the kerb and using cornflour in this curd. It's the perfect filling for bomboloncini or cannoli (page 149), it's the topping freshly fried French toast and pancakes pang for, it's what you want oozing into your crumpets or out of your scones. You'll fall in love with the tang of this, so pucker up!

40 g (1½ oz) vegan butter
40 g (1½ oz) cornflour
  (cornstarch)
350 ml (12 fl oz) lemon
  juice
100 g (3½ oz) caster
  (superfine) sugar
pinch of fine salt

In a small saucepan, melt the butter until it's bubbling. Move the pan off the heat and whisk in the cornflour. Place back over low heat and whisk for a minute, to allow the cornflour to cook.

Add the lemon juice in splashes, whisking the liquid into the flour mixture and allowing it to absorb fully before adding more.

Whisk in the sugar and salt last. Simmer for 2 minutes or until the mixture is thick enough to coat the back of a spoon, then switch off the heat.

Your curd will keep sealed in the fridge for a week from creation.

Mango curd

This man go crazy for mango curd! Try spooning it over ice cream or serve with scones, cakes or crumpets.

50 g (1¾ oz) vegan butter
50 g (1¾ oz) cornflour
  (cornstarch)
80 ml (2½ fl oz) lemon
  juice or lime juice
100 ml (3½ fl oz) coconut
  cream (the solidified
  part in the tin)
350 ml (12 fl oz) pureed
  mango flesh (from
  about 2 mangoes)
80 g (2¾ oz) caster
  (superfine) sugar
pinch of fine salt

In a small saucepan, melt the butter until it's bubbling. Move the pan off the heat and whisk in the cornflour. Place back over low heat and whisk for a minute, to allow the cornflour to cook.

Add the lemon or lime juice in splashes, whisking the liquid into the flour mixture and allowing it to absorb fully before adding more.

Whisk in the coconut cream and pureed mango, then the sugar and salt last. Simmer for 2 minutes or until the mixture is thick enough to coat the back of a spoon, then switch off the heat.

Your curd will keep sealed in the fridge for a week from creation.

Mayonnaise

Egg in mayonnaise is there to emulsify the oil and fat into a thick sauce. Aquafaba (or soy milk) as the emulsifying agent instead makes marvellous mayonnaise that tastes infinitely better than store-bought at a fraction of the cost. Even though it's a fairly quick recipe, it's essential to slowly introduce the oil to the emulsion so that it doesn't split.

—

60 ml (2 fl oz) soy milk or 3 tablespoons aquafaba, plus 1 tablespoon tinned chickpeas (garbanzo beans)
¾ teaspoon apple cider vinegar or white vinegar
¼ teaspoon American or Dijon mustard
¼ teaspoon garlic powder
¼ teaspoon sea salt
185 ml (6½ fl oz) canola oil or other neutral-flavoured oil

Place all the ingredients except the oil in the bowl of a stick blender or plastic jug. Blend with a stick blender for 20 seconds or so, until frothy.

With the stick blender running, very slowly pour in the oil in a steady stream for 1–2 minutes, until you have an emulsified and thick mayonnaise. Taste, and adjust the seasoning if necessary.

The mayonnaise will keep in an airtight container in the fridge for up to 4 weeks.

Dairy

Whether you're a soyboy or edama'am, oat-presenting or simply nut-curious, alternative milks are no new fad. One huge benefit to plant-based milk is its adaptability, with brands and cooks able to vary their recipes to allow the non-dairy products to mimic all the different culinary uses of cow's milk. Many brands fortify their milk with calcium and other vitamins, so the milk often matches or exceeds the nutritional qualities of dairy.

When plant-based milk is called for in this book, you can use what is on hand, or preferably use the best milk for the job, as suggested in some recipes. Don't feel restricted to these milks, as they are not exhaustive of the array available on the shelves, all of which can be experimented with to introduce exciting flavours into baking that dairy milk could never.

Butter

This homemade butter has a light tang and can be used in place of store-bought vegan butter or margarine. Turmeric is optional, but even a tiny pinch can make a subtle yellowed effect that tricks your eyes, along with your tongue, into thinking it's really butter! Leave out the probiotic if you'll be using the butter within a few days, as it won't have much effect by then. Even without it, this butter will flake, spread and taste great wherever dairy versions are called for. Store-bought vegan butter or margarine can just as easily be used for the recipes in this book. Laminating recipes specify vegan block butter, which cannot be interchanged for this recipe or tub margarines.

—

1 probiotic capsule
   (optional)
2 tablespoons soy milk
230 g (8 oz) refined
   coconut oil (without
   flavour or odour)
50 ml (1¾ fl oz) canola oil
80 ml (2½ fl oz) aquafaba
1 teaspoon apple cider
   vinegar
¾ teaspoon granulated
   white sugar
⅛ teaspoon black salt
   (kala namak) or
   regular salt
pinch of ground turmeric

Sprinkle the contents of the probiotic capsule, if using, over the soy milk in a cup. Set aside for at least 2 hours (or overnight) before using.

Melt the coconut oil in a saucepan over low heat, then pour into a spouted mixing jug and stir in the canola oil.

Dig out a tall mixing jug that can hold a stick blender. Add the cultured soy milk, aquafaba, vinegar, sugar, salt and turmeric. Blast with the blender a few times to begin emulsifying.

Gradually beat in the coconut oil mixture over the next 2 minutes, as if you're making a mayonnaise, to allow the oil to incorporate into the emulsion slowly and not break the suspension.

Pour the mixture into a clean jar and place, uncovered, in the fridge overnight to solidify.

Alternatively, for an easy block of butter, line a container with baking paper or plastic wrap before pouring in the butter mixture. Once it has set in the fridge overnight, remove from the container and cover fully with plastic wrap to use as a butter substitute. It will keep for up to 1 month.

Cream

A waltz through the dairy-free aisle at the supermarket should come up with a few vegan cream options that a vegan baker can easily utilise. This recipe is for those whose local stores are dragging their feet on the way to the future, or who love the accomplishment of cooking from scratch. This cream is ready for whipping, and also neutral-flavoured to serve as a point of difference to coconut cream, which naturally comes able to be whipped, but at the compromise of overpowering flavour.

—

250 ml (8½ fl oz) soy milk
200 g (7 oz) refined
   coconut oil (without
   flavour or odour)
1 teaspoon natural
   vanilla extract
large pinch of xanthan
   gum

FOR WHIPPING
40 g (1½ oz) icing
   (confectioners') sugar

Pour the soy milk into a small microwave-safe bowl and blast in the microwave, stirring at 30-second increments, until uncomfortably warm to the touch.

Add the coconut oil to the jug of an efficient blender, then pour the warm milk and vanilla over the top. Sprinkle in the xanthan gum. Blend on high speed for 2 minutes or until thoroughly combined.

Pour into a clean jar and seal, then leave in the fridge overnight to get cold and thick. Use as whipping cream in recipes, adding the icing sugar to help the cream whip.

Crème pâtissière

Crème pâtissière (pastry cream) can be thought of as a sturdier custard. In contrast to custard, which is a pourable consistency, crème pât sets thick and pipeable, so is the best choice for injecting into donuts and pastries.

—

225 ml (7½ fl oz) soy milk
60 g (2 oz) granulated
   white sugar
30 g (1 oz) cornflour
   (cornstarch)
25 g (1 oz) vegan butter
1 teaspoon vanilla
   bean paste
pinch of fine salt
40 ml (1¼ fl oz) bourbon
   or rum (optional)

Thoroughly whisk the soy milk, sugar and cornflour in a saucepan. Place over medium heat and stir for about 5 minutes, until the mixture thickens. Switch off the heat. Mix in the butter, vanilla bean paste, salt and alcohol, if using. (If leaving alcohol out, double the quantity of vanilla.)

Pour the mixture into a bowl, leave to cool for 20 minutes, then directly cover the surface with plastic wrap to avoid a skin forming. Chill in the fridge for at least 2 hours, or even for a day or two before using.

Sour cream

(EASY) **MAKES: 200 G (7 OZ)**

If vegan sour cream hasn't infiltrated your local grocery store yet, other vegan-friendly products can be combined to make a quick and easy substitute for sour cream.

—

100 g (3½ oz) vegan plain
   yoghurt
100 g (3½ oz) vegan
   mayonnaise

Whisk together the yoghurt and mayonnaise in a bowl until smooth. It will keep in a sealed container in the fridge for up to a week.

Buttercream

(EASY) **MAKES: 425 G (15 OZ)**

The dairy industry went from 'I Can't Believe It's Not Butter!' to 'This Is A Legal Notice From The Dairy Industry To Stop Calling It Butter Because People Can't Tell The Difference'. You can use soft vegetable shortening instead of 'not butter' for a buttercream with a higher melting point and more resilience – or use vegan butter alternatives to get that flavour into your buttercream. Better yet, use a 1:1 combination for a flavourful *and* sturdy buttercream.

—

225 g (8 oz) fat – either
   vegetable shortening or
   vegan butter, or a mix,
   at room temperature
200 g (7 oz) icing
   (confectioners') sugar
1 teaspoon natural
   vanilla extract

Using a large mixing bowl and a hand-held electric mixer, or a stand mixer fitted with the whisk attachment, beat the shortening and/or butter for 2 minutes to soften.

Sift your icing sugar to make sure it doesn't have lumps, then spoon it in as the mixer runs. Finish by splashing in the vanilla. Continue beating for another 30 seconds until smooth.

Keep your buttercream in the fridge to firm up before using in recipes. Covered, it will keep for a few weeks in the fridge. If emerging from a long stint in the cold, allow the buttercream to warm up on the bench, then give it a quick stir before using.

Ganache

Ganache is a spreadable chocolate sauce made from equal parts crumbled dark chocolate and vegan cream (1:1 by weight). It's great for icing, filling or dipping into. If decorating cakes, make the ganache at a 2:1 ratio of chocolate to cream for a thicker, drippable consistency.

100 g (3½ oz) dairy-free chocolate, crumbled
100 ml (3½ fl oz) vegan cream or coconut cream

Add the ingredients to a small microwave-safe bowl and blast in the microwave, stirring at 15-second increments, until melted and dippable.

Cool in the fridge for at least 15 minutes, before using on cakes, pastries or as a dip for Churros (page 203).

The ganache will keep in an airtight container in the fridge for up to 2 weeks.

Condensed milk

Making condensed milk at home is much easier than you might think, as it's really just sweetened milk that has been condensed right down until thick and sweet – in this case, by the simple method of reducing the liquid on the stovetop.

800 ml (27 fl oz) coconut
    milk, or soy or oat milk
225 g (8 oz) caster
    (superfine) sugar
½ teaspoon baking
    powder

Combine the milk and sugar in a saucepan over medium heat. Whisk until the sugar has dissolved and the mixture comes to a gentle boil. Add the baking powder and mix through.

Reduce the heat to maintain a simmer and cook for about 45 minutes, or until thick enough to coat the back of a spoon, stirring every 5 minutes or so.

Cool fully, then refrigerate in an airtight container until needed. It will keep for up to 2 weeks.

Dulce de leche

MAKES: 200 ML (7 FL OZ)

This simple, South American–style caramel is as easy as cooking down condensed milk even further. I recommend using your own freshly made condensed milk, but you can also use a tinned version, at a pinch.

—

1 × quantity Condensed milk (see opposite)

Make the condensed milk as directed opposite, but don't refrigerate once it has thickened. Instead, continue to simmer for another 1 hour or so, scraping down the side of the pan and whisking frequently for even cooking. When it becomes sludgy, deep golden brown, is no longer separated and much harder to whisk from the base of the pan, you'll know you have dulce de leche, which will become thick and spreadable once cooled.

Sealed well in a jar, it'll last at least 2 months in the fridge.

Making dulce de leche using tinned plant-based condensed milk

If using a 320 g (11½ oz) tin of vegan condensed milk, bring a very large saucepan of water to the lowest boil possible. Peel the label off the tin, then lower it into the pan on its side, so it can roll around and not trap any air bubbles. Gently simmer for 3–4 hours – the longer you cook it, the thicker your dulce de leche will be. During this time, make sure the water level doesn't fall below the top of the tin, so it remains fully submerged. Also, roll the tin around occasionally using a pair of tongs, to remove any air bubbles from under the tin. Remove the pan from the heat and allow to cool to room temperature, before removing and opening the tin. Ta-dah! That's dulce de leche, although it won't get as thick as when making it from scratch.

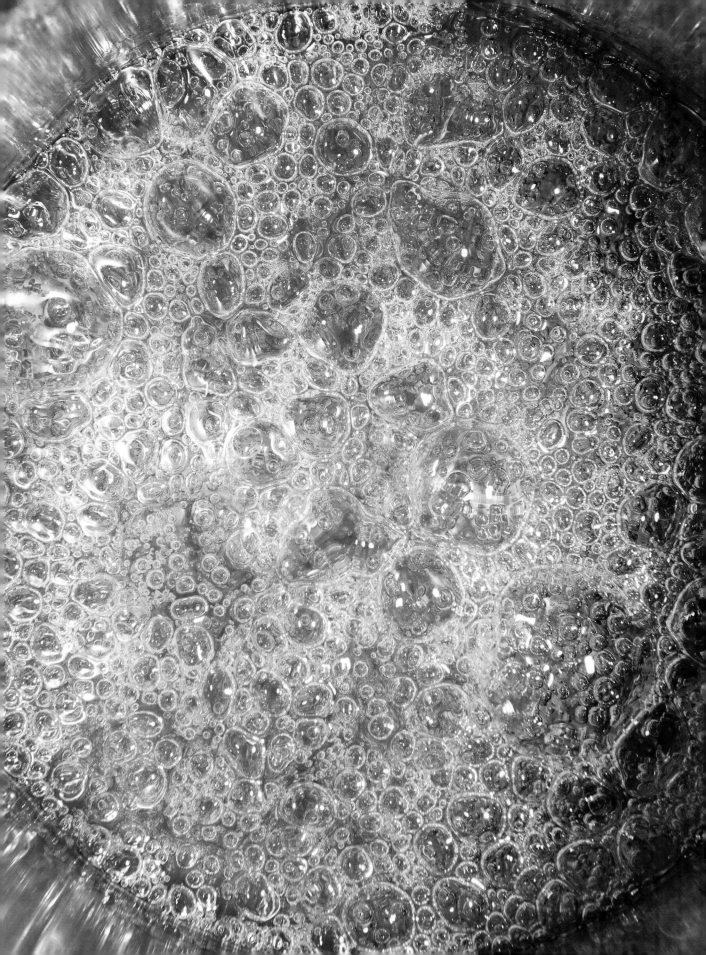

Sugar

Marshmallows, caramel, honeycomb and candies all start with the same basic concept of heating sugar and water. The resulting syrup is boiled and through evaporation becomes a supersaturated solution that, once cooled, is runny. Or soft. Or hard and crisp. The final form, whichever desired, is created by carefully monitoring the temperature of the solution. It's an exact science, but a cheap candy thermometer will make it like taking freshly made candy from a baby.

The various heat stages of candy-making occur within a small window and are named for the appearance the sugar takes on in each stage when dropped into a glass of cool water. Once the temperature hits 105°C (221°F) you've made a simple syrup; by the time it's about 112°C (234°F), you'll have reached the 'thread' stage; about 115°C (239°F) designates the start of the 'soft-ball' stage; and the 'firm-ball' stage occurs at 120°C (248°C). Higher temperatures (not used in this book) can achieve 'hard-ball', 'soft-crack' and 'hard-crack' stages.

Candied citrus zest & syrup

(EASY)   MAKES: 1 LARGE JAR

Here's a brilliant trick for citrus, which lets you use the juice for curds and drinks, while upcycling the peels into your new favourite cocktail syrup and candy all at once. Likely candidates for the candied zest or syrup are cannoli (page 149), wholemeal cinnamon fruit loaf (page 110), baklava (page 153) and galaktoboureko (page 154). They make fabulous gifts, too.

—

5–6 large oranges,
    lemons, limes or
    grapefruits – or a mix
400 g (14 oz) granulated
    white sugar
110 g (4 oz) caster
    (superfine) sugar,
    for tossing

Prepare a large bowl full of hot – but not boiling! – water. Wash the fruit well. Working with one piece of fruit at a time, slice off large strips of peel using a vegetable peeler (and avoiding too much of the white pith), until it has all been removed. Cut the peeled strips into thin slivers, adding them to the bowl of water as you go, to stop them browning.

Juice the fruit, reserving the juice for other recipes, or pouring it into a glass with ice and soda water for a baker's treat.

Add the granulated sugar and 250 ml (8½ fl oz) of water to a saucepan and stir briefly to dissolve. Bring to the boil.

Drain the citrus zest, then add it to the boiling syrup and reduce the heat to a simmer. Simmer for 45 minutes, swishing occasionally.

Strain the syrup, reserving it for other recipes. It'll keep in a sealed jar in the fridge for several weeks.

Spread the zest on a wire rack on the benchtop to dry out for a full day. (If you're a neat freak, place a sheet of baking paper underneath the rack, to catch the syrupy drips – or clean the bench well afterwards, as I do!)

Once they're no longer wet, toss the zest in the caster sugar and store in an airtight jar. They'll keep in the fridge for up to 3 months.

Caramel

Heating sugar, in cream, to high temperatures summons rich, complex flavours as the sugars break down. This is a wet caramel, which means the sugar is mixed with a liquid before cooking. Once mixed, it's a hand's off process ... but it likes to be watched. You must monitor closely as the sauce deepens in flavour and colour. You'll see the sugars go through all the candy-making stages; past the threads, over the balls and deftly slipping through the cracks.

But watch out! A basic, blonde caramel can, in seconds, rapidly sail past the point of no return and take on a burnt flavour. You can address this by taking the pot off the heat a few shades lighter, in anticipation of the fact that the sugars will continue to cook once off the stove. Or, prepare an ice bath in your sink to help halt the cooking process when it's the perfect amber colour. This caramel is made for drizzling, ideally over the warm sticky date pudding on page 259.

—

300 ml (10 fl oz) vegan cream
200 g (7 oz) brown sugar
60 g (2 oz) vegan butter
1 teaspoon natural vanilla extract

In a saucepan, whisk together the cream, sugar and butter over medium heat. Lightly slosh the liquid around the pan as it dissolves, then avoid stirring the solution once it comes to the boil. Maintain a simmer to keep it gently bubbling for 10-15 minutes, until the caramel turns from a light blonde to brown – don't make it too dark! – and begins to thicken.

Keep the caramel in a jar in the fridge for up to a month. Gently reheat and give it a good stir before using.

Raspberry or strawberry jam

EASY   **MAKES ABOUT 315 G (11 OZ)**

You'll never find yourself in a jam again when running out of toast condiments! When fresh berries hit that sweet spot where they're delicious but starting to get soft spots, this super-quick jam is the perfect way to use them up.

—

250 g (9 oz) raspberries
   or strawberries
   (fresh or frozen)
200 g (7 oz) caster
   (superfine) sugar
2 tablespoons lemon juice

Remove any stems that are still attached to the berries. Mash the berries in a large bowl.

Combine all the ingredients in a saucepan. Stir over low heat until the sugar has dissolved, then increase the heat to bring the mixture to the boil. While still stirring, maintain the boil until the mixture reaches 105°C (221°F) on a kitchen thermometer.

Refrigerate in an airtight jar and use within 1 week.

Vegan honey

There's no need to steal from bees and give them inferior sugar syrup, when it's perfectly possible to make this delicious honey-like sugar syrup that you'll love eating for yourself and using as a substitute in recipes, or as a finishing drizzle on toast and crumpets.

2 litres (68 fl oz) fresh, cloudy or long-life apple juice
880 g (1 lb 15 oz) granulated white sugar
4 teaspoons carob syrup

Place the apple juice in a saucepan and bring to the boil over medium heat. Simmer, maintaining a low boil, for about 45 minutes or until the apple juice has reduced by half. If using fresh or cloudy apple juice, frequently skim the surface to remove any sediment that rises to the top. Use this time to bask in how fantastic your kitchen smells right now.

In a separate saucepan, bring 1 litre (34 fl oz) of water to the boil over medium heat. Stir in the sugar and stir for 3 minutes or until the sugar has dissolved. Pour the sugar syrup into the reduced apple juice.

Keep the sweetened apple juice bubbling for 1–1½ hours, until the liquid has reduced to about 750 ml (25½ fl oz) and resembles a honey-like thickness. Use a kitchen thermometer to keep an eye on the temperature; if it goes over 112°C (234°F), the final product will be firmer than a syrup and it won't work as a pourable honey.

Remove the pan from the heat and stir in the carob syrup. Allow to cool before pouring into sterilised jars for storage. The honey will keep in the pantry for several months.

Pastries

Enriched doughs are made to look like paupers next to pastries, holding such a wealth of fat and flavour that they're practically rolling in the dough. Fat is either added to the dough first (such as shortcrust, hot water crust and pie pastries) to make sturdy filling-holders like tarts and pies, brushed on after the fact, as with crispy layers of filo sheets, or carefully folded into distinct strata stacked through the dough via a process called lamination.

The difficulty with creating perfect laminated layers comes down to temperature because laminated dough is a plump, picky winter baby who just can't get enough of the cold. Reach for rain-fed (not grain-fed!) dairy-free block butter which is imperative to creating the layers. Then, between each tour (folding) of the dough, the dough must be kept in the fridge, lest the butter layers melt before baking. Other approaches include taking advantage of winter months, or working in air-conditioned rooms and late at night to keep the dough as cold as possible. Put simply, the more uncomfortable you are, the happier the dough, the crisper the layers, and the faster you can laminate your way to homemade puff pastry or viennoiserie, such as croissants and danishes.

Shortcrust pastry

(EASY)   **MAKES: 6 INDIVIDUAL PIES OR 1 LARGE PIE**

350 g (12½ oz) plain
(all-purpose) flour
150 g (5½ oz) vegan
butter, chopped
2 teaspoons fine salt
2 teaspoons white
vinegar

Shortcrust is one of the easiest pastry doughs for novice bakers to begin with, as it doesn't rely on laminating or leavening for the final result. The high fat content in the dough stops the gluten strands in the flour from connecting into long strands, thereby shortening them – which is where the 'short' in the moniker comes from. The butter is 'cut' into the flour, so pockets of it end up in the dough, leading to flaky pastry. This base recipe tastes right at home in both savoury and sweet applications.

—

Place 90 ml (3 fl oz) of water, the flour and butter separately in the freezer for 30 minutes to get cold before you begin. (Cold ingredients = flakier pastry.)

Begin by 'cutting' the butter into the flour and salt. Ideally, a food processor will most efficiently distribute the fat by pulsing it with the flour and salt to make a crumb-like mixture. Pulse sparingly to ensure the butter blobs don't become too fine.

To do this process manually, you can use two knives or a pastry cutter to literally 'cut' the butter into the flour and salt until the blobs are pea-sized. (If you completely freeze your butter you can also grate it to get small, even pieces to distribute throughout the flour.) If you're going completely old-school, cut the butter into small pieces and just use your fingertips to rub it into the flour until crumbly.

Add the vinegar then the ice-cold water 1 tablespoon at a time, mixing it through thoroughly before adding any more (you may not need all of it). When the dough just comes together, knead it once or twice with your hands to create a dough ball. Secure inside plastic wrap and chill fully in the fridge for at least 2 hours and up to 3 days, or freeze for use within the next few months.

Use as directed in sweet dishes such as mini lemon meringue pies (page 184), or savoury ones like curried scallop pies (page 176). If blind-baking to fill with a no-bake pie filling, prick the dough all over with a fork and bake at 150°C (300°F) for about 30 minutes, until golden all over.

Pie crust

This is kinda like the American exchange student in the French pastry family, in that it comes from America and is almost identical to shortcrust pastry – except with double the fat! That extra fat helps protect the pastry from wet fillings, making it perfect for fruit pies.

A quick note on fat: vegan butter adds flavour to a pie crust, but extra moisture too. Vegetable shortening adds crispness to a crust, but no flavour. I often use a rough 50:50 split to get the best of both worlds, but you can use either or both to make pie crust.

—

230 g (8 oz) vegan butter or vegetable shortening (or a 50:50 split), chopped
320 g (11½ oz) plain (all-purpose) flour
1 teaspoon fine salt
80–100 ml (2½–3½ fl oz) ice-cold water (or a 50:50 split of cold water and vodka)

Place all the ingredients in the freezer separately for 30 minutes to get cold before you begin. (Cold ingredients = flakier pastry.)

Begin by 'cutting' the butter into the flour and salt. Ideally, a food processor will most efficiently distribute the fat by pulsing it with the flour and salt to make a crumb-like mixture. Pulse sparingly to ensure the butter blobs don't become too fine.

To do this process manually, you can use two knives or a pastry cutter to literally 'cut' the butter into the flour and salt until the blobs are pea-sized. (If your fat of choice can handle it, you can freeze your butter or shortening, then grate it to get small, even pieces to distribute throughout the flour.) If you're going completely old-school, cut your fat into small pieces and just use your fingertips to rub it into the flour until crumbly.

Add the ice-cold water 1 tablespoon at a time, mixing it through thoroughly before adding any more. When the dough just comes together, knead it once or twice with your hands to create a dough ball. Secure inside plastic wrap and chill fully in the fridge for at least 2 hours, or freeze for use within the next few months.

Use as directed in sweet dishes such as fruit pies (pages 178–179).

Filo pastry

(MEDIUM)   MAKES: 650 G (1 LB 7 OZ)

I adore the meditative practice of stretching out fresh filo on a giant table the traditional way, by hand, before industrial versions became commonplace. The tactile process of physically dragging the protein strands just about to their limit gives one enormous insight into the unique stretchability of gluten. You'd know it was thin enough when you could read a newspaper through the pastry sheet. Sadly, newspapers are harder to find by the day – but, gladly, store-bought filo that's vegan is commonplace, and reliably rolled thinner than many of us could.

For uber-thin layers and convenience, there's no shame in using store-bought versions; you'll find the best-quality filo in the chilled aisle, rather than the freezer section. After all, filo pastry takes patience, and thinly rolling it by hand is time consuming, as the gluten needs time to relax and stretch out without tearing. The reward for the wait? Beautifully rustic results, more control over pastry shaping, as well as fewer sheets drying out and ripping along the way. Basically, don't be hasty when rolling out this pastry ... you filo me?

400 g (14 oz) bread flour
1½ teaspoons fine salt
4 teaspoons white vinegar
2 tablespoons olive oil, plus 100 ml (3½ fl oz) extra, for brushing
30 g (1 oz) cornflour (cornstarch)

In the bowl of a stand mixer fitted with the dough hook, combine the flour, salt, vinegar and 200 ml (7 fl oz) of water on low speed until a loose dough forms. Increase the speed to medium for 5 minutes. Slowly pour in the 2 tablespoons of olive oil over the course of 2 minutes, then knead for a total of 10 minutes, until you have a smooth ball that pulls away from the side of the bowl.

The dough may be slightly sticky, so rub a small amount of olive oil over the surface with your hands, then form into a ball and wrap tightly with plastic wrap. Rest in the fridge for at least 4 hours (and up to 24 hours) to fully relax.

Prepare a large work surface to roll the dough out on. A flat, cleared table with all sides free is ideal, but home cooking is all about making do, so designate your largest free area for this task.

Divide the dough into 320 g (11½ oz) halves with a dough scraper. Cover one with plastic wrap and return it to the fridge. Take a second to familiarise yourself with the dimensions of your benchtop.

Using a pastry brush, coat the dough in oil, then use a rolling pin to begin pressing out the dough to lengthen it. ①

Flip the dough over and start rolling it out into a rectangle. Keep flipping the dough and re-oiling both sides as you go to prevent sticking.

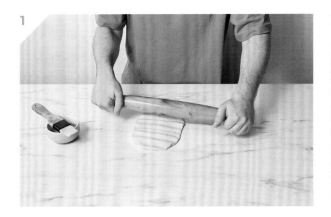

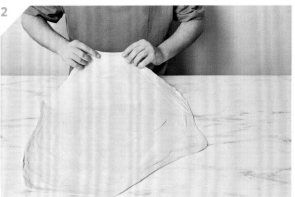

Finally, switch to hand-pulling the filo sheet by lightly pinching a section of the rolled dough, picking it up off the bench and 'walking it out' to a space on the bench further out. The dough should be sticky enough to stay in place as you move it out, and will start to become translucent. Continue around the dough until it is thin enough to see the pattern of the bench beneath you that you mentally noted earlier, and measures about 60 cm × 80 cm (24 in × 32 in). ②

Press together any small tears and forgive yourself for any large ones, as they'll likely be wrapped up in pastry layers and undetectable later on. Let it sit for 10 minutes so that the gluten doesn't try to retract the sheet back.

Wipe the pastry brush clean and lightly sprinkle half the cornflour over the filo. Dust off excess flour while brushing the cornflour evenly over the top. Use a pizza slicer to shape into sheets; I aim for about 30 cm × 40 cm (12 in × 16 in) each. Repeat with the remaining dough.

Use immediately to layer with fat for pastries, or store until needed as follows: lay a sheet of baking paper over each filo sheet, then gently roll it up from one end. These filo cylinders protect the layers from sticking together, and are efficient space savers in storage.

For best results, use the pastry immediately (after all, you've gone to the effort to make it fresh!). However, if you need to keep leftovers, wrap in plastic wrap to seal the roll, then store in the fridge for up to 2 days. Alternatively, freeze in the cylinder for up to 2 months, and gently thaw in the fridge or on the bench before use.

MORE IS MORE:

Homemade filo pastry will never be as thin as machine-manufactured, so when using homemade filo, you'll need to compensate with up to double the weight of the pastry asked for in a recipe. Don't be afraid to use fewer layers than called for in a recipe, as the extra thickness will make up for it. Double the amount of oil or vegan butter you'd use for store-bought filo.

This recipe will approximately do the job of 375 g (13 oz) of store-bought filo pastry.

Laminating dough

MEDIUM

Dough lamination is the excruciatingly slow process of folding cold butter and dough together, to create fine 'leaves' of pastry that can range in number from a few dozen to several hundred layers in a final product. During baking, the fat in the butter melts, which basically 'fries' the dough – and the water in the butter converts into steam, which expands and puffs the pastry layers before evaporating; the resulting expansion is the sole leavening agent behind puff pastry. This pedantic process ONLY works with vegan block butter (specifically not sold in a tub, but wrapped in foil) – otherwise the dough won't be able to retain its layers during repeated folding. Generally, their malleable solidity at cold temperatures is crucial to the process, something that spreadable margarine varieties can't yet replicate.

Refer to this helpful guide to enhance your understanding of the techniques called for in all recipes that require dough lamination.

—

To create a beurrage (butter block): spread a sheet of plastic wrap over your benchtop and sprinkle with flour. Place your cold butter on top, spread more flour over it and sandwich it all between another sheet of plastic wrap. Use a rolling pin to bash the butter into a smooth 15 cm (6 in) square. Proceed when your détrempe (pastry dough) and beurrage (bashed butter) have both spent several hours in the fridge.

Lightly flour the benchtop. Unwrap the chilled dough, then roll it out into a 20 cm (8 in) square. Score a square the same size as the beurrage in the centre of the dough, then use a dough scraper to cut lines from each corner of the square to the outer edge of the dough. Leaving the centre square intact, roll out the dough edges until they are large enough to fold over the centre square. Place the unwrapped cold butter block in the centre and fold each of the dough edges over the top, securely sealing the butter payload inside. Wrap in plastic wrap and return to the fridge for 15 minutes. ①

To prepare for a tour of the dough: unwrap the chilled dough, then place on a lightly floured benchtop. Always working either away from or towards you – not side to side – begin by pressing the rolling pin along the length of the dough. ②

Repeat by pressing down the spaces left between the rolling pin indentations, to flatten the whole thing, which will evenly begin to lengthen the dough in one direction. Check that both sides of the dough are adequately floured, then roll the dough carefully back and forth into a rectangle about 1 cm (½ in) thick, to give you more space to complete a fold.

Use a pastry brush to dust off the excess flour, then give the dough a quarter turn so the long side is facing you. If at any point the dough tears or butter is exposed, dust flour into the spot to 'repair' it, then return the dough to the fridge for at least 1 hour before picking up where you left off.

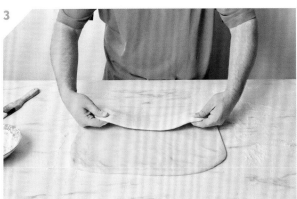

To perform a letter fold: fold the bottom third of the dough over, then fold the top third over this, as though you need to fit the dough into an envelope. Use a pastry brush to dust off any excess flour as you go. With the end of the rolling pin, tap lightly and evenly all over the top of the dough to secure the layers. ③

To perform a book fold: fold the right quarter of the dough into the middle, then fold the left quarter in so the ends meet. Fold over once more where the ends meet in the middle of the dough. Use a pastry brush to dust off any excess flour as you go. With the end of the rolling pin, tap lightly and evenly all over the top of the dough to secure the layers. ④

To complete a tour of the dough: this is the time to make sure that your dough edges are clean and perfectly rectangular, as this will carry through for each of your future folds. Dust off any excess flour with a pastry brush, flip the dough over and dust off again. Consider your future self and use the end of your rolling pin to make light indentations in the direction of the new top of the dough (the edge furthest from you), so you remember which way to roll for the next fold: 'against the grain' of the direction you folded the dough in. Make one, two, three, four, five or six indentations as a record of where you're up to, corresponding with which number fold you've completed, for when you inevitably forget this important detail while waiting between turns. Tightly seal in plastic wrap and refrigerate or freeze for at least 30 minutes before proceeding. Repeat from step 2 each time to complete the required number of folds specified in recipes.

Storing the pastry in the fridge will buy you at most 3 days, and the freezer a few months, with an overnight thawing in the fridge.

Puff pastry

While seemingly simpler than other laminated doughs, given there is no yeast to prove, puff pastry presents its own challenges by demanding hundreds of fine layers brought about by six different folds. Due to this high number of folds, when using more temperamental dairy-free butter it is especially important to fully chill the dough between each fold, and not attempt back-to-back passes, in order to preserve those pastry layers. When baking with puff pastry, make sure that the edges are always cut and not folded, nor coated with the wash applied to the rest of the pastry, as sealing the pastry edges will interfere with rising. Remember, the carefully rolled layers rely on heat to leaven them with steam, so make sure your oven is preheated adequately, to coax the pastry to puff!

—

DÉTREMPE
500 g (1 lb 2 oz) plain (all-purpose) flour, plus extra for dusting
100 g (3½ oz) cold vegan block butter, cut into cubes
2 teaspoons fine salt
200 ml (7 fl oz) almond milk, plus extra if needed

BEURRAGE
300 g (10½ oz) cold vegan block butter

To make the détrempe (dough), add the flour, butter and salt to a food processor and pulse until the butter is finely distributed. Continue to pulse while slowly pouring in the milk until it is all used – you may need to add more milk in small splashes until the dough begins to ball up. Using a food processor helps to slow the forming of gluten, making for crispier pastry. Wrap in plastic wrap and place in the fridge for 1 hour.

Prepare the beurrage (butter). Spread a sheet of baking paper over a large work surface that you can easily roll the dough out on later. Place the block of cold butter on top, and sandwich it between another sheet of baking paper. Use a rolling pin to gently bash and flatten the butter. Using a sharp knife, trim the edges to form a smooth 15 cm (6 in) square. Add the excess butter back on top, sandwich again between baking paper and beat the butter into the square, so it is nice and even. Move to the next step ONLY when the beurrage has had 1 hour to collect itself in the fridge.

Laminate the dough using the guide on pages 46–47, to complete six letter folds. If you aren't living in a cold environment, or your kitchen is warm, completely chill the wrapped dough for an hour in the fridge or freezer between each fold, aiming to keep the dough at all times below 10°C (50°F). When all the folds have been completed, seal the dough in a large zip-lock bag in the freezer and thaw overnight in the fridge as required. The fridge will buy you at most 3 days, and the freezer several months.

The fully chilled puff pastry should then be rolled out to a 5 mm (¼ in) thickness to use in recipes. If you cut the pastry into 24 cm (9½ in) squares after rolling – roughly the same size as a store-bought sheet of puff pastry – you'll easily be able to substitute your homemade pastry in recipes that use commercially made versions.

Rough puff

A hybrid of pie crust and puff pastry methods, this involves the roughest version of lamination to create a flaky crust. As with puff pastry, best results will come from keeping the dough as cold as possible – a cool room or generous rests in the fridge will help with this.

360 g (12½ oz) cold vegan block butter
520 g (1 lb 2 oz) plain (all-purpose) flour, plus extra for dusting
2 teaspoons fine salt
up to 240 ml (8 fl oz) ice-cold water

Divide the butter into quarters. Begin by 'cutting' one butter quarter into the flour and salt. Ideally, a food processor will most efficiently distribute the fat by pulsing it with the flour and salt to make a crumb-like mixture. Pulse sparingly to ensure the butter blobs don't become too fine.

To do this process manually, you can use two knives or a pastry cutter to literally 'cut' the butter into the flour and salt until the blobs are pea-sized. You can also freeze your butter, then grate it to get small, even pieces to distribute throughout the flour.) If you're going completely old-school, cut your butter into small pieces and just use your fingertips to rub it into the flour until crumbly.

Add the ice-cold water, one tablespoon at a time, mixing it through thoroughly before adding any more (you probably won't need all of the water). When the dough just comes together, knead it once or twice with your hands to create a dough ball. Secure inside plastic wrap and chill fully in the fridge for 30 minutes.

On a lightly floured work surface, roll the dough out to a 15 cm × 30 cm (6 in × 12 in) rectangle. Dot the surface of the rectangle with another quarter of the butter. (Alternatively, if your fat is frozen, grate it haphazardly over the dough.) Now perform a letter fold, by folding the bottom third of the dough over, then folding the top third over this, as though you needed to fit the dough into an envelope (see photo 3 on page 47). With the end of the rolling pin, tap lightly and evenly all over the top of the dough to secure the layers. Rest the dough in the fridge for 15 minutes, wrapped in plastic wrap.

Return the dough to the benchtop and rotate 90 degrees from where you last left off. Repeat the rolling out, butter dotting, letter folding and resting in the fridge twice more, to use up the remaining butter. (If the room you're working in and the dough remain cold enough, you can repeat these folds back-to-back, without resting in the fridge.)

When all the folds are complete, either roll the dough out one last time to use in recipes, or store in the fridge or freezer until ready to use. The fridge will buy you at most 3 days, and the freezer a few months, with an overnight thawing in the fridge.

Use in sausage rolls (page 284), rhubarb and strawberry handpies (page 183), or wherever you'd use puff pastry.

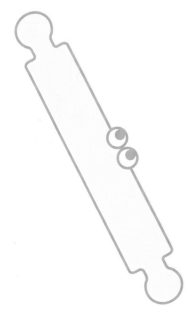

Dough

Grind up some grains, mix in a liquid and you've got yourself a rough dough. If you use wheat as the grain then you can say 'gluten morgen!' to a malleable ball with just about endless baking potential. Because of the unique elasticity of gluten, bakers can adjust the tension in a dough through kneading or resting for softer or firmer baked goods.

If a leavening agent is introduced, then the gluten network will trap gas bubbles and cause the dough to rise. An enriched dough throws sugar, eggs or fat into the mix on top of that. Increased sugar creates a more tender crumb, eggs contribute flavour, promote browning and add more rise to a baked good, and fat coats the gluten strands, preventing them from connecting, which forms softer breads. Striking a balance between these variables is how you turn a half-baked loaf into a bread-winner.

The difference in flour varieties often comes down to the protein percentage. A higher protein percentage means there's more gluten proteins available to form chewy strands in a dough, and the inverse is true, too. Cake or pastry flour has less than 10 per cent protein, which inhibits chewy texture. Plain (all-purpose) flour (10–12 per cent protein) aims to sit in the goldilocks zone, and bread flour (13 per cent–plus protein) leans on the additional gluten to provide structure in impressively large loaves. Double zero (00) flour is very finely milled Italian flour, perfect for pizzas and focaccias.

Kneading

Kneading is the mixing of a dough, which combines ingredients, introduces air and manually stretches and re-combines the gluten strands, which strengthens them into an ordered network. 'No knead' breads take advantage of high hydration, with the extra liquid swimming around meaning the gluten strands have more manoeuvrability, so they are able to arrange themselves autonomously over a long fermentation period. Similar to this, autolyse is the process of mixing flour and water together to begin the gluten-forming process during an initial resting period, before adding more ingredients and proceeding with kneading.

An electric stand mixer opens up the realm of possibilities for doughs for the home cook, while dramatically reducing hands-on effort and time expended. For hand kneading, you'll need to do this on a benchtop, and roughly double the kneading time asked for in stand mixer recipes. The recipes themselves will tell you whether or not you'll need to flour the bench first, depending on the kind of dough you're making. This hand kneading can be done with straight doughs (where all the ingredients are mixed at once before kneading), but is much more difficult for enriched doughs, such as brioche (page 100), where fat is added at a mid-point in the kneading process.

Basic kneading is a simple push–pull method, using the heel of your palm to push the dough down and out. Then, pull half the dough over to fold the lengthened strands of gluten. Continue this process for the duration asked for in each recipe (or double the timings of a stand mixer) to align the gluten strands.

High-hydration doughs, such as those favoured in sourdough recipes, use gentler folding practices that the dough responds better to. This book uses strong stretch-and-folds for this purpose, where you'll stretch out a portion of the soft dough and fold it over your dough ball. Rotating the dough, this step is repeated to create a rounded structure that increases the gluten connections while retaining the gases built up during the bulk fermentation.

The 'windowpane check' is the most reliable way to see if your dough has finished being kneaded. Thanks to the unique stretchy gluten network built through kneading, you can physically see when the gluten strands are strong enough. To check, take a small portion of kneaded dough and gently stretch it out. If the dough is ready, it will lengthen without breaking, to the point that the centre will spread out into a thin film. If you hold this stretched-out portion of dough up to a light source, properly kneaded dough will be thin enough to see the light through. You can consider the light shining through a windowpane-tested piece of dough your GO signal that it's ready to move to the rising stage.

Yeast & leavening

When you cut open a handmade loaf of bread, the crumb shot visible inside is almost like a fossil record of the gluten network you've built, and the yeast's reactions within the bread as it bakes. The yeast dines upon the sugars present in flour, digests it and burps out carbon dioxide in response. It's these little burps that are captured by the gluten network to form the holes in a bread crumb.

Historically, one of the first ways to propagate a yeast culture was to reserve a portion of dough from yesterday's baking to add into the next day's dough. This practice of handing down a dough's yeast legacy to the next day's generation is still carried out in some bakeries today. Sourdough starter keeps an active yeast culture alive through feeding the mother starter, or a portion of the starter after some has been discarded. The existing cultures feed on the new meal of flour and water, maintaining a leavening agent that can be employed on demand if you've kept your starter healthy.

Chemical leavening (baking powder) was realised at the turn of the 20th century, which gave bakers a quicker way to raise bread without the waiting, and opened the door to light, towering cakes such as the sponge. Both 'active' and 'instant' dried yeast were popularised in the following decades, which further simplified the leavening process for home bakes, sped up the process considerably and removed the need to actively keep your yeast alive.

Active dried yeast requires proving, which means you allow it to 'bloom' in lukewarm water or milk before adding to a dough, to quite literally 'prove' that the yeast is working. Instant dried yeast doesn't require this step, and can be added directly to dough mixes right at the start. This book celebrates all three (sourdough starters, baking powder and commercial dried yeast) to get our breads bubbling, as they all give different and valuable effects to baked goods.

Yeast is the support act to gluten's rockstar status in this book and, boy, are the dressing room rider demands extensive before they're willing to perform. If your bread doesn't behave the way you expect, the first thing to check is whether or not your yeast is still alive. The necessary proving step of active dried yeast does a great job of this, but you can also prove instant dried yeast to confirm its viability.

Doughs with high levels of added sugar, fat, salt or even cinnamon will slow (but not stop!) yeast growth, so more time may be needed for them to rise adequately.

When dispersed in the dough, yeast needs time to rise. It'll slowly do its job even if you keep it in the fridge, but for best results you should place yeasted dough somewhere between 25°C (77°F) and 40°C (104°F) as it rises. Rising dough in cooler environments is still possible, but you may need more time to let the yeast complete its job. Having a hot summer? Great! Get your well-covered doughs outdoors for a sunbake session that will speed them through leavening.

Sourdough starter

Sourdough is the last universal common ancestor of all breads, and the starter ('levain' in French, 'sponge' in old-timey speak) can be thought of as the single-cell precursor to that – as both a metaphor, and in the sense that a sourdough starter is quite literally a mixture of flour and water fed over time to make a symbiotic community of single-celled wild yeast strains and bacteria, all of which help ferment doughs and make them rise.

Rye flour is the Ferrari of starter food. It makes for a quality formula to feed your bacteria and yeast child as it's full of nutrients that'll make a noticeable boost in the size and speed of growth. When beginning your sourdough journey, I recommend beginning with rye before transitioning your starter to a white flour and rye blend for the quickest way to get to a healthy, bakeable starter. If rye is premium fuel, then bleached flour is running your car on rainwater. The bleaching process strips flour of the native yeasts needed to propagate your culture, so avoid it.

It's best to form a strong personal attachment to your starter right off the bat, lest you forget it and kill off your creation. I've named mine Nigel, after my father, so that there may be at least one cultured Nigel in the family. Once a starter starts, it will take 2–3 weeks of feeding until the right cultures have fought their way to the foreground for a viable loaf. Only then can you start making plans for your Nigel.

There's a great sense of pride in baking with ancient starters, as with age comes better-flavoured bread, but only to a point; this increasing quality doesn't go on infinitely. This is because sourdough starter is the ultimate Ship of Theseus. It is constantly having its components replaced until it is formed from none of the original pieces. Your local air, bacteria and water will influence the living yeast colony each time it is fed, and evolves again into a slightly new form in an ongoing process. So, don't be intimidated when you find yourself on day one of building a bacteria and yeast empire and realise its descendants might just outlive you. Your fermentorship is just beginning.

Raising your starter

On day 1, mix together the fruit and water in a jar no smaller than 500 ml (17 fl oz). Let it steep for a few minutes to introduce some wild yeasts right from the birth of your starter. Stir in the flour until no streaks are left. Use muslin (cheesecloth) or a loosely secured lid to cover the jar while allowing it to breathe.

Tie a rubber band around the outside of the jar to mark where your starter comes up to. Each time you feed your starter, move the rubber band so that you can monitor how much growth the starter goes through each time. Leave it at room temperature for a full day to begin souring. For the next three days, at the same time each day, stir in the daily feeding amount, then cover the jar again.

On day 5, add 50 g (1¾ oz) of your starter to a fresh jar and discard the starter fruit and remaining starter. Stir the daily feeding of flour and water into your fresh starter, before loosely sealing the jar again. Continue this process of discarding and feeding for 10 days while keeping at room temperature.

DAY 1
2–3 raisins, sultanas
(golden raisins) or
blueberries (unwashed)
25 ml (¾ fl oz) warm
water
25 g (1 oz) rye flour

DAYS 2–4
25 g (1 oz) rye flour
25 ml (¾ fl oz) warm
water

DAYS 5–14
50 g (1¾ oz) starter
(from above)
50 g (1¾ oz) rye flour
50 ml (1¾ fl oz) warm
water

DAY 14 ONWARDS
50 g (1¾ oz) starter
25 g (1 oz) rye flour
25 g (1 oz) unbleached
white flour
50 ml (1¾ fl oz) warm
water

After the full 14 days, you can start transitioning your starter's diet from rye flour to white or wholemeal (whole-grain) flour or a blend. Rye helps the starter grow up quicker, but isn't necessary for regular feedings if you don't normally use rye in your kitchen. A sourdough starter fed on unbleached plain (all-purpose) or bread flour is generally the most versatile. I use a 1:1 rye and bread flour mix for my starter in most recipes.

Using your starter
While you may see bubbling and lots of growth during this initial period, the competing yeast and bacteria strains are fighting it out for dominance still. Depending on the temperature, local bacteria and yeasts, water quality and frequency of feeding, your unique starter may take more or less time to be ready to bake with. It may take up to 3 weeks until your sourdough starter has strengthened the right strains to produce a delicious loaf of bread, and will continue to improve as it ages further. Making a great sourdough loaf takes a few practices, so I recommend trying your first loaf after 2 weeks so your technique mastery and sourdough culture reach maturity at the same time.

To check if the starter is ready, add a spoon of visibly bubbly starter 'at peak' (doubled in size) to a bowl of warm water. If it floats, it should be good to go. When mature, sourdough starter should be fed once every 1–2 days if kept at room temperature, and baked with several times a week. A healthy starter that doubles in size within 4–8 hours (the warmer, the faster) of feeding is generally a positive omen for making leavened loaves.

When you get an understanding of how fast your starter doubles, plan ahead to feed the starter so that it is at its peak when added to doughs.

Keeping your starter
When it's not in active use, you should place your starter into hibernation. Feed the starter and place in an airtight container in the fridge. A healthy starter should keep for several weeks in the fridge before needing a maintenance feed. To do so, remove the starter from the fridge and discard the excess. Feed as normal, then allow it to rest at room temperature for a few hours to work up an appetite. Re-seal back into the fridge and feed every 1–2 weeks.

Starters that have gone too long between feeds will form a clear liquid on top (hooch). Just stir it back in to preserve the hydration ratio of the starter. If the liquid has darkened or hardened, discard the entire top half of the starter and only use the preserved amount below it.

You can also use this method to store an emergency back-up of your starter in the freezer, which is your best way to secure the lineage of your yeast offspring should any mishaps happen to the original. Feed as normal, then allow it to rest at room temperature for a few hours to work up an appetite. Pour into a zip-lock bag and seal, then freeze for up to a year.

When you're ready to wake your Lazarus, return the starter to room temperature, feed as normal for 2–3 days, and leave to double in size within 4–8 hours before using to bake with.

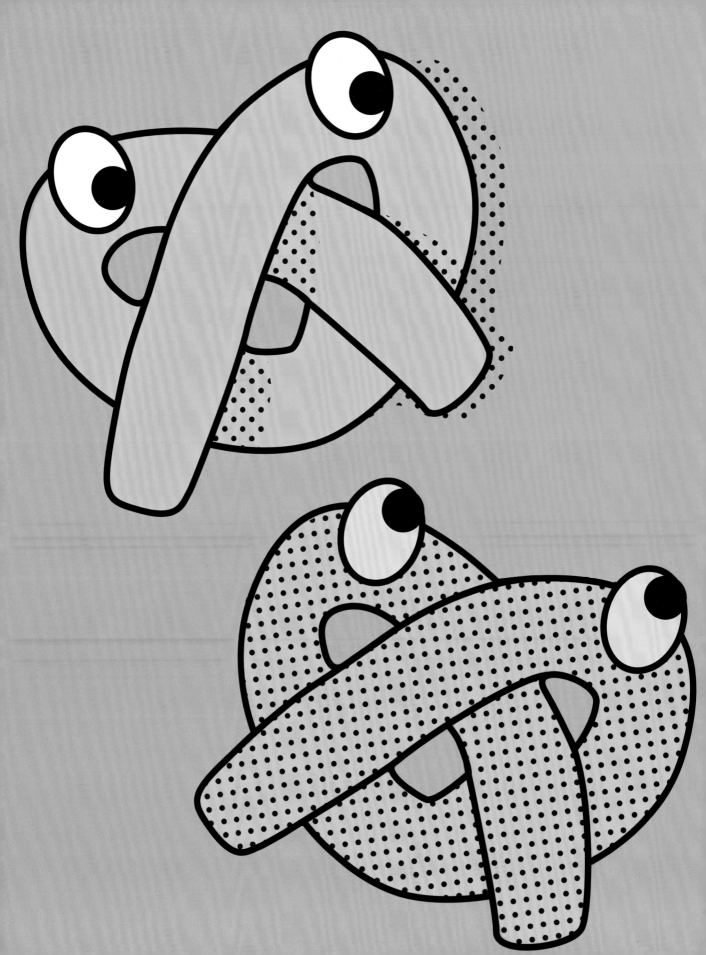

Savoury Breads

Sourdough loaf

(MEDIUM)   **MAKES: 1 BOULE OR BATARD**

The art of sourdough is baking brilliant bread with little more than good-quality flour, labour and patience. Where chemical leavening and instant yeast only entered the field about the same time as the advent of photography, sourdough baking boasts seniority over some of the oldest pyramids. The bakers of human history have refined this wild-yeast leavening concept into loaves of all shapes and sizes. Two of the most common, and the first you should try to master are boules (round loaves) and batards (longer, oval loaves).

It's a general rule of thumb that the less ingredients a dish has, the higher quality those ingredients should be; so choosing fancy bread flour is a must here. For the sourdough methods in this book to be successful, I highly recommend a stand mixer to adequately knead the high-hydration doughs. Mechanical kneading is vital to develop the gluten enough so that only a few simple stretch and folds are required for shaping, instead of needing to spend hours returning to the dough during bulk fermentation.

In addition to strong and unbleached bread flour, you will also need a banneton, or a baker's couche, for proving, and a baker's lame with a sharp razor to score beautiful shapes on your boules and batards (see page 10 for more information). When risen, these loaves demand a well-preheated oven with boiling water added to a baking tray to mimic the steam-injecting ovens that professional bakers use for best results. A hot cast-iron Dutch oven with a lid also produces this effect by retaining the bread's moisture as steam while baking.

Learning the art of hand-raising yeast with the culture of your local area, then using it to craft your own artisanal sourdough won't happen overnight. Your first few loaves definitely won't be perfect, but it's really failing upwards when every single one will be damn delicious anyway. So crack out your yeasty boys and let's get down to the business of building the bubbles in bread the good old-fashioned way.

—

Add the water, instant dried yeast, if using, and sourdough starter to the bowl of a stand mixer fitted with the dough hook. (If the starter floats in the water, it's ready to bake with; if not, you may need more feedings and time to get it ready.) Add the flour and salt on top, then knead on medium speed for 16–18 minutes, until the marshmallowy dough pulls away from the side of the bowl. Transfer the dough to a floured benchtop.

Pinch a piece of the edge of the dough, then drag it to the opposite side of the dough and press down. Rotate the dough and continue the process until you create a taut, smooth ball that pulls away from the benchtop. ①

390 ml (13 fl oz) warm
water
3 g (1 teaspoon) instant
dried yeast (optional;
see Notes on page 61)
100 g (3½ oz) Sourdough
starter, at peak
(page 54)
500 g (1 lb 2 oz) bread
flour, plus extra for
dusting
2 teaspoons fine salt
rice flour, for dusting
semolina, for dusting

Lightly flour, flip seam side down, then cover with a tea towel and rest on the bench for 45 minutes to 1½ hours (depending on the ambient temperature), until significantly risen. Repeat the pinching and dragging process twice more, with covered rests in between. This is the bulk ferment step, and the goal is to promote gluten development and connectivity, while shaping the dough in the way we want as it begins to rise.

To make a boule (rounded ball loaf)

Flip the ball seam side down onto a very lightly floured work surface. Slightly cup a hand against the base of a ball to push it to the side, from left to right. Use the same process and drag the ball towards you to create tension, round the ball out and smooth out any seams. Continue working around the ball, allowing the dough to balloon out as it rolls, then round it out and smooth out any seams. Continue for about a minute until smooth, using a dough scraper to turn it slightly as you go, to round out and apply more pressure inside the dough ball. Make sure the seam is on the bottom of the loaf. ②

To make a batard (long loaf)

Flip the ball seam side down onto a lightly floured work surface. Begin to roll out under your palms to slightly lengthen the dough, then fold the dough over itself lengthways away from you. Use the palm of your hand to smack along the seam to seal it together. ③

Repeat this process twice more, lengthening the dough each time. Flour and roll lightly to adjust the loaf into a neat and even shape, seam side down.

Final temperate rising

Choose a long banneton for a batard, or a round one for a boule. Dust the banneton with rice flour – don't use normal flour, or the gluten will begin to form and attach the loaf to the banneton. Use the dough scraper to flip the dough into the banneton, ugly side up with the seam exposed. Lightly brush rice flour over the top. Place the whole thing inside a plastic bag and seal completely. Leave to rise for 1 hour on the bench.

Plus a cold, slow ferment

Move the dough to the fridge overnight for at least 8 hours, or up to 48 hours. The dough should double in size. The delayed additional rise is important to encourage a deeper sourdough flavour. Baking cold dough straight out of the fridge makes scoring easier, and can also help with 'oven spring' (the rapid rise when high heat hits a loaf, before the crust sets), as the yeast is shocked into rapid action.

Get ready to bake

Select an appropriate cast-iron dish with a fitted lid, or scatter semolina all over a baking tray. Preheat the oven to 250°C (480°F), or to its highest setting, placing the cast-iron dish or baking tray inside for at least 45 minutes, until it's swelteringly hot inside. Crumple a square of baking paper under running water and lay it out on the benchtop. Sprinkle semolina generously over the top (but actually, eventual bottom) of your dough. Holding a dough scraper over the dough, up-end the banneton and guide the dough onto the baking paper, seam side down.

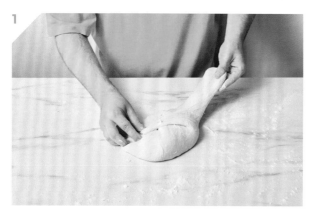

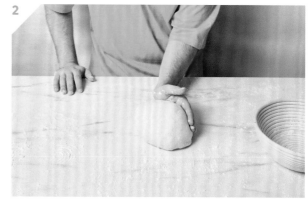

Scoring and decorating

You will need to score the dough with a baker's lame or sharp kitchen scissors to allow steam to escape during baking. For successful slashing, practice is key to achieve firm, confident motions to slice the dough without dragging on it. (The process is called 'slashing', after all – not 'bluntly hacking'!) You may have to further pronounce your slash with a second run through the first cut to make sure it is deep enough to expose the under-surface of the dough. Try to hold the lame almost flush with the surface (sideways) when cutting, and use the corner of the blade. ④

FOR A SIMPLE BOULE

Use water in a spritz bottle to coat the top of the loaf. Use the lame to cut three or four even, medium-deep slashes across the surface of the dough. Alternatively, 'cut' a large square out of the centre, like you're drawing a big hashtag.

FOR A SIMPLE BATARD

Your slash can be as simple as one deep, well-placed steam ventilation point. Use your hand to gently rub an even but light dusting of rice flour over the dough – then, with the lame, make a deep off-centre slash across the surface of the dough, about 1 cm (½ in) to the right of the centre.

FOR A MOUNTAIN LOAF BOULE

Get artistic with your scoring. Use your hand to gently rub an even but light dusting of rice flour over the surface of the dough. Use the lame and a pair of scissors to cut fir trees around the base of a boule. Use a wet finger to draw in clouds around the top. With the lame, cut a cross directly in the centre on top of the boule.

FOR A LEAF BATARD

Use your hand to gently rub an even but light dusting of rice flour over the dough. Make a few medium slashes distributed across the surface of the dough, then make many small secondary cuts to create a leafy pattern stemming off your first cuts.

To bake in cast iron (boules only)

Carefully remove the dish from the oven, then use the baking paper to lower in the dough, leaving the loaf on the paper. Put the lid on and transfer to the oven. Bake, covered, for 30 minutes. Reduce the heat to 220°C (430°F). Carefully remove the dish from the oven, and the bread from the dish. Peel the paper off and bake the bread directly on the oven rack for another 10 minutes. Leave to FULLY COOL on a wire rack before approaching it with a bread knife or your crumb won't set properly. Eat fresh within 48 hours – the sooner the better.

To bake on a baking tray

Carefully remove the baking tray from the oven, then use the baking paper to transfer the dough to the tray, leaving the loaf on the paper. Add 100 ml (3½ fl oz) of boiling water to an oven-friendly dish and place it in the bottom of your oven to introduce steam. Bake for 20 minutes, then open the oven door slightly for a few seconds to release the steam. Reduce the heat to 220°C (430°F). Peel the paper off and bake the bread directly on the oven rack for another 5–10 minutes for a batard, and 10–15 minutes for a boule. The loaf should be a deep, gorgeous brown and sound hollow when tapped. Cool off on a wire rack until every skerrick of oven warmth has dissipated before approaching it with a bread knife. Eat fresh within 48 hours – the sooner the better.

Rustic goodness

For an earthier texture and flavour, use only 450 g (1 lb) bread flour, and add 25 g (1 oz) rye flour and 25 g (1 oz) wholemeal (whole-wheat) flour.

NOTES

When beginning your sourdough journey, your starter may need a boost to achieve ballooned-out loaves. Add up to 3 g (1 teaspoon) of additional instant dried yeast to the dough when starting sourdough loaves, and gradually reduce this amount, until your sourdough starter is doing all the heavy lifting by itself.

Depending on your oven and your environment, your perfect loaf may need a slightly different temperature or baking time. Adjust these elements slightly for each bake until you find your sweet spot.

Batard

Sourdough olive demi-baguettes

(MEDIUM) **MAKES: 4**

If your oven is large enough to hold truly long baguettes, good on you for baguetting your shit together. For the rest of us, we generally need to switch to making demi-baguettes at home to accommodate the length of a domestic oven. If you want a simple bread, leave out the olives – but definitely try serving with fresh tomatoes as bruschetta. For this recipe, a baker's cloche (a special cloth for rising dough on) and baguette baking trays aren't necessary, but will make your job easier and results more traditional. If you've got a rad vegan feta alternative in your area, sprinkling it in with the olives will take these breadsticks to the next level. Try to keep your mix-ins no more than 10 per cent of the total dough weight.

360 ml (12 fl oz) warm water
3 g (1 teaspoon) instant dried yeast (optional; see Notes on page 61)
60 g (2 oz) Sourdough starter, at peak (page 54)
500 g (1 lb 2 oz) bread flour, plus extra for dusting
1 tablespoon fine salt
200 g (7 oz) pitted black olives
rice flour, for dusting (optional)

Add the water, yeast, if using, and sourdough starter to the bowl of a stand mixer fitted with the dough hook. (If the starter floats in the water, it's ready to bake with; if not, you may need more feedings and time to get it ready.) Add the flour and salt on top, then knead on medium speed for 16–18 minutes, until the marshmallowy dough pulls away from the side of the bowl.

Transfer the dough to a floured benchtop. Divide into four dough balls with a dough scraper, about 200–250 g (7–9 oz) each. Pinch a piece of the edge of one of the balls, then drag it to the opposite side of the ball and press down. Rotate the dough and continue the process until you create a taut, smooth ball that pulls away from the benchtop. Lightly flour, flip seam side down, and set aside on the bench (using a dough scraper if needed) while you work on the others. Cover with a tea towel and rest on the bench for 30 minutes.

Repeat the pinching and dragging process twice more, with covered rests in between.

On a lightly floured work surface, press out each portion into a rough rectangle with a long edge facing you. Arrange one-quarter of the olives over each. Working with one piece of dough at a time, fold the dough over, away from you, to seal the olives inside. Use the palm of your hand to smack along the seam to seal it together.

Begin to roll the dough under your palms to slightly lengthen it, then fold the dough over itself lengthways away from you. Use the palm of your hand to smack along the seam to seal it together, then repeat this process one more time to make a 30 cm (12 in) long baguette. Roll under your palms to smooth out and taper the ends.

Use a dough scraper to transfer the baguettes to a perforated baguette tray fitted with strips of baking paper (recommended), seam side down, stretching and adjusting the baguettes so they evenly fill the tray. Alternatively, place in a long baker's couche or several tea towels lightly dusted with rice flour, ensuring they're totally covered. Leave to rise for 2–3 hours at room temperature, or overnight in the fridge, until doubled in size.

Now we're baguettin' somewhere! Preheat the oven to 250°C (480°F), or to its highest setting. Add 100 ml (3½ fl oz) of boiling water to a baking tin and place in the bottom of the oven just before baking. If using a perforated baguette tray, gently flip the baguettes out, remove the baking paper and sit them back in the tray. Alternatively, use a dough scraper to transfer the baguettes from the couche or tea towel to a baking tray.

Use a sharp razor or baker's lame to slash three diagonal cuts across each baguette, holding the blade at a 45-degree angle and using the corner to make the cuts. Use a spray bottle to lightly and evenly spritz the baguettes with water.

Place the baguettes in the oven. Reduce the heat to 220°C (430°F) and bake for 22–24 minutes, opening the oven door slightly for a few seconds halfway through, to let the steam out.

Cool the baguettes off on a wire rack until every skerrick of oven warmth has dissipated before approaching with a bread knife. Eat fresh within 48 hours – the sooner the better.

To extend the freshness window, keep the baguettes wrapped in a tea towel in the fridge. To bring them back to life, spritz with water and bake for up to 10 minutes at 180°C (350°F).

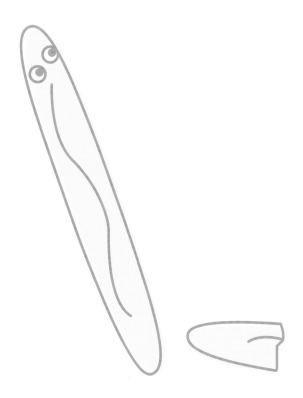

Sourdough olive demi-baguettes

10th circle loaf

10th circle loaf

(MEDIUM) **MAKES: 2 MINI LOAVES**

Dante Alighieri passed the ninth circle of Hell on his way to Lucifer, but if he'd only looked to his left he might've spotted the lesser known 10th circle. In it, atop a podium, sits only a loaf of this blazing boule engorged with sweet, slow-cooked shallots ... and an aggressive, spiteful volume of chilli – fittingly, about 10 bird's-eye chillies, actually. If you're a glutton for punishment, this is torture your tastebuds wouldn't mind an eternity of.

Experiment with different fresh chillies to play with the flavour and heat level in this recipe. Or, worst-case scenario, just wait outside the gates of Hell and use whatever variety you can handle. Save the leftover aromatic confit oil for cooking with, making vinaigrettes or dipping the fresh bread slices into. Stale cuts of this loaf make for fabulous croutons once diced, soaked in the confit shallot oil and baked in an oven inferno for 10–20 minutes, until crispy.

rice flour, for dusting
semolina or coarse
 cornmeal, for dusting

CONFIT SHALLOTS
450 g (1 lb) shallots
2 garlic bulbs
350–400 ml (12–13½ fl oz)
 olive oil

DOUGH
400 ml (13½ fl oz) warm
 water
100 g (3½ oz) sourdough
 starter, at peak
 (page 54)
1½ teaspoons ground
 turmeric
3 g (1 teaspoon) instant
 dried yeast (optional;
 see Notes on page 61)
500 g (1 lb 2 oz) bread
 flour, plus extra for
 dusting
2 teaspoons fine salt

Preheat the oven to 115°C (240°F). Peel the shallots and garlic. Halve the larger shallots, then add them to a baking dish (preferably cast-iron or metal). Pour the olive oil over to cover. Put the lid on (or cover tightly with foil) and bake for about 3 hours. Halfway through, give the shallots a good stir and toss in the garlic. Remove from the oven when lovely, golden and aromatic, and a fork easily glides through both the shallots and garlic. Leave to cool, then bottle the alliums and oil together in the one jar, to use as desired. Store in the fridge and consume within 2 weeks.

Add the water, sourdough starter, turmeric and yeast, if using, to the bowl of a stand mixer for a quick status report. (If the starter floats in the water, consider it a divine sign to continue on your journey. If not, you may need more feedings and time to get it ready.) Add the flour and salt on top. Attach the dough hook, then knead on medium speed for 16–18 minutes, until the marshmallowy dough pulls away from the side of the bowl.

Transfer the dough to a floured benchtop. Divide into two even balls with a dough scraper.

Begin the torture by pinching a piece of the edge of one of the balls, then dragging it to the opposite side of the ball and pressing down. Rotate the dough and continue the process until you create a taut, smooth ball that pulls away from the benchtop. Lightly flour, flip seam side down, and set aside on the bench (using a dough scraper if needed) while you work on the other one. Cover with a tea towel and leave to rest on the bench for 30 minutes.

To resume your journey, prepare the devilishly good additions by using a sharp knife and careful hand to finely chop the confit shallots until they're almost a mush. Chop the chillies into 1 cm (½ in) chunks.

DEVILISHLY GOOD
ADDITIONS
5 confit shallots
10 red bird's-eye chillies
3 tablespoons confit
shallot oil

Press out each dough ball into a rough rectangle and smear each with the mushy shallots. Scatter the chilli over and sprinkle with the confit shallot oil. Roll up the dough from one of the short ends to laminate the fillings inside. Use the palm of your hand to smack along the seam to seal it together, then pull the sides of the resulting cylinder around to fashion a ball.

Repeat the pinching and dragging process five times, with 30-minute covered rests in between. You shouldn't need very much extra flour across the bench for the additional folds – only enough to remind any fillings that try to leave that there is no escape.

After the last fold, flip the balls seam side down onto a very lightly floured surface. Slightly cup a hand against the base of a ball to push it to the side, from left to right. Use the same process and drag the ball towards you to create tension, round the ball out and smooth out any seams. Continue for about a minute until smooth, using a dough scraper to turn it slightly as you repeat to round out and apply more pressure inside the dough ball. Make sure the seam is on the bottom of the loaf. Repeat with the remaining dough ball.

Dust two round bannetons with rice flour (do not use normal flour, or the gluten will begin to form and the loaf will be condemned to eternity in the banneton). Use the dough scraper to flip the loaves into the bannetons, ugly side up with the seam exposed. Lightly brush rice flour over the top.

Place each banneton inside a plastic bag and seal completely. Leave to rise for 2–4 hours at room temperature on the bench, until doubled in size. Depending on the warmth of the room, the rising time will vary season to season for you.

Preheat the oven to 220°C (430°F). Prepare two 20 cm (8 in) cake tins by sprinkling water over, lining the bases with baking paper and sprinkling semolina inside each.

Sprinkle semolina generously over the top of your loaves. Holding a dough scraper over the dough, up-end the bannetons and guide the dough into the cake tins, seam side down. Envision two lines separating your boules into thirds, then use a very sharp knife or baker's lame to slash the dough, holding the blade at a 45-degree angle and using the corner to make the cuts, in a confident motion along one of the imaginary lines to make an off-centre steam exit strategy.

Just before baking, spritz the outside of the loaves with unholy water (from a tap is fine) in a spray bottle. Add 100 ml (3½ fl oz) of boiling water to a baking tin and place in the bottom of the oven. Bake the loaves for 20 minutes, then open the oven slightly for a few seconds to release the steam and screams.

Turn the bread out of the tins, then bake the loaves directly on the oven racks for another 10–15 minutes. The loaves should be a deep, gorgeous brown and sound hollow when tapped.

Cool off on a wire rack until every skerrick of oven warmth has dissipated, before approaching with a bread knife. Slices can be frozen for a few months, or eat fresh within 48 hours and pray for mercy.

Épi de blé

(HARD) MAKES: 2

One of the first ever bakes I learned and one of the last I ever mastered, there's a certain *je ne sais quoi* about baguettes shaped like blades of wheat. Tearing off a fresh dinner roll from the bready stem made from little more than milled wheat and skilled technique is the farm-to-table moment in which you'll know you've truly mastered artisanal breads on your sourdough journey. Serve your épi de blé with fougasse (page 74), another French bread inspired by the shape of wheat.

—

180 ml (6 fl oz) warm
    water
50 g (1¾ oz) Sourdough
    starter, at peak
    (page 54)
3 g (1 teaspoon) instant
    dried yeast (optional;
    see Notes on page 61)
240 g (8½ oz) bread flour,
    plus extra for dusting
3 teaspoons flaxseed
    (linseed) meal
1 teaspoon fine salt
rice flour, for dusting
semolina or coarse
    cornmeal, for dusting

Add the water, sourdough starter and yeast, if using, to the bowl of a stand mixer fitted with the dough hook. (If the starter floats in the water, it's ready to bake with; if not, you may need more feedings and time to get it ready.) Add the flour, flaxseed meal and salt on top, then knead on medium speed for 16–18 minutes, until a marshmallowy dough pulls away from the side of the bowl.

Transfer the dough to a floured benchtop. Using a dough scraper, divide the dough into two balls, about 200–250 g (7–9 oz) each. Pinch a piece of the edge of one of the balls, then drag it to the opposite side of the ball and press down. Rotate the dough and continue the process until you create a taut, smooth ball that pulls away from the bench. Lightly flour, flip seam side down, set aside on the bench (using a dough scraper if needed) and cover with a tea towel. Repeat with the other dough ball, then leave to rest on the bench for 30 minutes.

Working with one dough ball at a time, fold the dough over, away from you, to lengthen and add gluten tension. Use the palm of your hand to smack along the seam to seal it together. ① ②

Fold the dough over again, lengthening it as you do it. Smack together the seam, then repeat this process one more time to make a 40 cm (16 in) long baguette. Roll under your palms to smooth out and taper the ends.

Use a dough scraper to transfer the baguettes to a baker's couche or a few tea towels lightly dusted with rice flour, ensuring they're totally covered. Leave to rise for 2 hours at room temperature, or overnight in the fridge until doubled in size.

Preheat the oven to 220°C (430°F). Sprinkle semolina over two wide baking trays, then use a dough scraper to carefully guide each baguette onto the trays, seam side down.

Starting at the top of one of the baguettes, use a sharp pair of kitchen scissors to cut almost entirely through a piece of the dough at an angle, to form a leaf shape. Continue working down the baguette, cutting at 7.5 cm (3 in) intervals. ③

Splay each leaf out at alternating angles to form the wheat stalk shape, pushing them together to form a strong 'stem' in the middle that will ensure the baguette can be picked up after baking. ④

Use a spray bottle to lightly and evenly spritz the dough with water.

Add 100 ml (3½ fl oz) of boiling water to a baking tin and place in the bottom of the oven. Transfer the loaves to the oven and bake for 20–25 minutes, until the ends are charring and crispy, with a lovely brown crust all over the bread.

Cool completely on a wire rack. If you cut into them too early, the inside will prematurely crumb and you'll spoil the potential texture with gumminess. Eat fresh within 48 hours – the sooner the better.

To extend the freshness window, keep the épi de blé wrapped in a tea towel in the fridge. To bring them back to life, spritz with water and bake for up to 10 minutes at 180°C (350°F).

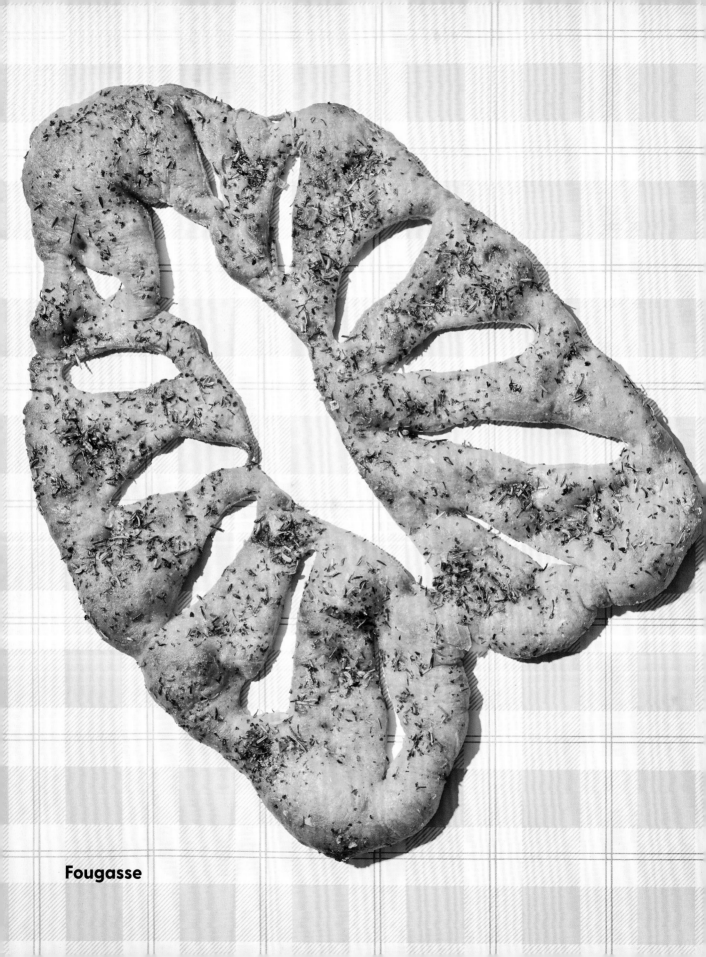

Fougasse

Épi de blé

Fougasse

(HARD)   MAKES: 4

The lesser-known French cousin of focaccia, fougasse is a flatbread named for the squashing of the dough ahead of baking, to look like an ear of wheat – like the épi de blé on page 70, but to a very different effect. The final shape, inspired by mother nature, is just as eclectic as she – one of my fave fougasses I've found in the wild is stretched to be torso size and resembles an errant bread handlebar you have to proudly lug home. If it's squashed, slashed and fits your baking tray, then you can expect some pretty fabulous fougasse once the herbs and garlic oil are splashed over the top. By using long-cooked garlic or shallot confit oil in the dough, some garlic powder, and then fresh toum for the outside coating post-bake, you can expect deep and complex garlic in every bite.

—

semolina or coarse
   cornmeal, for
   sprinkling
Toum (page 272) or Confit
   garlic oil (page 76), for
   coating

DOUGH
350 ml (12 fl oz) warm
   water
75 g (2¾ oz) sourdough
   starter, at peak
   (page 54)
pinch of instant dried
   yeast (optional; see
   Notes on page 61)
450 g (1 lb) bread flour,
   plus extra for dusting
50 g (1¾ oz) rye flour
2 teaspoons caster
   (superfine) sugar
1½ teaspoons fine salt
1 teaspoon garlic powder
50 ml (1¾ fl oz) Confit
   garlic oil (page 76)
   or Confit shallot oil
   (page 68)

To make the dough, add the water, sourdough starter and yeast, if using, to the bowl of a stand mixer fitted with the dough hook. (If the starter floats in the water, it's trying to say, 'Come bake with me!') If not, you may need more feedings and time to get it ready, so don't begrudge its final wish.) Add the flour, rye flour, sugar, salt and garlic powder on top. Knead on medium speed for 10 minutes. Slowly pour in the confit garlic oil and knead for another 5 minutes, until the marshmallowy dough pulls away from the side of the bowl.

Lightly oil a large bowl, transfer the dough to it, cover tightly with plastic wrap and put the dough in the fridge and out of your mind for 48 hours.

Cover four large baking trays with baking paper or silicone baking mats and sprinkle with semolina. (If you don't have four baking trays, use two baking trays, and leave half the dough in the fridge to make more fresh bread tomorrow.)

Transfer the dough to a floured benchtop. Divide into two balls with a dough scraper. Using your hands, flatten each into a thick round, then use a pizza cutter to cut each round in half, into two half-circles, giving you four semicircles.

Fold the two ends of each half-circle into the centre to form a triangle. Press down to secure, cover with a tea towel and leave to rest on the bench for 1 hour to come back to room temperature.

Re-flour the bench sparingly. Working with one at a time, roll out a dough triangle until it is 2.5 cm (1 in) thick, then use your hands to finish stretching the dough into a large triangle with rounded edges. ①

Transfer the dough triangle to a baking tray and pull the fougasse edges to spread it out nicely. With a pizza cutter, make a vertical slice through the centre of the triangle, leaving the edges attached at both ends. As you cut into the fougasse, use your fingertips to spread the gap apart and adjust the fougasse to maintain symmetry. ②

Leaving space at the edges and between other cuts, make a series of shorter cuts on either side of the central cut. ③

HERBS DE PROVENCE
1 tablespoon dried
    rosemary
1½ teaspoons fennel
    seeds
2 tablespoons flaky salt
1 tablespoon dried thyme
1 tablespoon dried basil
1 tablespoon dried
    marjoram
1 tablespoon dried
    parsley
1½ teaspoons dried
    oregano
1½ teaspoons dried
    tarragon

Use your hands to adjust the final shape of the bread, fanning and dragging out all the cuts to ensure they won't close up as the dough rises. ④

Repeat with all the dough portions, then cover securely with plastic wrap or tea towels and leave to rise on the bench for a further 1 hour.

Preheat the oven to 240°C (465°F). Get your herbs de Provence ready. Using a mortar and pestle, finely grind the rosemary and fennel seeds. Add the remaining ingredients and mix with the pestle until combined. Brush each fougasse with toum or confit garlic oil, then lightly sprinkle with some of the herbs de Provence.

Add 100 ml (3½ fl oz) of boiling water to a baking tin and place in the bottom of the oven just before baking. Turn the oven temperature down to 210°C (410°F) and immediately move the fougasse to the oven. Bake for about 20 minutes, drizzling on more toum or oil and another sprinkle of herby salt in the last 5 minutes for extra luck and flavour dimension. The bread will be browned and crispy when it's ready to leave the oven. Brush them one more time with any toum or oil and sprinkle with any herbs that may have tried to exit the vehicle before pulling to a complete stop. Carefully stack the fougasse to cool on top of each other so any excess oil flows to their downstairs neighbour. Patiently let them cool almost completely before moving, to preserve their delicate structure.

Your fougasse are best served warm on the day of baking. Keep leftovers in the freezer for up to 2 months and thaw wrapped in a tea towel in the fridge to replenish their freshness, before reheating in the oven.

Focaccia

This has been my most popular recipe in recent years, probably due to it sitting at the intersection of no-knead and garlic-doused breads. What sets this recipe apart is the attention to flavour. Fresh confit garlic is studded into the dough, then the infused oil is whisked with kalamata olive brine and poured over the top to add flavour, salt and moistness as the bread bakes.

—

275 g (9½ oz) 00 flour
275 g (9½ oz) bread flour
   or plain (all-purpose)
   flour
4 g (1 slightly heaped
   teaspoon) instant
   dried yeast
2 teaspoons fine salt
500 ml (17 fl oz) warm
   water
150 g (5½ oz) mashed
   potato (optional)
120 ml (4 fl oz) kalamata
   olive brine
1 teaspoon coarse
   salt, plus extra for
   sprinkling

CONFIT GARLIC OIL
2 garlic bulbs, peeled
120 ml (4 fl oz) olive oil

TOPPINGS
rosemary leaves
cherry tomatoes
kalamata olives
pickled peppers
1 small onion, sliced
   into thin rounds

IMPORTANT!
Garlic confit, the oil, and any focaccia using either of them MUST be stored in the fridge, or they can become a health hazard. (Specifically, botulism. No fun.)

To make the confit garlic oil, preheat the oven to 130°C (265°F). Place the garlic cloves in a small baking dish, cover with the oil and bake for 1½–2 hours, checking after the 1-hour mark to make sure the garlic is still submerged in the oil, until the garlic is soft. Pour the oil and garlic into a clean jar and keep in the fridge until needed; it will keep for up to 2 weeks (see Note).

Combine the flours, yeast and fine salt in a large mixing bowl. Add the warm water and potato, if using, and stir until incorporated; you should have a sticky, slightly runny dough that can still be manoeuvred by hand. Pour 2 tablespoons of the confit garlic oil over the dough, then flip the dough over a few times to coat fully in the oil. Cover the bowl securely with plastic wrap and store in the fridge for at least 6 hours, and up to 72 hours – the longer, the better!

On the day you want to bake the focaccia, grease a 28 cm × 40 cm (11 in × 16 in) baking tray with another 2 tablespoons of the confit garlic oil. Deflate the dough by grabbing a piece and folding it into the middle of the dough ball, then rotate and repeat this action until the dough is more manageable. Place the dough in the middle of the baking tray and use your fingertips to prod and push the dough into the edges of the tray.

Cover with plastic wrap to avoid a skin forming, then move to a warm spot and leave to rise for at least 2 hours. When risen, the dough should have bubbles throughout, and any coldness from the fridge should have been warmed away.

To get it ready for baking, preheat the oven to 220°C (430°F). Use your fingertips to prod all over the top of the risen focaccia, through to the base of the baking tray, to create the signature dimples. Scatter the confit garlic and your chosen toppings all over the focaccia, then go in with a second dimpling to push them in. Doing this makes even more room for a second scattering of toppings if you're keen for an overloaded version. Whisk together most of the remaining garlic oil and the olive brine (I use a 1:2 ratio of oil to brine) then pour this over the top of the focaccia. Finish with a scattering of coarse salt.

Bake the focaccia for about 30 minutes, rotating the tray halfway through cooking. Brush any remaining garlic confit oil over the top and sprinkle with more coarse salt to make every bite perfect from the get-go.

Cool the focaccia on the tray for 20 minutes, then transfer to a wire rack or chopping board, ready for slicing and serving. Alternatively, you can store it in the fridge for 3–4 days to slice and reheat as desired.

Irish soda bread

(EASY)   **MAKES: 1 LOAF**

No yeast proving, no dough rising, and no micromanaging the leavening member of your group bread-making project who just won't do their part. Baking soda, for which the bread is named, reacts with the acidity of a quickly curdled buttermilk to just about instantly spit out all the carbon dioxide bubbles we need to get the loaf to rise. What comes out of the oven is a dense, gigantic scone-like quick-bread that's on your dinner table with less than an hour's notice. This recipe teaches you how to use two cake tins as an impromptu Dutch oven, but if you've already invested in a cast-iron casserole dish with a tightly fitting lid, here's the perfect use for it.

—

olive oil, for greasing
480 g (1 lb 1 oz) plain
   (all-purpose) flour, plus
   extra for dusting
360 ml (12 fl oz) soy milk
2 tablespoons vinegar
1 slightly heaped
   teaspoon baking soda
1 teaspoon fine salt
large pinch of caster
   (superfine) sugar
1 tablespoon nutritional
   yeast (optional, for
   extra flavour)
30 g (1 oz) vegan butter
aquafaba or soy milk,
   for brushing

Preheat the oven to 210°C (410°F). You'll need two 20 cm (8 in) cake tins for this recipe. Lightly grease and sparingly flour one of them, shaking the flour around to fully coat the side. Dump the excess flour onto a work surface to use for kneading later.

In a small bowl, combine the milk and vinegar. Leave to sit for 5 minutes to thicken and curdle into buttermilk.

In a large bowl, sift together the flour, baking soda, salt, sugar and nutritional yeast, if using.

'Cut' the butter into the flour using two knives or a food processor, until the butter looks like pea-sized blobs. If you're going completely old-school, cut the butter into small pieces and just use your fingertips to rub them into the flour until crumbly.

Stir in the buttermilk, then finish by kneading on the pre-floured benchtop for 1 minute to bring the scraggly dough together and round it out into a ball as best you can. Rustic (read: sloppy) Irish soda loaves are perfectly fine.

Wet your hands, then transfer the dough to the greased and floured cake tin. Use a sharp knife or baker's lame to score a deep cross across the centre, then slather aquafaba or soy milk over the top with a pastry brush. Sit the second tin on top, upside down, bum up, to create more space for the loaf to rise, and to jury-rig a sealed baking environment, and then put the whole thing in the oven. (If using a Dutch oven, simply put the lid on.)

Bake for 30 minutes, then remove the top cake tin (or casserole lid) and bake for another 10 minutes.

As this is a fresh, preservative-free loaf, it can dry out quickly. Given how speedy it is to put together, just bake it fresh each time to eat the same day.

MORNING GLORY
Add a cup of raisins to the flour for a sweeter, breakfast-friendly loaf.

Shokupan

(MEDIUM) **MAKES: 1 LOAF**

Shokupan dough relies on Asian baking techniques where a portion of the flour is super-hydrated with hot water (which flour can absorb more efficiently than cool water) before mixing in other ingredients. This leads to a longer shelf-life, better rising and a sweeter bread. The popular Chinese tangzhong method makes a roux in a saucepan with the flour, but I prefer the original Japanese yudane method, which uses a higher portion of the flour (about 20 per cent), with boiling water simply stirred through.

Acclaimed by my mother as the 'best bread ever', this dairy-free milkbread recipe is impossibly soft and errs a little on the sweeter side. It's perfect for sandwiches such as the iconic Japanese katsu sando, or French toast. This recipe fills one small pullman-style bread tin, but will also go great in any bread tin, although it won't achieve the perfectly squared aesthetic shokupan has come to be known for.

vegan butter, softened, for brushing

YUDANE
75 g (2¾ oz) bread flour
100 ml (3½ fl oz) boiling water

DOUGH
180 ml (6 fl oz) plant-based milk
30 g (1 oz) granulated white sugar
2 tablespoons plant-based milk powder (optional)
9 g (2¾ teaspoons) instant dried yeast
300 g (10½ oz) bread flour, plus extra for brushing
2½ teaspoons fine salt
25 g (1 oz) vegan butter, at room temperature, plus extra for greasing

To prepare the yudane, measure the flour into a small bowl, then stir through the boiling water until completely combined into a stiff mixture. Cover with plastic wrap and set aside for at least 2 hours before proceeding – ideally overnight in the fridge for best results.

To make the dough, add the milk, sugar, milk powder, if using, yeast and flour to the bowl of a stand mixer fitted with the dough hook. Begin kneading on medium speed for 16–20 minutes. Tear off small pieces of the yudane and gradually add it to the dough as it is being kneaded, until all the yudane has been incorporated. Add the salt, then the butter, teaspoon by teaspoon, and continue to knead.

When the dough passes the windowpane test (page 52), cover the bowl with a tea towel and leave to rise in a warm spot for 1–2 hours, until doubled in size.

Lightly grease a 23 cm × 4 cm (9 in × 1½ in) pullman baking tin. On a lightly floured workbench, roll the dough into a rectangle the same length as the bread tin. Tightly roll the dough into a cylinder, then place in the baking tin, seam side down. Allow to rise for another 1 hour, until the dough doubles in size again.

Preheat the oven to 180°C (350°F). Put the lid on the bread tin and bake the loaf for 30–35 minutes. Liberate the loaf from the tin and transfer to a wire rack to cool.

While the bread is still hot, brush some vegan butter over the surface for an extra shiny loaf. Cool fully before slicing. Thanks to the yudane method, your loaf should keep fresh for up to 1 week in an airtight environment.

ON A ROLL
Make eight rolls, following the shaping guide for the Fennel seeded dinner rolls on page 268. Bake for 25–30 minutes at 180°C (350°F), then go wild by brushing the rolls with vegan butter as they leave the oven.

English muffin toasting loaf

(EASY)   **MAKES: 1 LOAF**

Baking a batch of English muffin batter into an entire loaf is a remarkably quicker process than fashioning it into individual muffins, and also saves you monitoring them on the griddle. Pop the whole thing in the oven instead, and you'll end up with perfectly toastable slices, filled with all those signature nooks and crannies, in half the time.

—

cooking spray, for
   greasing
220 ml (7½ fl oz) plant-
   based milk
30 g (1 oz) vegan butter
360 g (12½ oz) plain
   (all-purpose) flour
1 tablespoon granulated
   white sugar
1¼ teaspoons fine salt
½ teaspoon baking soda
7 g (2 teaspoons) instant
   dried yeast
semolina or coarse
   cornmeal, for dusting

Lightly grease a standard loaf (bar) tin. Warm the milk, butter and 180 ml (6 fl oz) of water in a saucepan (or with a few short blasts in a microwave) until comfortably warm to the touch, like you're preparing it for a baby. Aim to get the liquid to about 50°C (120°F).

Using a stand mixer fitted with the paddle attachment, begin mixing together the flour, sugar, salt, baking soda and yeast on medium speed. Pour in the warm liquid in a thin, constant stream. Increase the mixer speed to high and continue beating for 3 minutes, to make a sticky batter.

Pour the batter into the loaf tin and smooth the top with the back of a spoon. Use cooking spray to generously coat the top in oil, then lay a sheet of plastic wrap over the surface to prevent a skin from forming. Leave to bask somewhere warm for 1–2 hours, until the batter has risen dramatically and just reaches the top of the tin.

Preheat the oven to 180°C (350°F). Carefully remove the plastic wrap, to avoid deflating the risen batter, and sprinkle semolina all over the top.

Transfer to the oven and bake for about 25 minutes, until a gorgeous crust has formed on top, and the loaf sounds hollow when tapped. Cool in the tin for a few minutes, then transfer to a wire rack to cool completely.

Slice up and toast your new favourite breakfast loaf, storing the excess slices in the freezer for when they're required.

Rye crispbread

EASY   **MAKES: A LOT**

Cure the wasteful guilt pang that hits when you discard excess sourdough starter on your sourdough journey. Try using it instead to create these crispbreads that belong right on an antipasto platter. Cut into long strips for giftable crackers, medium strips for the perfect length to scoop all kinds of dips while keeping your fingers clean, or short strips for a crunchy vessel to mount plant-based cheeses onto.

180 ml (6 fl oz)
   plant-based milk
1 teaspoon rice
   malt syrup
120 g (4½ oz) Sourdough
   starter discard
   (page 54)
30 g (1 oz) sunflower
   seeds
2 teaspoons fennel seeds
2 teaspoons caraway
   seeds
175 g (6 oz) rye flour
125 g (4½ oz) bread flour,
   plus extra for dusting
1 teaspoon fine salt

Warm the milk in a saucepan (or with a few short blasts in a microwave) until comfortably warm to the touch, as if preparing it for a baby. Pour into a large bowl, whisk in the rice malt syrup, then add the sourdough discard and leave for a few minutes to start enjoying its meal.

Mix together the seeds, then add three-quarters to the sourdough mixture, along with the rye flour, bread flour and salt. Stir until combined, then turn the dough out onto a lightly floured benchtop and knead for 5 minutes.

Transfer the dough to a large bowl, cover with plastic wrap and rest for 1–2 hours in a warm place to lightly ferment.

Line two large baking trays with baking paper or silicone baking mats. Re-flour the benchtop, more generously this time. Tip the dough onto the flour and use a dough scraper to divide it into quarters. Working with one quarter at a time, roll the dough out to about 1 cm (½ in) thick. Use your fingertips to dab water over the surface, then scatter with one quarter of the remaining seeds. Continue to roll the dough out until it is 5–7.5 mm (¼ in) thick, pressing the seeds into the dough as you go. Repeat with the remaining dough and seeds.

Use a pizza slicer to cut the dough into 5–6 cm (2–2½ in) wide strips, then cut the strips to your desired length of crispbread crackers, keeping in mind that you can break them up further (but less neatly!) after baking. Transfer to the baking trays and leave to rest, just while the oven heats up.

Preheat the oven to 200°C (400°F). Slide the crispbreads in and bake for about 10 minutes, until browned.

Switch off the oven. Open the oven door slightly for a few seconds to lower the heat, then close again and leave the crispbreads in the oven to finish drying out until completely cool (overnight works!).

Keep the crispbreads in an airtight container in the pantry for up to 1 week.

Grissini

(EASY) MAKES: 32

I like making my breadsticks extra long for the drama of it all. They tower over my antipasto platters like a lighthouse-tower beacon of hope for vegans seeking snacks. Tie them up with a pretty ribbon and you've got a lovely homemade gift to take to friends' houses to force them to get the nice dips out while you're there.

200 ml (7 fl oz) warm water
5 g (1½ teaspoons) active dried yeast
300 g (10½ oz) plain (all-purpose) flour, plus extra for dusting
1½ teaspoons fine salt
80 g (2¾ oz) vegan parmesan, finely grated
2 teaspoons mixed dried Italian herbs
3 tablespoons extra-virgin olive oil, plus 2 tablespoons extra for brushing
cooking spray, for greasing

HERBED SALT MIX
1 tablespoon flaky salt
1 teaspoon finely chopped rosemary leaves
½ teaspoon fennel seeds
½ teaspoon caraway seeds

Mix together the warm water and yeast in a small bowl, then sprinkle in a small pinch of the flour and set aside to bloom for 5 minutes.

In a large bowl, combine the flour, salt, parmesan and herbs. Make a well in the middle.

Whisk 2 tablespoons of the olive oil into the yeast mixture, then pour into the well. Gradually mix together to form a semi-sticky dough, then knead for 1 minute. Pour the remaining tablespoon of oil over the dough, then flip the dough to coat both the bowl and dough in the oil. Fashion the dough into a rough ball, cover with a tea towel, then leave to rise for 2 hours in a warm spot until tripled in size.

Preheat the oven to 200°C (400°F). Line two or three baking trays with baking paper or silicone baking mats. Grease the paper or mats with cooking spray.

On a lightly floured work surface, punch down the dough, then roll into a 20 cm × 30 cm (8 in × 12 in) rectangle. With a dough scraper, cut a cross sign through the centre of the dough, then cut along to make four quarters. Use the scraper to cut eight even strips out of each quarter.

Pick up a strip of dough and begin to stretch it out with your hands, into a long, thin strand, almost as long as your baking tray. Twist it around slightly and place it on one of the prepared baking trays. Repeat with the remaining dough. You may need to bake these in two batches, depending on the size of your trays and your oven.

Using a small blender or a mortar and pestle, grind the herbed salt mix ingredients together. Brush the extra oil over the grissini, then carefully sprinkle the salt mix over the top. Bake the grissini for about 25 minutes, until golden, rotating the trays halfway through cooking.

Switch on the oven grill (broiler) for the last few minutes of cooking, to make sure the grissini are crispy and golden all over. Leave to cool before serving.

The grissini will keep in an airtight container in the pantry for up to 1 week.

Bagels

(HARD) MAKES: 6

A durable bread made for smearing, scattering and precariously balancing toppings onto. You'll definitely want to keep extra everything bagel seasoning on hand because, as advertised, it goes on EVERYTHING. Bagels go through both boiling (to gelatinise the starches in the crust) and baking (to cook the bread through and brown the crust) to get their signature dense and chewy crumb, sturdy enough to hold your entire breakfast.

—

300 ml (10 fl oz) warm water
2 teaspoons rice malt syrup
8 g (2½ teaspoons) instant dried yeast
500 g (1 lb 2 oz) bread flour, plus extra for dusting
1¾ teaspoons fine salt
olive oil, for greasing
60 ml (2 fl oz) aquafaba

FOR BOILING
2 tablespoons rice malt or barley malt syrup

EVERYTHING BAGEL SEASONING
2 tablespoons poppy seeds
2 tablespoons sesame seeds
4 teaspoons garlic granules
4 teaspoons onion granules
2 teaspoons caraway seeds
2 teaspoons flaky salt

In a small bowl, whisk together the warm water and rice malt syrup. Add the yeast and leave to bloom for 5 minutes.

Mix the flour and salt in the large bowl of a stand mixer with the dough hook attached. Make a well in the centre, slowly pour in the yeasty liquid and stir it through. Knead on medium speed for 5 minutes. Alternatively, lightly flour a work surface and knead vigorously by hand for 10 minutes.

Lightly oil a large bowl, then add the dough. Cover with plastic wrap and leave to rise in a warm place for 1 hour.

Lightly flour the benchtop and punch down the dough. Use a dough scraper to divide the dough into six pieces. Take one piece and pinch a bit of the edge of the dough, then drag it to the opposite side of the dough and press down. Rotate the dough and continue the process until you create a taut, smooth ball that pulls away from the bench. Lightly flour the dough, flip seam side down, and set aside on the bench (using a dough scraper if needed) while you work on the remaining pieces of dough.

Take one of the balls of dough, cup a hand around one side of the dough and push the ball from side to side, left to right and towards you to round the ball out, smooth out any seams and create tension. Act on the tension now existing between you and the bagel dough; flour the tip of your index finger, hold the dough in your other palm and poke it through the centre. Swirl your finger around the dough to create a smooth ring. Put the dough on the bench, then use both index fingers to stretch out the ring. Continue until your ring is about a third of the size of your dream bagel, or until the hole is about as wide as a golf ball. Repeat this filth with the remaining dough balls.

Transfer the bagels to individual squares of baking paper and space them out on a wide baking tray. Cover well with plastic wrap and leave to cold ferment in the fridge for 12–24 hours, until at least doubled in size. Note that once they go through the next step (boiling), they won't rise much further.

Remove the bagels from the fridge 2–3 hours ahead of boiling and baking, to let them return to room temperature.

Prepare to boil and bake the bagels. Pour 2 litres (68 fl oz) of water into a large saucepan, add the rice malt syrup and bring to a rolling boil.

Preheat the oven to 230°C (445°F).

In a wide bowl, stir together the 'everything bagel seasoning' ingredients. Pour the aquafaba into a cup.

Transfer the bagels, still on their baking paper squares, into the boiling water in small batches. After a few seconds, you'll be able to easily peel the paper away to discard. This is the best way to make sure they don't deflate or lose their smooth shape prior to the crust setting during boiling.

Boil the bagels for 30–60 seconds on each side, then remove to a wire rack to drain while you cook the next batch of bagels. The longer you boil, the chewier your bagels will be.

While they're still hot and damp, quickly splash some aquafaba over one side of the bagels, then firmly press the bagels into the seasoning to adhere. Return the bagels to the baking tray, now lined with fresh baking paper, seedy side down.

Get the bagels straight into the screaming hot oven for 20–25 minutes, flipping them over halfway through. Turn on the oven grill (broiler) for the last 2 minutes of baking and monitor carefully until the tops are golden brown and just about beginning to char.

Cool the bagels on a wire rack, then slice in half with a bread knife and crack in.

Eat your bagels fresh within 2 days, or rinse under water briefly and toast within 5 days to bring them back to life. They are best stored at room temperature in an airtight container.

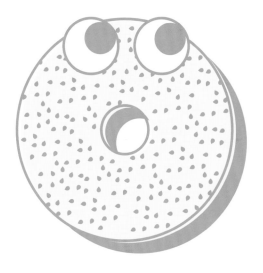

Pretzels

Pretzels

(HARD) **MAKES: 6**

Breadsticks ... but on a yoga kick. This recipe is listed as hard, not for the technique, but because of the fridge space you'll need to clear for their overnight rise. A baking soda solution is the home baker's remedy to not having the traditional (and potentially dangerous!) lye bath for the pretzels to gain their signature browning and flavour.

360 g (12½ oz) bread flour, plus extra for dusting
4 g (1 slightly heaped teaspoon) instant dried yeast
1 teaspoon fine salt
large pinch of granulated white sugar
30 g (1 oz) vegan butter
olive oil, for greasing
150 g (5½ oz) baking soda
pretzel salt or flaky salt, for sprinkling

Mix the flour, yeast, fine salt and sugar in the bowl of a stand mixer fitted with the dough hook attachment. Knead on low speed as you pour in 240 ml (8 fl oz) of water, followed by the butter, teaspoon by teaspoon. Increase the speed to medium and knead for 8–10 minutes, until the dough pulls away from the side of the bowl. Lightly oil a large bowl, add the dough and cover with plastic wrap. Leave to rise in a warm place for 1 hour, until almost doubled in size.

On a lightly floured benchtop, punch down the dough. Use a dough scraper to divide the dough into six pieces, weighing about 100 g (3½ oz) each. Working with one piece of dough at a time, pinch a piece of the edge of the dough, then drag it to the opposite side of the ball and press down. Rotate the dough and continue the process until you create a taut, smooth ball that pulls away from the bench. Lightly flour, flip seam side down, and rest under a tea towel while you continue with the remaining dough.

Flatten a ball under your palm, then use a rolling pin and your hands to roll and stretch the dough into a 10 cm × 20 cm (4 in × 8 in) rectangle. Roll from one of the long ends to make a tight and well-sealed cylinder, pressing down with your fingertips to seal together. Now use both of your palms to roll the dough into a 60–65 cm (24–26 in) rope. The ends should taper slightly, and the rope should have a slightly thicker centre. You may need to rotate through the ropes a few times to allow the gluten time to relax and stretch out fully.

To shape the pretzels, place one rope parallel to you on a wide expanse of work space. Drag the two ends towards you to form a U-shape. Cross the ends over where they meet in the centre, then cross the rope ends a second time to form a twist. ①

Drag the crossed ends up over the top of the loop and firmly press them into the pretzel base at about the 2 o'clock and 10 o'clock points. ②

Transfer the pretzels to individual squares of baking paper and space them out on a wide baking tray. Cover well with plastic wrap and leave to cold ferment in the fridge for 12–24 hours, until at least doubled in size. Note that once they go through the next step (boiling), they won't rise much further at all.

Remove the pretzels from the fridge 1 hour ahead of boiling and baking, to let them return to room temperature.

Pour 2 litres (68 fl oz) of water into a large saucepan. Add the baking soda and stir to dissolve. Bring to a rolling boil, then reduce the heat to a simmer.

Preheat the oven to 220°C (430°F).

Take this one pretzel at a time as you begin your pretzel conquest to get used to the rhythm. The pretzels are meant to be tied in knots, not you! Add a pretzel, still on its baking paper square, to the simmering water. After a few seconds, you'll be able to easily peel the paper away and discard. This is the best way to make sure the pretzel doesn't deflate or lose its knot prior to the crust setting during boiling.

Boil the pretzel for 15–20 seconds on each side, holding it under the water with a wide slotted spatula or skimmer to keep it fully submerged. Remove to a wire rack to drain and quickly sprinkle with salt while it's still hot and damp. Repeat with the remaining pretzels.

Line the baking tray with fresh baking paper or a silicone baking mat and use the spatula to return the pretzels to it.

Get them straight into the screaming hot oven for 16–22 minutes, until deep and gorgeously browned all over. Celebrate any diversity in your pretzel shapes and take them out of the oven individually as they each come to perfection, so none over-cook as the others catch up.

Cool the pretzels on a wire rack, then eat fresh and warm, ideally within 5 days, if stored properly in an airtight container in the pantry.

Crumpets

(MEDIUM) **MAKES: 6**

From giant crumps to classic crump-ettes, this batter made with sourdough discard has the perfect amount of tang to add complexity to your crumpets, compensating for the absence of cultured dairy butter. My father has been caught admitting to having a greater love for his morning crumpets than any of his actual progeny, and who can blame him?

Nothing compares to a freshly made, hand-raised sourdough crumpet still hot from being forged in the pan. Especially when the raising agent is repurposed from discarded sourdough starter. That's free yeast! The flavour is butter but better: loads of it to fry in so that the bottom remains soft enough for toasting, and then even more to feed the insatiable holes cursed with a thirst that only vegan butter can quench.

Purists can purchase crumpet rings for cooking, but you could also repurpose those old egg rings you stopped needing when you turned vegan, or grab large metal cookie cutters to make do. It's not the size or style of the crumpet ring that matters, it's how you use it.

—

220 g (8 oz) Sourdough starter (page 54)
150 g (5½ oz) plain (all-purpose) flour
90 ml (3 fl oz) plant-based milk
1 tablespoon granulated white sugar
½ teaspoon fine salt
½ rounded teaspoon baking soda
loads of vegan butter, for frying
maple syrup, to serve (optional)

In a mixing jug, whisk together the sourdough starter, flour, milk, sugar, salt and 90 ml (3 fl oz) of water until no streaks of flour remain. Cover with muslin (cheesecloth) or a tea towel and leave to rest on the bench for about 8 hours, until almost doubled in size. It doesn't need to completely double, but it'll certainly make a good crack at it. Depending on the temperature of your kitchen and the health of your starter, this time can vary.

When you're ready to proceed, whisk the baking soda with 2 tablespoons of water, then thoroughly whisk it through your batter to encourage even more bubbles. It should look like a pit of lava, lightly frothing at the prospect of good crumpets for breakfast.

Heat a wide frying pan or crepe pan over medium–low heat. Liberally grease your crumpet rings and pan with butter. Place the rings in the hot pan and add about 1 tablespoon of butter to each ring. When melted and bubbling, pour in the batter, filling each ring about 2.5 cm (1 in) high. Increase the heat slightly, cover the pan with a lid and cook the crumpets for 6–8 minutes, until the batter fills with bubbles that pop and leave canyons for butter in their place. Once the tops are no longer moist, remove the rings and add more butter to the pan. Use a spatula to flip the crumpets and cook for another 1–2 minutes.

Serve the crumpets while still warm, absolutely flooding 'em with vegan butter. (Don't be shy to drizzle maple syrup on top, too!)

If not eating within a day, freeze the crumpets in an airtight container for up to 3 months, and enjoy your entry into the sourdough crumpet club where the perfect breakfast is always as easy as popping these beauties into the toaster for the crumpteenth time.

Garlic naan

A quick and easy vegan garlic butter is the perfect dressing for naan, but you could also use toum (page 272) or confit garlic oil (page 76) for different garlic notes. Better yet, combine them to form the holy garlic trinity! I like to (blasphemously) also use Chinese-style crispy chilli oil on top, because this hearty Indian flatbread is just too perfect when every inch is coated in fat and flavour.

—

125 ml (4 fl oz) warm water
3 g (1 teaspoon) instant dried yeast
300 g (10½ oz) plain (all-purpose) flour, plus extra for dusting
1 tablespoon granulated white sugar
1 tablespoon baking powder
2 teaspoons garlic powder
2 teaspoons fine salt
60 g (2 oz) vegan yoghurt
2 tablespoons melted vegan butter, plus 90 g (3 oz) extra, for frying

NAAN TOPPING
90 g (3 oz) vegan butter
4 tablespoons finely chopped garlic
3 tablespoons finely chopped parsley
large pinch of sea salt
crispy chilli oil, for drizzling (optional; make sure it doesn't contain shrimp or anchovy!)

Combine the warm water and yeast in a small bowl and leave to bloom for 5 minutes.

In a large bowl, mix together the flour, sugar, baking powder, garlic powder and salt.

Add the yoghurt and melted butter to the yeast mixture and stir to combine, then stir the mixture into the flour. Knead for 1 minute in the bowl, until a dough ball comes together. Cover with a tea towel and leave to rise in a warm place for 1 hour.

Dust a work surface with flour, then divide the dough into six pieces. Working with one piece of dough at a time, use your hands and your fingertips to push and stretch the dough into an elongated flat and tantalisingly large naan. Cover with a tea towel and leave to rise for about 30 minutes.

Add a tablespoon of butter to a large frying pan and set over medium heat. Fry your first naan for 5 minutes on each side or until brown spots begin to appear. To avoid catastrophe when flipping, place a plate over the uncooked side, place your hand on top to secure it, then carefully flip the pan upside down to remove the naan. Slide the naan from the plate back into the pan, re-buttering the pan if needed. Rotate all six naan through this process and let them rest on paper towel to drain off some of the butter.

Meanwhile, prepare the topping. In a small saucepan, melt the butter and sauté the garlic over low heat for 10 minutes. Switch off the heat and stir in the parsley.

Brush the garlic mixture over both sides of the freshly cooked naan and sprinkle with a hearty amount of sea salt. Try splattering some crispy chilli oil over, if you dare.

The naan breads will keep for up to 1 week in an airtight container in the fridge. Reheat in the microwave, between lightly dampened paper towels, for about 30 seconds at a time.

Sweet Breads

Brioche

There's enriched dough, and then there's filthy rich dough. Brioche is of French origin, so it's no surprise there's so many animal products (eggs, milk, butter) squeezed into the dough – so much so that brioche is a bread that flirts with being a pastry. Here, aquafaba takes on the job of eggs, but you will need to use loads of vegan butter to replicate the wealth of a true brioche dough.

cooking spray, for greasing

DOUGH

180 ml (6 fl oz) plant-based milk

7 g (2 teaspoons) active dried yeast

90 ml (3 fl oz) aquafaba, plus 2 tablespoons extra for brushing

500 g (1 lb 2 oz) bread flour, plus extra for dusting

1½ teaspoons fine salt

80 g (2¾ oz) granulated white sugar

120 g (4½ oz) vegan butter, at room temperature

2 tablespoons mixed sesame seeds (if making rolls or burger buns)

FOR SWEET BRIOCHE (OPTIONAL)

80 ml (2½ fl oz) simple syrup, Rum syrup (page 249), Finger bun glaze (page 116) or Citrus syrup (page 36)

FOR SAVOURY BRIOCHE (OPTIONAL)

1 tablespoon vegan butter, melted

To make the dough, place half the milk in a microwave-safe bowl and blast in a microwave, stirring at 15-second increments, until warm. Add the yeast and leave for a few minutes, until frothing with excitement to become brioche.

Add the yeast mixture, aquafaba, flour, salt, sugar and remaining milk to the bowl of a stand mixer fitted with the dough hook. Begin kneading on slow speed for 2–3 minutes, then increase the speed to medium and knead for 5 minutes. Add the butter, tablespoon by tablespoon, over the course of another 3 minutes or so of kneading, occasionally scraping down the side of the bowl if needed. Continue to knead until the dough is smooth and just passes the windowpane test (page 52).

Cover the bowl with plastic wrap and let the dough rise in a warm spot for 1–3 hours, until doubled in size. (Alternatively, keep the covered dough in the fridge for at least 8 hours for a slow rise, and allow it to come to room temperature before proceeding.)

To make brioche loaves

Lightly mist two loaf tins, each measuring about 12 cm × 22 cm (4¾ in × 8¾ in), with cooking spray, then line with baking paper, allowing some overhang.

Use a dough scraper to split the dough into two equal balls. On a lightly floured benchtop, roll each ball into a 1 cm (½ in) thick rectangle, about 20 cm (8 in) long on the short side (nearly the length of your bread tin). From the short side, tightly roll each dough rectangle into a cylinder and use a dab of water to seal. Transfer the dough cylinders to the bread tins, seam side down. Cover with a tea towel and leave somewhere warm for another 1–2 hours of rising to the challenge, until roughly doubled in size.

Preheat the oven to 180°C (350°F).

Brush the tops of the loaves with 2 tablespoons aquafaba, then transfer to the oven and bake for about 30 minutes, until the tops are golden brown.

Allow the loaves to cool in the tin for 10 minutes, before removing and glazing with syrup (for a sweet brioche), or brushing with melted butter (for a savoury brioche), for eye-catchingly shiny loaves. Eat fresh within 3 days, or pop into the freezer to defrost on demand.

To make brioche rolls or burger buns

Line two baking trays with baking paper or silicone baking mats. Punch down the dough, then divide into 12 pieces, weighing about 80 g (2¾ oz) each. Flatten each piece into a round with your palms. Fold pieces of the edge over the top and pinch to gather them together to create a smooth ball. Flip the ball seam side down onto a very lightly floured workbench. Cup a hand around one side of the dough and push the ball from side to side, left to right and towards you to round the ball out, smooth out any seams and create tension. Repeat with the other pieces of dough, then evenly space them out on the baking trays so they don't pick territorial fights with each other as they rise. Cover with a tea towel and leave somewhere warm for another 1½–2½ hours of rising.

Preheat the oven to 180°C (350°F).

Brush the rolls with the aquafaba, then sprinkle with the sesame seeds. Bake for 20–25 minutes, until the tops are golden brown. (If you're feeling extra, brush with melted butter as they leave the oven to create a glossy look.) Allow to cool for 10 minutes before tearing off a bun and enjoying warm, cutting them in half with a bread knife to use for sandwiches or burgers.

Eat fresh within 3 days, or pop into the freezer to defrost on demand.

Brioche

Chocolate hazelnut babka

Chocolate hazelnut babka

The debate over whether cinnamon or chocolate babka reigns supreme is one we may never find peaceful resolution to. This dough creates two babkas so you can spread chocolate and hazelnut – *my* favourite! – throughout the swirls of one loaf, and opt for cinnamon in the other. Whichever filling you choose, babka is a delicious braided bread where you won't know where one part starts and the other ends. She's quirky, y'know, a real weirdough.

—

cooking spray, for
  greasing

DOUGH
180 ml (6 fl oz) warm
  plant-based milk
7 g (2 teaspoons) active
  dried yeast
90 ml (3 fl oz) aquafaba,
  plus extra for brushing
500 g (1 lb 2 oz) bread
  flour, plus extra for
  dusting
80 g (2¾ oz) granulated
  white sugar
1½ teaspoons fine salt
120 g (4½ oz) vegan
  butter, at room
  temperature
80 ml (2½ fl oz) simple
  syrup, Rum syrup
  (page 249), Finger bun
  glaze (page 116) or
  Citrus syrup (page 36)

To make the chocolate hazelnut spread, spread the hazelnuts on a baking tray and bake in a preheated 180°C (350°F) oven for 10–12 minutes, until aromatic. Remove from the oven and cover with a tea towel to steam for a few minutes. Either keep the nuts enclosed in the towel, or transfer to a metal colander, and use the towel to vigorously rub the bitter skins off. Scavenge out the skinned hazelnuts as you go, until most of the skin has been removed.

While the hazelnuts are still warm, so they release their oils more quickly, begin grinding them in a food processor. Process for a good 15 minutes or so, scraping the bowl occasionally, until the hazelnuts have formed into a hot liquidy butter. It should be smooth and not at all grainy. Blend in the cocoa powder, milk powder, if using, and salt. With the processor running, slowly add the icing sugar. The mixture will create something like a dough ball.

Add the coconut oil in small increments until you're satisfied with the consistency, noting that the final product will be slightly less runny once it has fully cooled. Store in a jar in the pantry until needed; it will keep for up to 3 months.

To make the dough, place half the milk in a microwave-safe bowl and blast in a microwave, stirring at 15-second increments, until warm. Add the yeast and leave for a few minutes, until frothing with excitement to become babka.

Add the yeast mixture, aquafaba, flour, sugar and milk to the bowl of a stand mixer fitted with the dough hook and knead on slow speed for 2 minutes. Add the salt, then increase the speed to medium and knead for 5 minutes. Add the butter, tablespoon by tablespoon, over the course of another 3 minutes or so of kneading, occasionally scraping down the side if needed, until the dough just passes the windowpane test (page 52).

Cover the bowl with plastic wrap and let the dough rise in a warm spot for 1–3 hours, until doubled in size. (Alternatively, keep the covered dough in the fridge for at least 8 hours for a slow rise, and allow it to come to room temperature before proceeding.)

Line two loaf tins, each measuring about 12 cm × 22 cm (4¾ in × 8¾ in), with baking paper, allowing some overhang. Lightly mist the tins with cooking spray, then line with more baking paper (the spray will help it stick).

CHOCOLATE HAZELNUT SPREAD
225 g (8 oz) hazelnuts
40 g (1½ oz) Dutch
   (unsweetened)
   cocoa powder
2 tablespoons soy milk
   powder (optional)
⅛ teaspoon fine salt
90 g (3 oz) icing
   (confectioners') sugar
1½ teaspoons refined
   coconut oil

CINNAMON TWIST
Use the filling from the Cinnamon scrolls (page 113) instead of the chocolate hazelnut spread to make one or both babkas.

Lightly flour a work surface. Use a dough scraper to split the dough into two equal balls, then roll each ball into a 1 cm (½ in) thick rectangle, that's 20 cm (8 in) long on the short side (nearly the length of your bread tin). Spread a generous 150 g (5½ oz) of the chocolate hazelnut spread over each rectangle, leaving a 2 cm (¾ in) border around the edges. ①

From the short side, tightly roll each rectangle into a cylinder and use a dab of water to seal the end. Use a bread knife or dough scraper to trim the ends of each cylinder, and rotate so one of the short ends is facing you. Working with one cylinder at a time, cut through the centre of the log, leaving it attached at the end furthest from you. ②

Pull the two new strands apart to form a vegan 'wishbone' shape. Spread more chocolate hazelnut spread over the naked parts of each strand. Twist each strand in position to create texture, then cross the strands over each other a few times to form a twisted dough. ③ ④

Transfer the babkas to the prepared tins, coiling each babka so that the dough fills the tins as evenly as possible. Cover with tea towels and leave them somewhere warm for another 2–3 hours, until roughly doubled in size.

Preheat the oven to 190°C (375°F). Brush the top of the babkas with the aquafaba. Bake for 30–35 minutes, until the tops are golden brown.

Allow the babkas to cool in the tins for 10 minutes, then turn out onto a wire rack and glaze with your chosen syrup for an eye-catchingly shiny loaf. Slice up, shut your agape jaw and marvel at that marble, and eat the lot within 3 days.

Challah

(MEDIUM) MAKES: 1 LOAF

Traditionally served for Jewish holidays, challah is an enriched dough similar to brioche, but one that is dairy free, as it is made using olive oil instead of butter. Egg-free challah has a rich history, too – so this braided loaf is perfect for serving on a vegan holiday table. There's six ropes in the braid, so it makes for a centrepiece you'll keep around because she ain't no challahback, girl.

—

200 ml (7 fl oz) warm water
60 ml (2 fl oz) rice malt syrup
10 g (3 teaspoons) active dried yeast
375 g (13 oz) bread flour, plus extra for dusting
1 teaspoon fine salt
60 ml (2 fl oz) olive oil or canola oil
aquafaba, for brushing
1 tablespoon poppy seeds, for sprinkling (optional)

Combine the water and rice malt syrup in a bowl, add the yeast and leave for a few minutes, until frothing with excitement to become challah.

Add the yeast mixture and flour to the bowl of a stand mixer fitted with the dough hook and knead on slow speed for 2 minutes. Add the salt, then increase the speed to medium and knead for 5 minutes. Slowly drizzle in the olive oil over the course of another 3 minutes or so of kneading, occasionally scraping down the side if needed, until the dough just passes the windowpane test (page 52).

Cover the bowl with plastic wrap and let the dough rise in a warm spot for 1–3 hours, until doubled in size. (Alternatively, keep the covered dough in the fridge for at least 8 hours for a slow rise, and allow it to come to room temperature before proceeding.)

Line a baking tray with baking paper or a silicone baking mat. Lightly flour a workbench. Punch down the dough, then divide into six pieces. Roll each piece under your palms to make six long, even strands about 30 cm (12 in) long. Connect all the strands at one end, then splay them out in front of you so you can keep track of each as you braid. Take the strand furthest to your right, lay it over the top of the two strands directly to its left, weave it under the next strand, then over the last two strands. ①

Grab the strand furthest to your right again and repeat the same step: skipping two strands, weaving under the third and skipping the last two. Continue braiding in this manner while slightly turning the dough each time until the strands have been used up. ②

Tuck the final pieces underneath, then unravel the pinched together strands at the other end of the loaf. Re-braid them neatly and tuck under as well to complete the loaf. Transfer the challah to the prepared tray, cover with a tea towel and leave somewhere warm for another 1½–2½ hours of rising, until roughly doubled in size.

Preheat the oven to 180°C (350°F). Brush the challah with aquafaba, then sprinkle poppy seeds over the top, if desired. Bake for about 30 minutes, until the top is a deep golden brown, then cool on a wire rack. If you're feeling extra, brush the top with extra oil as it leaves the oven for a glossy finish.

Eat fresh within 3 days, slicing up or tearing the braids apart to get at that soft bread inside. L'Chaim!

GET LIT
Use this dough to braid smaller rounds that can hold a candle for decorating your feasting table, using the directions in the Tsoureki recipe on page 109.

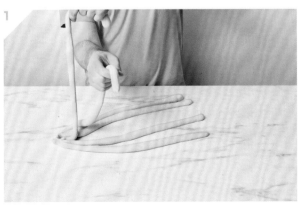

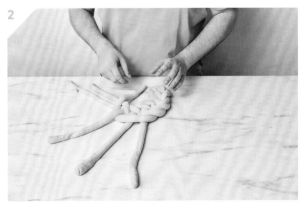

Tsoureki

A much more heavily flavoured brioche dough that on the outside looks closer to challah, tsoureki is like a hot cross bun whose older sister braided their hair before school one day. It's normally served for Easter and, as such, uses three strands in the braid to represent the holy trinity. I like to wrap the braided dough rope into a wreath that can hold a candle, to double up as the decoration, lighting and dessert for meals year round. If you can't easily get hold of mahlepi or mastic for the signature flavour, replace them with cardamom and cinnamon.

plain (all-purpose) flour
   for dusting
½ × quantity Brioche
   dough (page 100)
1 tablespoon aquafaba
50 g (1¾ oz) slivered
   almonds
80 ml (2½ fl oz) Rum
   syrup (page 249) or
   simple syrup (optional)

FLAVOUR MIX

1 tablespoon brown sugar
1½ teaspoons mahlepi
   (or ground cardamom)
1 teaspoon vegan butter
1 teaspoon vanilla bean
   paste
¼ teaspoon ground
   mastic (or ground
   cinnamon)
grated zest of 1 orange

Line two baking trays with baking paper or silicone baking mats. Combine the flavour mix ingredients in a small bowl.

On a lightly floured work surface, punch down the dough, then hand knead or use a stand mixer fitted with the dough hook to knead in the flavour mix for a few minutes, until dispersed. Divide the dough into six pieces, then leave to sit for 15 minutes to relax the gluten (and the baker!).

Roll each dough portion under your palms to make six long, even strands about 30 cm (12 in) long.

Connect three strands at one end, then splay them out in front of you, so you can keep track of each as you braid. Take the strand furthest to your left, lay it over the middle strand so it becomes the new middle strand, then bring the furthest right strand in to become the new middle strand. Continue braiding, letting the strands fight for middle position in alternating order, until you come to the end of the strands. Tuck the final pieces underneath to complete. If making a wreath, drag the ends around and adhere together to make a ring. Check the candle you'll be using and make sure there's a 3 cm (1¼ in) clearance around the width of the candle for the dough to rise, or the candle won't fit once the wreath is baked. Or, just leave it as a braided mini-log.

Repeat with the remaining three dough strands to form a second log or wreath.

Transfer the tsoureki to the prepared tray. Cover with a tea towel and leave them somewhere warm for another 1½–2½ hours of rising, until roughly doubled in size.

Preheat the oven to 180°C (350°F). Brush the tsoureki with the aquafaba, then sprinkle the slivered almonds over the top. Bake for 25–30 minutes, rotating the trays halfway through baking, until the tops are golden brown. Glaze with rum syrup as they leave the oven if you'd like to really get festive.

Cool on a wire rack. Eat warm and fresh within 3 days, or pop into the freezer to defrost on demand.

LIGHT UP THE ROOM

Ahead of guests arriving, place the tsoureki on the dining table on a nice plate, insert a candle in the centre and light. Once the conversation and candles dim, serve ice cream to accompany the tsoureki and announce that the decorations are really the dessert.

Wholemeal cinnamon fruit loaf

(MEDIUM)   **MAKES: 1 LARGE LOAF FOR TOASTING**

This makes an enormous loaf of wholesome goodness that's perfect for thick, jumbo slices that'll just barely fit into the toaster.

cooking spray, for
    greasing
70 g (2½ oz) Cinnamon
    sugar (page 198)
3 tablespoons aquafaba
200 g (7 oz) Rum-soaked
    raisins (page 156)
2 tablespoons wholemeal
    (whole-wheat) flour
vegan butter, for
    brushing and serving
1 × quantity Rum syrup
    (page 249; optional)

FRUIT DOUGH
100 ml (3½ fl oz) plant-
    based milk
14 g (5 scant teaspoons)
    instant dried yeast
300 ml (10 fl oz) warm
    water
2 tablespoons granulated
    white sugar
15 g (½ oz) vegan butter
1 teaspoon fine salt
200 g (7 oz) wholemeal
    (whole-wheat) flour
400 g (14 oz) bread flour,
    plus extra for dusting

BACK TO BASICS
Want a textbook loaf of wholemeal sandwich bread? You're in the right place. Make this recipe without adding the cinnamon sugar and raisins to the second dough portion in the rolling step. Brush with vegan butter 10 minutes after the loaf leaves the oven and you've got yourself a loaf of the good-old wholemeal faithful.

To make the dough, warm the milk in a saucepan (or with a few short blasts in a microwave) until comfortably warm to the touch, as if preparing it for a baby. Add the yeast to the milk and sit for 5 minutes to prove that it's working.

Add the warm water, yeast mixture, sugar, butter, salt and most of the wholemeal and bread flours to the bowl of a stand mixer fitted with the dough hook. Knead for 8 minutes on medium speed, then add the remaining flour, until the dough has completely pulled away from the bowl. Hooray! It'll be easier to clean now.

Spray the top of the dough with cooking spray, flip over and spray again. Cover with a tea towel and leave to rise in a warm spot, for at least 1 hour, until doubled in size.

Lightly mist a standard loaf tin with cooking spray. Place the dough on a lightly floured work surface. Press down lightly to remove air pockets, then divide in half with a dough scraper.

Knead the cinnamon sugar into one dough portion to disperse it. Roll each portion into a 20 cm × 30 cm (8 in × 12 in) rectangle, with the shorter end no wider than the length of your loaf tin. Place the cinnamon dough on top of the other piece of dough and brush the top with 1–2 tablespoons of the aquafaba.

Drain the soaked raisins, reserving the rum. Evenly scatter the raisins over the dough and sprinkle with some of the rum for good luck, before thoughtfully disposing of the remaining rum in whatever tipple you prefer. Dimple the raisins into the dough with your fingers, as you would with focaccia dough. Finish by sifting the wholemeal flour over the top.

From the short side, tightly roll the dough into a cylinder and use a dab of water (or rum, you cheeky thing!) to seal the end. Place in the tin, seam side down, and tuck the ends under. Cover with a tea towel and leave somewhere warm for another 1–2 hours of rising to the challenge, until roughly doubled in size.

Preheat the oven to 180°C (350°F). Brush the top of the loaf with the remaining aquafaba. Bake for 30–35 minutes, rotating the tin halfway through baking, until golden brown on top.

Turn the loaf out onto a wire rack to cool for 10 minutes, before brushing melted butter over the top for an eye-catchingly shiny loaf. Or, generously brush the rum syrup over the loaf, then return to the oven for another 5 minutes before turning out onto a wire rack to cool.

Eat fresh within 3 days, or slice into toast-able portions and freeze, popping the slices straight into the toaster. Slather in vegan butter before serving.

Cinnamon scrolls

EASY   MAKES: 12

Finally, endless scrolling I can get into! The crusty abomination of a cinnamon scroll I posted as my first ever vegan social media post may never leave my nightmares or the archives of the internet, but at last they get their redemption here in the softest scrolls ever, which I offer up as penance. Eggs are replaced with juicy applesauce, and the entire tray of scrolls is drowned in vegan cream, which they soak up every drop of. Oh, and the classic cream cheese glaze has been veganised, too, if you simply can't do without. Nor should you.

250 ml (8½ fl oz) plant-based milk
8 g (2½ teaspoons) instant dried yeast
100 g (3½ oz) granulated white sugar
½ teaspoon ground cardamom
80 g (2¾ oz) vegan butter, softened
90 g (3 oz) applesauce
500 g (1 lb 2 oz) plain (all-purpose) flour, plus extra for dusting
1 teaspoon fine salt
cooking spray, for greasing
160 ml (5½ fl oz) vegan cream

CINNAMON FILLING
225 g (8 oz) vegan butter, softened
200 g (7 oz) dark brown sugar
3 tablespoons ground cinnamon
1 teaspoon fine salt

CREAM CHEESE GLAZE
100 g (3½ oz) icing (confectioners') sugar
100 g (3½ oz) vegan cream cheese
50 g (1¾ oz) vegan butter
1 teaspoon natural vanilla extract

Place the milk in a microwave-safe bowl and blast in a microwave, stirring at 15-second increments, until warm. Add the yeast, sugar and cardamom and leave to bloom for a few minutes until frothy. Mix together the butter and applesauce, then stir into the yeast mixture.

Add the flour and salt to the bowl of a stand mixer fitted with the dough hook. Pour in the yeast mixture. Knead the dough for about 4 minutes on medium speed, keeping in mind it will be very sticky, even when done. (Alternatively, stir together with a wooden spoon and hand knead for 8 minutes. If needed, lightly spray the benchtop with cooking spray after the flour is used up to prevent sticking.)

Grease a large bowl with cooking spray, add the dough, then cover with a tea towel and leave to sit somewhere warm for 1 hour to double in size.

Line a lamington or brownie tin with baking paper or a silicone baking mat. Place the dough on a floured work surface, flouring the top of the dough as well. Roll the dough into a 40 cm × 60 cm (16 in × 24 in) rectangle, with the long end towards you. Evenly spread the softened butter over the top. Mix together the sugar, cinnamon and salt, then sprinkle over the dough.

From the edge closest to you, tightly roll the dough into a long tube. Use floss to cut into 12 pieces, about 7.5 cm (3 in) thick, then space them out in the prepared tin. Cover with plastic wrap and leave in the fridge overnight (8–12 hours), until considerably risen and fighting for real estate on the tray.

About 1 hour before baking, leave the scrolls and the cream on the bench to come to room temperature.

Preheat the oven to 200°C (400°F). Waterboard the scrolls with the cream, then bake for 25–30 minutes, until lovely and golden on the outside.

Whisk together the cream cheese glaze ingredients until smooth then pour the glaze over the warm scrolls. They'll keep in an airtight container for up to 2 days.

Banana bread

(EASY) **MAKES: 1 LOAF**

A good banana bread is made with bananas so over-ripened that they're ready for their last rites. Don't call a priest though! That cloying sweetness contrasted with earthy-bitter walnuts and tangy vegan sour cream in the batter will resurrect even the most borderline-necrotic piece of fruit into a loaf worthy of ascension to your lips.

cooking spray, for greasing
4 very ripe bananas (420 g/15 oz peeled flesh)
120 g (4½ oz) vegan sour cream or vegan Greek-style yoghurt
120 g (4½ oz) vegan butter
100 g (3½ oz) brown sugar, plus extra for sprinkling
100 g (3½ oz) granulated white sugar
1 teaspoon natural vanilla extract
250 g (9 oz) plain (all-purpose) flour
2 teaspoons baking powder
1 teaspoon ground cinnamon
⅔ teaspoon sea salt
60 g (2 oz) small walnut pieces

Preheat the oven to 170°C (340°F). Lightly grease a 24 cm × 13 cm × 6.5 cm (9½ in × 5 in × 2½ in) loaf tin with cooking spray.

Say a few brief words of respect about the bananas, then mash them in a bowl with a fork. Stir in the sour cream.

Using a large mixing bowl and a hand-held electric mixer, or a stand mixer fitted with the paddle attachment, cream together the butter, sugars and vanilla for 3 minutes. With the mixer running, pour in the banana mixture and mix for another minute.

In a separate bowl, mix together the flour, baking powder, cinnamon, salt and walnuts, then stir through the batter to only just combine – don't overmix (a Danish dough whisk is great for this). The batter should be fluffy, with no dry parts.

Pour the mixture into the prepared tin and smooth the top with the back of a spoon. Bake for 60–70 minutes, until a skewer inserted in the middle of the bread comes out clean.

Turn the banana bread out onto a wire rack and allow to cool. Eat, digest and crave more, then make another loaf and enjoy both loaves for up to 1 week out of the fridge, or a few months if frozen in slices.

Toast and heap on vegan butter while still warm, or slather with your favourite breakfast spreads.

SLICE IT UP NICE
For easy slicing, freeze the bread for 1 hour, then turn the bread on its side on a chopping board and slice into hearty, thick pieces using a bread knife.

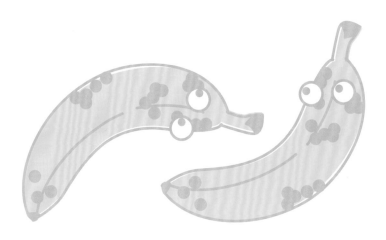

THE VEGAN BAKER

Finger buns

(EASY) MAKES: 6

The best kind of bun is a fingered one. These long buns defy convention, and instead read like a sweet hot dog bun. For Kiwi and Aussie kids, the garish pink icing smeared along the top and dipped in coconut is an after-school siren for the sugar rush that'll get you through to dinnertime. The sultanas in the dough are there just so you can say yes when Mum asks if you ate some fruit today.

160 ml (5½ fl oz) plant-based milk

7 g (2 teaspoons) instant dried yeast

250 g (9 oz) bread flour, plus extra for dusting

1 teaspoon baking powder

½ teaspoon fine salt

30 g (1 oz) vegan butter, softened

25 g (1 oz) caster (superfine) sugar

cooking spray, for greasing

40 g (1½ oz) sultanas (golden raisins)

2 tablespoons desiccated coconut

FINGER BUN ICING

120 g (4½ oz) icing (confectioners') sugar, sifted

2 teaspoons vegan butter, melted

1 teaspoon plant-based milk

few drops vegan red food colouring

FINGER BUN GLAZE

1 tablespoon caster (superfine) sugar

sprinkle of agar agar powder

1 tablespoon boiling water

Place the milk in a microwave-safe bowl and blast in a microwave, stirring at 15-second increments, until warm. Add the yeast and leave to bloom for a few minutes until frothy.

Add the yeast mixture, flour, baking powder, salt, butter and sugar to the bowl of a stand mixer fitted with the dough hook. Knead on medium speed for 10 minutes to develop the gluten.

Remove the dough from the bowl, oil the bowl with cooking spray, then place the dough back in. Cover with plastic wrap and leave to rise in a warm spot for 1–3 hours, until doubled in size.

Spray an 18 cm × 28 cm (7 in × 11 in) baking tray with cooking spray. Punch down the dough in the bowl and toss in the sultanas. Knead by hand just enough to disperse the sultanas throughout. Divide the dough into six pieces, weighing about 85 g (3 oz) each.

Roll each dough portion on a lightly floured work surface under your palms to make 15 cm (6 in) long fingers that are even in width, and taper only very slightly at the ends. Space the dough fingers evenly apart on the baking tray, so they fill the tray. Cover with a tea towel and leave to rise for another 1 hour in a warm spot, until the fingers are touching each other.

Preheat the oven to 220°C (430°F). Bake the buns for 8–12 minutes, until evenly golden brown, covering with foil if they are browning too quickly. Move to a wire rack to cool. (It's important that the buns are totally chilled out before approaching with any toppings, or they'll buck them off.)

Meanwhile, to make the icing, sift the icing sugar into a bowl, then whisk in the remaining ingredients until smooth. Transfer to the freezer to get cold.

To make the glaze, whisk together the sugar and agar agar powder very well, then stir in the boiling water. Brush the glaze over the cooled finger buns, then let the glaze set.

Spoon the icing in an even strip over the tops of the glazed buns. Use your finger to smooth out the icing, then sprinkle the coconut over the top.

Keep the buns in an airtight container in the pantry and give yourself the finger as much as you want for up to 3 days.

Schiacciata all'uva

(EASY)   **MAKES: 1 GIANT FLATBREAD TO SHARE, OR 2 MEDIUM**

Schiacciata (ski-a-chi-atta), named for the squashing of the dough before baking, is an Italian flatbread-like focaccia – or to be more precise, like two focaccias baked atop each other, with grapes sandwiched inside. I use a medley of white and black grapes, but this version is all about celebrating when grapes are in season, so use what's local and fresh. Pips in the grapes are okay, too! What you'll end up with feels like a rustic raisin loaf that is equally at home as a breakfast, after-dinner treat or even paired with really good vegan cheeses. If you prefer, split this recipe across two smaller baking trays: one for you and one for a mate.

9 g (2¾ teaspoons)
   active dried yeast
210 ml (7 fl oz) warm
   water
375 g (13 oz) bread flour,
   plus extra for dusting
80 g (2¾ oz) granulated
   white sugar, plus
   50 g (1¾ oz) extra for
   sprinkling
1¼ teaspoons sea salt
3½ tablespoons olive oil,
   plus extra for greasing
   and drizzling
1 kg (2 lb 3 oz) grapes
1 rosemary sprig, plus
   2 scant tablespoons
   very finely chopped
   rosemary leaves
flaky salt, to serve
icing (confectioners')
   sugar, for dusting
   (optional)

Add the yeast and warm water to a large bowl with a pinch of the flour, then leave for a few minutes to get frothy.

Add the yeast mixture, flour, 80 g (2¾ oz) of sugar and the salt to the bowl of a stand mixer fitted with the dough hook. Knead for 4–5 minutes, then slowly pour in 1½ tablespoons of the olive oil and knead for another 3 minutes. Fashion the dough into a ball and place in a large lightly oiled bowl. Leave to rise somewhere warm for 2 hours or until tripled in size.

Pour the remaining 2 tablespoons of oil onto a very large baking tray to coat it. Place the grapes in a large bowl and press down with your hands to slightly squish them.

Punch down the dough to release the air bubbles, then turn out onto a lightly floured work surface. Cut the dough in half. Roll out one portion into a 20 cm × 45 cm (8 in × 18 in) oval, then spread it out on the baking tray. Evenly sprinkle half of the 50 g (1¾ oz) of sugar and half the grapes over the dough, leaving a 2 cm (¾ in) border. Dip the rosemary sprig in the olive oil in the baking tray to brush the dough border.

Roll out the remaining dough in the same fashion, then place it over the grape-covered dough. Pull the border of the bottom dough up over the edges and press down to seal the filling. Arrange the remaining grapes over the top, drizzle with extra olive oil and scatter with the remaining sugar. Artfully place the chopped rosemary among the grapes. Cover with plastic wrap and leave to rise for another 1 hour somewhere warm.

ALL'UVA PUDDING!
Take a schiacciata that's a few days old and slice into chunks. Add to a baking dish, pour brandy-spiked vegan custard over the top and bake until lightly golden, to make a particularly breathtaking bread and butter pudding.

Preheat the oven to 180°C (350°F). Just before baking, use your fingertips to prod the dough and squash it down. Bake for 45–50 minutes, until golden on top.

Scatter flaky salt over the top of the schiacciata and allow to cool fully, so the grapes get nice and jammy. You may like to dust icing sugar over the top.

Cut into slices and eat fresh, or toasted like a rustic raisin loaf. It is best eaten on the day of baking.

Anpan

MAKES: 12

I have a lot to thank anpan for. When I was a young exchange student in Japan, the only dish I could trust was truly vegetarian were these buns stuffed with a sweet paste made from adzuki beans. I might not be here without anpan's ubiquity as a go-to snack in Japan, which are so popular they just might be the only bread in the world with a dedicated superhero. That's Japan for you! In this naturally sweet milkbread dough, any doubts you might have about the idea of beans in dessert will be banished on first nibble. You'll find the paste in Asian or Japanese supermarkets; look for either koshian (fine paste) or tsubuan (coarse paste). If you can, buy the ones that come in a tube for easy filling.

1 × quantity Shokupan
 dough (page 80)
500 g (1 lb 2 oz) adzuki
 paste (Japanese red
 bean paste)
black sesame seeds, for
 topping
vegan butter, for
 brushing
coarse salt, for topping

Prepare the shokupan dough as directed on page 80.

Line a baking tray with baking paper or a silicone baking mat. Divide the dough into 12 balls, weighing about 55 g (2 oz) each. Press one between your palms, then scoop 1 tablespoon of the bean paste into the centre of the dough. Make a letter fold by folding one side into the centre, followed by the opposite side. Rotate 90 degrees and roll up tightly, then pinch the seams together. Roll and shape the ball between your palms to smooth it out. Place on the prepared tray and repeat with the remaining dough. Cover with a tea towel and leave to rise for 1 hour in a warm spot.

Preheat the oven to 180°C (350°F).

Dab a small amount of water on the very top of the risen buns and sprinkle with a few sesame seeds. Bake for 16–18 minutes, until golden brown. Transfer to a wire rack to cool.

In a microwave, soften (don't melt!) a small amount of butter and liberally brush it over the hot buns for extra-shiny anpan. Sprinkle salt on top.

Eat warm after a 10-minute rest – or rest safe knowing your milkbread-based dough will buy you a few days before the anpan begin to seem stale.

Melonpan

Soft milkbread rolls that come with a cookie crust on top! These ones have matcha powder added to the cookie crust for colour and extra flavour, but if it's not to your taste, just leave it out. Cut the rolls open and add a scoop of vegan ice cream (vanilla, coconut, mango or matcha-flavoured) for a texture experience you won't forget.

—

1 × quantity Shokupan
  dough (page 80)
2 tablespoons caster
  (superfine) sugar
plain (all-purpose) flour,
  for dusting

COOKIE CRUST
100 g (3½ oz) granulated
  white sugar
50 g (1¾ oz) vegan butter
  or vegan shortening
150 g (5½ oz) plain
  (all-purpose) flour
  or 00 flour
2 teaspoons matcha
  powder
½ teaspoon baking
  powder
½ teaspoon fine salt
60 ml (2 fl oz) plant-based
  milk or water

Prepare the shokupan dough as directed on page 80.

To make the cookie crust, using a large mixing bowl and a hand-held electric mixer, or a stand mixer fitted with the paddle attachment, cream together the sugar and butter for 2 minutes or until well combined. Sift in the flour, matcha powder, baking powder and salt and continue to beat together. Pour in some of the milk and use your hands to briefly knead until a homogenous dough ball comes together. You may need more or less milk than directed – just enough to bring the dough together. Cover with plastic wrap and refrigerate for 2 hours or until fully chilled.

Line a baking tray with baking paper or a silicone baking mat. Divide the dough into eight balls about 80 g (2¾ oz) in weight each. Press one between your palms. Make a letter fold by folding one side into the centre, followed by the opposite side. Rotate the dough 90 degrees and roll up tightly, then pinch the seams together. Roll and shape the ball between your palms to smooth it out. Flatten very slightly, then place on the prepared tray and repeat with the remaining dough.

Spread the caster sugar on a plate. On a well-floured benchtop, roll the cookie crust dough out until 5 mm (¼ in) thick. Cut out eight rounds using a 10 cm (4 in) cookie cutter. Place a dough ball in the centre of each round, then fold the cookie crust dough around, to nearly meet on the other side. Round out the covered ball with your hands. Dip the cookie-crusted parts in the caster sugar, then flip back onto the baking tray, with the cookie crust on top.

Taking care to not slice through the layers, use a dough scraper to press a diamond grid into the top of each melonpan. Cover with a tea towel and leave to rise in a warm spot for another hour or so, until almost doubled in size.

Preheat the oven to 175°C (345°F).

Bake the melonpan for about 20 minutes, until beginning to brown on top. Transfer to a wire rack to cool and eat within 3 days, storing them in an airtight container in the pantry. Cut them half and add a scoop of your fave vegan ice cream, and it's turtles all the way down.

Anpan

Melonpan

Coconut scones

EASY   MAKES: 6

It's hard to stand out in a country where everyone's grandmother has an innate knack for turning out the perfect scone, but my nana's scones are infamous for being simply the better among the best. Betty's unique step, honed over thousands of morning teas, is introducing a resting period before the scones hit the oven. Even without dairy, this update to her classic method will have you making these absolutely smashing jam and cream delivery vehicles with ease.

—

220 g (8 oz) plain (all-purpose) flour, sifted, plus extra for dusting
50 g (1¾ oz) vegan butter
4 teaspoons baking powder
1 tablespoon caster (superfine) sugar
pinch of sea salt
100 g (3½ oz) coconut yoghurt
50 ml (1¾ fl oz) vegan cream, plus extra for brushing
1 teaspoon white vinegar or lemon juice

TO SERVE
your favourite jam
whipped vegan cream

Add the flour, butter, baking powder, sugar and salt to a food processor and pulse until the butter is finely distributed. Tip into a bowl and make a well in the centre.

In a microwave-safe bowl, whisk together the coconut yoghurt, cream and vinegar. Blast in the microwave for 45 seconds until the mixture is very warm.

Slowly pour the warm liquid into the well of the dry ingredients, in a slow, thin stream, using a spatula or dough scraper to fold in the liquid.

Turn the dough out onto a work surface and gently knead together just until it forms a fluffy dough. (Using warm liquid makes it easier to handle, before it cools into a stiff dough.)

Very lightly flour the bench (with a mere wafting!) if needed, then tenderly pat the dough into a rough round about 2.5 cm (1 in) thick. Don't pat too hard! The more scarcely held together the dough, the better your scones will be.

Use a sturdy wine glass, mug or cookie cutter about 6 cm (2½ in) in diameter to cut out the scones. Press down firmly without twisting. Pull away the dough on the outside of the scones like a sculptor removing clay to reveal their vision. Bunch together the remaining dough and cut again to total six scones. You might even get seven if the scone gods look favourably upon you!

Very scarcely cover the tops and bottoms with flour, and flip so the pretty side is on top. Cover the scones with a tea towel and allow to rest for 30 minutes to calm down.

Preheat the oven to 200°C (400°F). Place a baking tray inside to heat up.

Brush the top of the scones with extra cream. Bake for about 12 minutes, checking from 10 minutes, until they're getting nice and golden.

Pull them out of the oven, leave them on the baking tray and throw a tea towel over them. After a 10-minute cooling session, slice them in half with a butter knife and serve immediately, with jam and cream! Give your gorgeous scones the respect they deserve by eating them fresh, within a day.

Double-choc hot cross buns

(MEDIUM)   **MAKES: 12**

These buns aren't just cross. They're positively seething. With double chocolate flavouring, sourdough starter to raise the dough, and totally vegan the whole way through, there's not a thing that's traditional about 'em. And given that supermarkets have been making hot cross buns earlier each year until they're no longer just an Easter treat anymore, you don't need to feel weird about making these year round.

—

cooking spray, for
    greasing
vegan cream, for
    brushing
Citrus syrup (page 36),
    for brushing

HOT CROSS BUN DOUGH
250 ml (8½ fl oz) plant-
    based milk
150 g (5½ oz) Sourdough
    starter, at peak
    (page 54)
100 g (3½ oz) granulated
    white sugar
480 g (1 lb 1 oz) bread
    flour
35 g (1¼ oz) Dutch
    (unsweetened)
    cocoa powder
1½ teaspoons psyllium
    husk powder
1 teaspoon sea salt
80 g (2¾ oz) vegan butter
125 g (4½ oz) vegan dark
    chocolate (preferably
    one with nuts), roughly
    chopped

CROSS PASTE
60 g (2 oz) plain
    (all-purpose) flour
2 teaspoons neutral-
    flavoured oil

Warm the milk in a saucepan over low heat to the temperature of a room in a hot and sunny holiday house, then add it with the starter and sugar to the bowl of a stand mixer fitted with the dough hook. Stir together the flour, cocoa powder, psyllium husk powder and salt and dump it on top.

Begin kneading on medium speed for 5 minutes. Add the butter, tablespoon by tablespoon, over the course of another 3 minutes or so of kneading, occasionally scraping down the side if needed. Leave the dough to knead for a total of 18 minutes, until it is the rough consistency of playdough. During the last minute, add the chocolate chunks to the dough so that they disperse.

Lightly mist a rectangular baking tray with cooking spray, then line with baking paper (the spray will help it stick).

Move the dough to an unfloured workbench and knead by hand a few times to form a ball. Now smoosh it! Divide the flattened ball into 12 pieces. Press one of the portions into a rough square, then make a letter fold by folding one side into the centre, followed by the opposite side. Rotate 90 degrees and roll up tightly. Pinch together the seams, then roll and shape the ball between your palms.

Cup the bun in one hand and squeeze gently between your palm and fingertips, pressing down on top with your other hand, to square it off. Place on the prepared tray and repeat with the remaining dough portions, evenly spacing them out. Once done, press them all down slightly to fill in any glaring gaps. Seal tightly with plastic wrap and rest in the fridge overnight (8–12 hours). Remove from the fridge to a warm location for 2–4 hours, until doubled in size.

Preheat the oven to 230°C (445°F). Whisk the paste ingredients and about 60 ml (2 fl oz) of water in a small cup until smooth and pipeable. Transfer to a zip-lock bag and seal shut. Snip a small hole in one of the bottom corners. Use your impromptu piping (icing) bag to pipe a cross on top of each bun, then brush generously with the cream.

Reduce the oven temperature to 180°C (350°F). Bake the buns for 22–25 minutes. A skewer inserted should come out clean, but watch out for chunks of delightfully melted chocolate, which may deceive you, so check in a few spots.

Brush the hot (cross) buns with citrus syrup, then cool slightly on a wire rack. Each bun should tear off cooperatively and send you straight to heaven. Keep the buns in an airtight container in the pantry for up to 3 days, after which time they will be unable to be resurrected.

Orange & poppyseed muffins

It's the low-waste dessert for wide waists. Using up just about every bit of citrus fruit means there'll be no left-over crumbs to be found on plates, either. Sourdough discard without a home can rest easy for it has a zesty refuge right here. The candied orange zest and citrus syrup are the secret to packing big flavour into these glorious muffins.

—

25 g (1 oz) semolina, for sprinkling
275 g (9½ oz) plain (all-purpose) flour
1 teaspoon baking powder
½ teaspoon fine salt
2 tablespoons poppy seeds, plus extra for sprinkling
100 g (3½ oz) vegan butter, softened
220 g (8 oz) Sourdough starter discard (page 54)
120 ml (4 fl oz) soy milk
180 ml (6 fl oz) Citrus syrup (page 36), plus extra for brushing
60 ml (2 fl oz) orange juice or water
40 g (1½ oz) Candied orange zest (page 36), finely chopped, plus extra for sprinkling

Preheat the oven to 175°C (345°F). Lightly grease a 12-hole muffin tin. Sprinkle the semolina into each muffin hole.

In a large bowl, mix together the flour, baking powder, salt and poppy seeds.

Whisk together the butter, sourdough starter discard, milk, citrus syrup and orange juice. Pour the mixture into the flour mixture, add the candied orange zest and fold through until just combined.

Scoop just over 2 tablespoons of batter into each muffin hole. Smooth the tops and add an extra sprinkle of poppyseeds and candied orange zest. Bake for 22–25 minutes, until a skewer inserted in the middle of a muffin comes out clean. While still warm, brush a generous amount of extra syrup over the muffins.

The muffins will keep in an airtight container in the pantry for up to 5 days.

DOUBLE WHAMMY
Pour the batter into a 24-hole mini-muffin tin, bake for only 10–13 minutes, and you'll get double the muffins in half the time!

Jumbo blueberry muffins

(EASY) **MAKES: 6 HUGE MUFFINS**

Sad little homemade versions ain't got muffin' on these jumbo, juicy blueberry beauties. They're made cafe-style, with a secret ingredient: ground coriander. Surprisingly, blueberries and coriander seeds share many flavour compounds, so the finely ground powder is there to help the blueberries taste more like themselves! Using both fresh *and* frozen blueberries in these muffins offers up a medley of blueberry textures, flavour and maximum satisfaction!

375 g (13 oz) plain (all-purpose) flour, plus 20 g (¾ oz) extra
175 g (6 oz) granulated white sugar
3¼ teaspoons baking powder
¾ teaspoon fine salt
240 ml (8 fl oz) plant-based milk
100 g (3½ oz) vegan sour cream or vegan Greek-style yoghurt
zest of 1 lemon, plus 1 tablespoon juice
60 ml (2 fl oz) olive oil
1½ teaspoons natural vanilla extract
170 g (6 oz) fresh blueberries (see Tip)
170 g (6 oz) frozen blueberries
¾ teaspoon ground coriander
icing (confectioners') sugar, for dusting (optional)

Preheat the oven to 220°C (430°F). Lightly grease a large six-hole muffin tin.

In a large bowl, mix together the flour, sugar, baking powder and salt.

In another bowl, whisk together the milk, sour cream, lemon zest and juice, olive oil and vanilla. Pour the mixture into the flour mixture and fold through until just combined.

Mash the fresh blueberries in a bowl, then add the frozen blueberries, coriander and extra flour. Toss to coat the berries, then fold them through the batter until dispersed.

Divide the batter among the muffin holes. Smooth the tops with the back of a spoon as best you can, as they should be slightly overfilled. I like to make sure a few blueberries are peeking out the top.

Reduce the oven temperature to 180°C (350°F) and slide the muffins into the oven. Bake for 25–30 minutes, until a skewer inserted in the middle of a muffin comes out clean.

Cool the muffins in the tin for a few minutes, then transfer to a wire rack to cool fully. Once cooled, you may like to dust icing sugar over your muffins so they look like ones you'd pluck from a cafe window.

The muffins will keep in an airtight container for up to 5 days. They won't just go with your morning coffee, they'll eclipse it.

BLUEBERRY BLUES?
If you can't get fresh blueberries, just use a double quantity of frozen ones. Fully thaw half of them, then mash before mixing them through the batter.

Pastries

Croissants

(HARD) **MAKES: 8**

This is a project, but a glorious one. Croissant-making isn't a fleeting impulse, it's a lifestyle choice. One that invites you to take your time with a recipe that can take up to three days (*oui! Trois jours!*) before bearing its heavenly fruit. This behemoth of baking is just that, because croissants combine the perfection demanded by laminating fat with introducing yeast to make the dough swell up in a honeycomb-style crumb.

The key is keeping the pastry – and specifically, the fat in it – as cold as possible to preserve the individual layers as the folding steps happen. That means emerging at night like a raccoon, baking these in the cool months, switching on the air conditioner in the hot months, and anything that helps the dough stay cold. Your best bet – hence the agonising amount of wait time – is to rest the dough in the fridge between every action, which also serves the dual purpose of giving the gluten in the flour time to relax between rolls.

Every seemingly bewilderingly specific step is for good reason, to turn out perfect pastry. Most of the recipe time, thankfully, is passive. Planning ahead means you can use the wide stretches of rest time to make croissants alongside all sorts of other things while you're already in the kitchen. As an example, were you to make the dough before bed tonight, you could then expect to have fresh croissants for breakfast the morning after tomorrow! You can also start to plan your victory tour, because mastering a homemade vegan croissant will give you bragging rights for life.

—

plain (all-purpose) flour, for dusting
2 tablespoons vegan cream or plant-based milk, for brushing

DÉTREMPE
240 ml (8 fl oz) warm almond milk
14 g (5 scant teaspoons) active dried yeast
500 g (1 lb 2 oz) bread flour
40 g (1½ oz) granulated white sugar
2 teaspoons fine salt
50 g (1¾ oz) vegan block butter, cut into cubes
110 ml (4 fl oz) aquafaba

1 Start with the détrempe (dough). Place the warm milk in a bowl and add the yeast to get ready for a long day at work, sitting in a bowl for a few minutes until frothy. Add the flour, sugar, salt and butter to the bowl of a stand mixer fitted with the paddle attachment. Mix on medium speed for 1–2 minutes, until the mixture is finely distributed into crumbs. Add the aquafaba to the milk mixture, then slowly pour into the bowl as the mixer runs. When the dough comes together, switch to the dough hook attachment and knead for another 5 minutes. Wrap the dough in plastic wrap so that it is sealed, but not too tightly, as it will begin rising in the fridge. Leave to rest in the fridge for 6–12 hours.

2 Prepare the beurrage (butter). Spread a sheet of baking paper over a large work surface that you can easily roll the dough out on later. Place the block of cold butter on top, and sandwich it between another sheet of baking paper. Use a rolling pin to gently bash and flatten the butter. Using a sharp knife, trim the edges to form a smooth 15 cm (6 in) square. Add the excess butter back on top, sandwich again between baking paper and beat the butter into the square, so it is nice and even. Move to the next step ONLY when the beurrage has had at least 1 hour to collect itself in the fridge.

BEURRAGE
350 g (12½ oz) fridge-cold
vegan block butter

3 Sprinkle flour over your benchtop. Unwrap the chilled dough, then roll it out into a 20 cm (8 in) square. Score a square the same size as the beurrage in the centre of the dough, then use a dough scraper to cut lines from each corner of the square to the outer edge of the dough. Leaving the centre square intact, roll out the dough edges until they are large enough to fold over the centre square. Place the unwrapped cold butter block in the centre and fold each of the edges over the top, securely sealing the butter payload inside. Flip the dough over. Press or lightly beat all along the length of the dough with a rolling pin to squash it down and secure the layers. Wrap in plastic wrap and return to the fridge for 1 hour.

4 Flour the benchtop again, ready to begin your first tour of the dough. You'll need to complete three tours, each consisting of one letter fold. Unless your kitchen is really cold, completely chill the dough for 1 hour in the fridge or freezer between each tour, aiming to keep the dough at all times below 10°C (50°F). Use a pastry brush to dust excess flour from the pastry as you go, to keep an even dusting as you roll. If you're more of a visual person, turn to page 47 for a photographic guide to your laminating dough journey.

5 Working either away from or towards you – not side to side – begin by pressing the rolling pin along the length of the dough. Repeat by pressing down the spaces left between the rolling pin indentations, to flatten the whole thing, which will evenly begin to lengthen the dough in one direction. Check that both sides of the dough are adequately floured, then roll the dough carefully back and forth to give you more space to complete a fold. The more precise and neat you are at forming this rectangle and performing the first fold, the better your internal structure will be.

6 Use a pastry brush to dust off excess flour, then give the dough a quarter turn so the long side is facing you. (If at any point the dough tears or butter is exposed, dust flour into the spot to 'repair' it, then return the dough to the fridge for at least 1 hour before proceeding.) Now perform the first letter fold. Fold the bottom third of the dough over, then fold the top third over this, as though you needed to fit the dough into an envelope. Quelle surprise: you should still use a pastry brush to dust off excess flour! With the end of the rolling pin, tap lightly and evenly all over the top of the dough to secure the layers, completing the tour of the dough. Cover in plastic wrap and get the dough straight back in the fridge for at least 1 hour to cool back down.

7 Repeat steps 5 and 6 twice more to complete three full tours.

8 Complete a final dusting off of any excess flour, tap the top of the dough with the rolling pin to slightly lengthen, trim the very outer folded edges with a pizza cutter – and then the dough is finally ready … tomorrow! Cover in plastic wrap and refrigerate for at least 2 hours, or even overnight, as yet another test of your patience.

9 Return the dough to the bench. Press the rolling pin along the length of the dough. Repeat for the spaces left between. Throughout this process, generously pour flour over the dough several times, dusting off just about completely. Now roll the dough in all directions into about a 45 cm × 60 cm (18 in × 24 in) rectangle, 5 mm (¼ in) thick. Flip the dough regularly and re-flour as you do so, using your forearm to flip the dough over and guide it back to the benchtop when it is getting thin and large. Rest the dough for 5 minutes before proceeding.

NOTES:

To stave off forgetfulness, you can use the end of your rolling pin to make light indentations in the direction of the new top of the dough (the edge furthest from you) so you remember which way to roll for the next fold: 'against the grain' of the direction you folded the dough in. Rotating the dough between folds is important to achieve the 'honeycomb' crumb inside the croissants. Make one, then two, then three indentations, corresponding with which number fold you've just completed, for when you inevitably forget that, too.

10 Use a pizza cutter to trim the dough edges, then divide the dough in half lengthways. Mark off small cuts, 10 cm (4 in) apart, along one edge of each dough half – then do the same on the other side, but mark in between the first cuts. Using these points as a guide, cut diagonally across the dough to make long triangles. Gently pull the edges out to make them even. ①

11 Line two baking trays with baking paper or silicone baking mats. Form the croissants. With the pizza cutter, make a small incision on the fat end of a dough triangle. ②

12 Gently stretch apart the two edges to form an adorable little Eiffel Tower! Each tip of your tower will be visible as the outside edges of your croissants, so go easy to preserve the lamination as much as possible while doing this step. ③

13 Roll up each side of the tower's base to meet at the end of the incision, then use your palm to gently begin rolling the croissant up. You want to be firm, but not too tight in the roll, so the layers have room to rise. Use your hand or a rolling pin to hold the thinner end of the tower and gently pull towards you to stretch out the pastry as you roll it up. ④

14 When you come to the top of the tower, lightly pinch the top and roll the croissant over to adhere it on. (A dab of water can help if needed to reinforce it!) Position the croissant on a baking tray, with the tip side down. Drag the edges around to form a crescent shape. Repeat until you've used up all the croissant dough, making sure they're generously spaced out on the tray. (If you want to freeze some or all of the croissants for later, do so now.)

15 I'm so sorry to say, you're not done yet. Cover the croissants with plastic wrap and allow to rise, at a room temperature no higher than 25°C (77°F), for 3–12 hours, until ballooned out and almost doubled in size. The rising time will vary depending on your home conditions, so check hourly during your first attempt, and remember that future croissant endeavours should be fairly consistent with how long that takes. When the croissants are ready for baking, you should be able to see the separate layers between the risen dough, when looking at the sides of the croissants.

16 Preheat the oven to 200°C (400°F) and clear it of other baking trays. Brush the top of the croissants with cream or milk, trying to avoid the laminated edges of the croissants. Place the croissants in the oven, reduce the temperature to 180°C (350°F) and bake for 25–30 minutes, until gorgeously golden, rotating the trays halfway through cooking, brushing extra cream or milk on any spots that aren't browning fast enough and monitoring closely towards the end (smaller croissants may need to be removed from the 15-minute mark).

17 Remove from the oven and leave to cool for 10 minutes on the trays, then move to wire racks to cool fully before slicing, so the crumb can set properly. Félicitations, c'est la fin! Eat within 2 days, or use old croissants to make almond croissants (see opposite).

ALMOND CROISSANTS:
Repurpose croissants that have passed the two-day event horizon of freshness by halving them, smearing Crème d'amande (page 246) in the middle and closing them up again. Dunk the croissants in Rum syrup (page 249). Smear a small amount of crème d'amande on top of each croissant, and press flaked almonds on top. Resuscitate in a preheated 160°C (320°F) oven for 20–25 minutes, turning on the oven grill (broiler) for the last few minutes, until the almonds are gorgeously toasted.

Croissants

Cruffins

Almond cruffins

(HARD) **MAKES: 10**

Invented only recently in Melbourne by Kate Reid of Lune Croissanterie, cruffins are a croissant-muffin hybrid phenomenon in which fresh creams are piped into the top of croissant dough. Even though every morsel of a well-made cruffin is already a celebration on its own, this recipe is flavoured with crème d'amande, a classic French bakery cream designed to be baked into pastries – making it the perfect use for a slightly stale cruffin that could use a second bake anyway. This recipe asks for your commitment and quality time to prepare, but promises sensory delights like no other.

—

1 × quantity Croissant
  dough (page 134)
plain (all-purpose) flour,
  for dusting
2 tablespoons vegan
  cream or plant-based
  milk, for brushing
60 ml (2 fl oz) Rum syrup
  (page 249)
1 × quantity Crème
  d'amande (page 246,
  chilled for at least
  1 hour
30 g (1 oz) slivered
  almonds

Prepare the croissant recipe as directed on pages 134–35, to the end of step 8.

Flour your benchtop and rolling pin, and place the dough on the bench. Press the rolling pin along the length of the dough. Make a second pass of the rolling pin, pressing down the ridges left between the rolling pin indentations, which will evenly begin to elongate the dough in one direction. Throughout this process, generously pour flour over the dough several times, dusting off just about completely. Now roll the dough in all directions into a 40 cm × 70 cm (16 in × 28 in) rectangle, 5 mm (¼ in) thick. Flip the dough regularly and re-flour as you do so, using your forearm to flip the dough over and guide it back to the benchtop when it is getting thin and large. Fully dust off with a pastry brush. Rest the dough for 5 minutes before proceeding.

Lightly grease ten holes of two six-hole muffin tins. Use a pizza cutter to trim the dough edges, reserving the offcuts. Divide the dough into thirds lengthways. Cut each third into 15 equal-sized strips. Lay a strip in front of you, add another strip overlapping by 1.5 cm (½ in), then a third overlapping the same sway. ①

Starting from the bottom strip of dough, roll up the pastry (firmly but not too tightly) into a swirly round. As the roll comes to the end of the first strip, stretch the end out and tuck under the cruffin. Do the same for the second end, and lay it over the first end piece. Stretch out the third end, wrap it under and tuck it in. You should have a swirly, open top and sealed pastry bottom. ②

Place the cruffin in the muffin tin and repeat with the remaining strips to make 10 cruffins. Dip your finger into flour and press into the centre of each coil, to make an indentation. Jiggle your finger to loosen the layers so they have more stretching room.

Stretch out the dough offcuts left over from trimming the dough rectangle and wrap them around the cruffins. Cover the cruffins with plastic wrap and allow to rise, at a room temperature no higher than 25°C (77°F), for 3–12 hours, until they've made a good attempt at doubling in size. The rising time will vary depending on your home conditions, so check hourly during your first attempt, and remember that future cruffin endeavours should be fairly consistent with how long that takes.

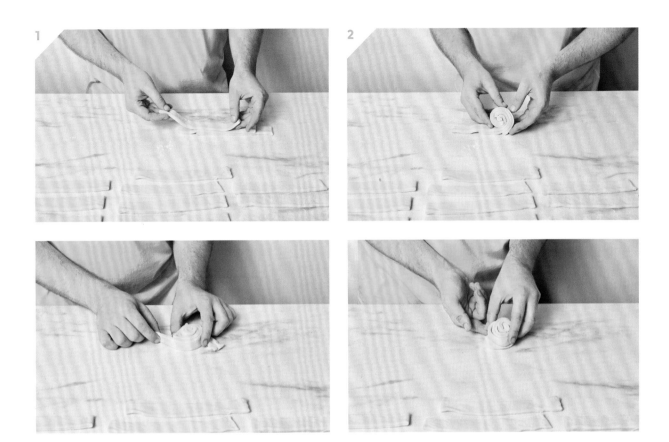

Preheat the oven to 200°C (400°F) and clear it of other baking trays. Use a pastry brush to coat the top of the cruffins with cream or milk. Place the cruffins in the oven, reduce the temperature to 180°C (350°F) and bake for 25–30 minutes, until gorgeously golden, rotating the trays halfway through cooking, brushing extra cream or milk on any spots that aren't browning fast enough and monitoring closely towards the end.

Remove from the oven and leave to cool for 10 minutes on the trays, then move to wire racks to cool fully. You'll be delighted to know that you can definitely tuck into those cruffins right now – or proceed with the rest of the recipe.

Reduce the oven temperature to 160°C (320°F). Pour the rum syrup into a dish. Spoon the crème d'amande into a piping (icing) bag fitted with a star nozzle at least 1 cm (½ in) thick. Use a chopstick to pierce the centre of a cruffin, then insert the piping bag nozzle. Generously fill the centre by forcefully squeezing in the crème d'amande. With tongs, dunk the cruffin in the syrup and turn to coat. Place back in the muffin tin. Stingily pipe or smear a small amount of crème d'amande in a ring around the top. Press slivered almonds on top to form a triumphant crown – you're almost done! Repeat with all the cruffins.

Transfer to the oven and bake for a final 22–25 minutes. Turn on the oven grill (broiler) for the last few minutes, until the almonds are just beginning to get scorched around the edges. Remove from the oven, leave to cool in the tins for about 10 minutes, then turn out onto wire racks to cool.

Keep in an airtight container on the bench and eat within 2 days, reheating briefly in the oven before getting stuck in.

Apricot danishes

(HARD)   MAKES: 18

Danishes use a similar technique to croissants, with a different combination of laminating folds in the dough. A pizza cutter is ideal for trimming or cutting laminated pastries when forming these danishes, as it won't apply the downward pressure that a knife would, which compresses the dough and makes you lose some of the lamination you worked so hard on!

plain (all-purpose) flour, for dusting

DÉTREMPE
240 ml (8 fl oz) warm almond milk or plant-based milk
14 g (5 scant teaspoons) active dried yeast
550 g (1 lb 3 oz) bread flour
50 g (1¾ oz) vegan block butter, cut into cubes
50 g (1¾ oz) granulated white sugar
3 teaspoons fine salt
½ teaspoon ground cardamom
¼ teaspoon ground nutmeg
120 ml (4 fl oz) aquafaba
1 teaspoon natural vanilla extract

BEURRAGE
350 g (12½ oz) fridge-cold vegan block butter

1   Start with the détrempe (dough). Place the milk in a small bowl and add the yeast to get ready for the long haul, sitting for a few minutes, until frothy. Add the flour, butter, sugar, salt, cardamom and nutmeg to the bowl of a stand mixer fitted with the paddle attachment. Mix on medium speed for 3 minutes or until the mixture is finely distributed into crumbs. Add the aquafaba and vanilla to the milk mixture, then slowly pour into the bowl as the mixer runs. When the dough comes together, switch to the dough hook attachment and knead for another 5 minutes. Wrap the dough in plastic wrap so that it is sealed, but not too tightly, as it will begin rising in the fridge. Leave to rest in the fridge for 6–12 hours.

2   Prepare the beurrage (butter). Spread a sheet of baking paper over a large work surface that you can easily roll the dough out on later. Place the block of cold butter on top, and sandwich it between another sheet of baking paper. Use a rolling pin to gently bash and flatten the butter. Using a sharp knife, trim the edges to form a smooth 15 cm (6 in) square. Add the excess butter back on top, sandwich again between baking paper and beat the butter into the square, so it is nice and even. Move to the next step ONLY when the beurrage has had 1 hour to collect itself in the fridge.

3   Sprinkle flour over your benchtop. Unwrap the chilled dough, then roll it out into a 20 cm (8 in) square. Score a square the same size as the beurrage in the centre of the dough, then use a dough scraper to cut lines from each corner of the square to the outer edge of the dough. Leaving the centre square intact, roll out the dough edges until they are large enough to fold over the centre square. Place the unwrapped cold butter block in the centre and fold each of the edges over the top, securely sealing the butter payload inside. Flip the dough over. Press or lightly beat all along the length of the dough with a rolling pin to squash it down and secure the layers. Wrap in plastic wrap and return to the fridge for 1 hour.

4   Flour the benchtop again, ready to begin your first tour of the dough. You'll need to complete two letter folds and one book fold. Unless your kitchen is really cold, completely chill the dough for 1 hour in the fridge or freezer between each fold, aiming to keep the dough at all times below 10°C (50°F). Use a pastry brush to dust excess flour from the pastry as you go, to keep an even dusting as you roll. If you're more of a visual person, turn to page 47 for a photographic guide to your laminating dough journey.

200 ml (7 fl oz) vegan
    cream or plant-based
    milk,
120 g (4½ oz) granulated
    white sugar
60 g (2 oz) cornflour
    (cornstarch)
250 g (9 oz) vegan cream
    cheese
40 g (1½ oz) vegan butter
60 ml (2 fl oz) rum or
    bourbon
pinch of sea salt
2 teaspoons vanilla
    bean paste

TO FINISH
2 tablespoons aquafaba
18 tinned apricot halves
2 tablespoons vegan
    cream or plant-based
    milk
2 tablespoons apricot jam
½ teaspoon vanilla bean
    paste

5   Working either away from or towards you – not side to side – begin by pressing the rolling pin along the length of the dough. Repeat by pressing down the spaces left between the rolling pin indentations, to flatten the whole thing, which will evenly begin to lengthen the dough in one direction. Check that both sides of the dough are adequately floured, then roll the dough carefully back and forth to give you more space to complete a fold. The more precise and neat you are at forming this rectangle and performing the first fold, the better your internal structure will be.

6   Use a pastry brush to dust off excess flour, then give the dough a quarter turn so the long side is facing you. (If at any point the dough tears or butter is exposed, dust flour into the spot to 'repair' it, then return the dough to the fridge for at least 1 hour before proceeding.) Now perform the first letter fold. Fold the bottom third of the dough over, then fold the top third over this, as though you needed to fit the dough into an envelope. Quelle surprise: you should still use a pastry brush to dust off excess flour! With the end of the rolling pin, tap lightly and evenly all over the top of the dough to secure the layers, completing the tour of the dough. Cover in plastic wrap and get the dough straight back in the fridge for at least 1 hour to cool back down.

7   When it's time to perform the second fold, begin by repeating step 5 to roll the dough back out again. This time, make a book fold. Give the dough a quarter turn so the short side is facing you. Fold in the left quarter of the dough, then fold in the right quarter over so the ends meet. Fold over once more where the ends meet in the middle of the dough. Dust off excess flour. With the end of the rolling pin, tap lightly and evenly all over the top of the dough to secure the layers. Cover in plastic wrap and return the dough to the fridge for another hour.

8   Repeat step 5 to prepare for the third and final tour. Repeat step 6 to perform another letter fold. Dust off excess flour, tap the top of the dough with the rolling pin to slightly lengthen, trim the very outer folded edges with a pizza cutter – and then the dough is finally ready … tomorrow! Cover in plastic wrap and refrigerate for at least 2 hours, or overnight.

9   To make the vanilla cream filling, whisk together the cream, sugar and cornflour in a small saucepan. Place over medium heat and whisk for about 5 minutes, then turn the heat down to low. When the mixture starts to thicken rapidly, remove from the heat entirely. Stir in the cream cheese, butter, rum, salt and vanilla bean paste. Leave to cool slightly, then cover the surface directly with plastic wrap to avoid a skin forming. Cool in the fridge as you continue your mission.

10 Return the dough to the bench. Press the rolling pin along the length of the dough. Repeat for the spaces left between. Throughout this process, generously pour flour over the dough several times, dusting off just about completely. Now roll the dough in all directions into about a 30 cm × 60 cm (12 in × 24 in) rectangle, 1.5 cm (½ in) thick. Flip the dough regularly and re-flour as you do so, using your forearm to flip the dough over and guide it back to the benchtop when it is getting thin and large. Rest the dough for 5 minutes before proceeding.

TUTTI FRUITY
Swap the apricots in the centre of half the danishes with whatever berries are in season right now, or other rounds of tinned stonefruit.

11 Line two baking trays with baking paper or silicone baking mats. Use a pizza cutter to trim the dough edges, then cut the dough into 10 cm (4 in) squares; you should end up with 18 of them. Use a pastry brush to dab aquafaba in the centre of each square. Fold each corner into the middle, then gently press down with your fingers to attach them there. This should help fan out the laminated edges, which will rise higher than the centre, holding the apricot topping in place. ①

12 Spread the pastries out on the baking trays. Cover with plastic wrap and leave at a room temperature no higher than 25°C (77°F) for 2–4 hours, until they've risen considerably.

13 Fit a piping (icing) bag with a nozzle and place it in a tall jug, furling the edges over the rim to hold it in place. Spoon the cold cream filling into the bag, but don't overfill, so you can twist the bag tightly shut. Press a finger into the centre of each danish to create space for the cream. Pipe it into the centre of each, then add an apricot half. Whisk together the cream and remaining aquafaba, then brush onto the un-topped parts of the pastry. ②

14 Preheat the oven to 200°C (400°F) and clear it of other baking trays. Place the danishes in the oven, reduce the temperature to 170°C (340°F) and bake for 25–30 minutes, until gorgeously golden, rotating the trays halfway and monitoring closely towards the end.

15 While the danishes are baking, mix the apricot jam and 4 teaspoons of water in a small saucepan over medium heat for 2 minutes. Stir in the vanilla bean paste.

16 Brush the pastries with the apricot liquid as they come out of the oven, then move them to wire racks to cool fully. Store on the bench in an airtight container and devour within 2 days.

Pain au chocolat

(HARD) MASKES: 8

1 × quantity Croissant
    dough (page 134)
plain (all-purpose) flour,
    for dusting
150 g (5½ oz) dairy-free
    chocolate
2 tablespoons vegan
    cream or plant-based
    milk

It can be a real pain au pain in the ass to find a measly wedge of chocolate hidden in your pain au chocolat. This recipe refuses to be stingy on chocolate, so squeeze as much as you can into these glorious hunks of croissant pastry. Those yet unsatisfied are directed to the revelation I enjoyed at Zest, in the Balinese hill town of Ubud, where the entire pastry is dunked in melted chocolate instead.

—

Prepare the croissant recipe as directed on pages 134–135, to the end of step 8.

Flour your benchtop and rolling pin, and place the dough on the bench. Press the rolling pin along the length of the dough. Make a second pass of the rolling pin, pressing down the ridges left between the rolling pin indentations, which will evenly begin to elongate the dough in one direction. Throughout this process, generously pour flour over the dough several times, dusting off just about completely. Now roll the dough in all directions into about a 45 cm × 60 cm (18 in × 24 in) rectangle, 5 mm (¼ in) thick. Flip the dough regularly and re-flour as you do so, using your forearm to flip the dough over and guide it back to the benchtop when it is getting thin and large. Fully dust off with a pastry brush. Rest the dough for 5 minutes before proceeding.

Line two baking trays with baking paper or silicone baking mats. Use a pizza cutter to trim the dough edges, reserving the offcuts, then cut the dough in half, into two large rectangles. Cut each portion into quarters to form eight rectangles. Stretch each rectangle so the centre is thinner than the ends.

Chop the chocolate into long chunks. Place at least two rows of chocolate (be as generous as you can without ruining the smooth rolling of the pastry) along one of the short ends of each rectangle. Fold the pastry over the chocolate. Make sure the chocolate is totally nestled in the pastry, not peeking out the edges. Continue to fold the pastry over, rolling loosely to leave voids between the layers. Place the pain au chocolat on the baking trays, seam side down, spacing them apart. Press down lightly with your palm to make a slightly squashed roll.

Cover with plastic wrap and allow to rise at a room temperature no higher than 25°C (77°F) for 3–12 hours, until they've nearly doubled in size.

Preheat the oven to 200°C (400°F) and clear it of other baking trays. Use a pastry brush to coat the tops of the pastries with cream or milk, avoiding the exposed laminated layers where possible. Place them in the oven, reduce the temperature to 180°C (350°F) and bake for about 25 minutes, until gorgeously golden, rotating the trays halfway through cooking, brushing extra cream or milk on any spots that aren't browning fast enough and monitoring closely towards the end.

Remove from the oven and leave to cool for 10 minutes on the trays, then move to wire racks to cool fully before eating, so the crumb can set properly.

FEELING HORNY?

If you've invested in cream horn moulds for the Cream horns on page 159, they'll also work in place of cannoli tubes. Your cannoli will be more like ice-cream cones, but will still hold the fillings just as well.

Cannoli

Cannoli tubes are generally inexpensive to buy, and are essential for making these cigar-shaped pastries, which are generally filled with ricotta. Homemade and store-bought vegan ricotta just doesn't cut it yet for me. As an apology, I've provided as many alternatives as I can, so you can find the cannoli of your dreams. A simple vanilla or lemon filling with pistachio is pretty reliable, though.

neutral-flavoured oil, for
  deep-frying
melted dark or white
  dairy-free chocolate,
  for dipping (optional)
icing (confectioners')
  sugar, for dusting

CANNOLI SHELLS
240 g (8½ oz) plain
  (all-purpose) flour,
  plus extra for dusting
20 g (¾ oz) caster
  (superfine) sugar
1 teaspoon Dutch
  (unsweetened) cocoa
  powder
½ teaspoon fine salt
40 ml (1¼ fl oz) vegetable
  oil
2 teaspoons vinegar

FILLINGS
White chocolate ganache
  cream (page 186)
Thick custard (page 150)
Chocolate custard
  (page 150)
Crème pâtissière
  (page 29)
Quick rum-whipped
  cream (page 249)
Lemon curd (page 24)
Mango curd (page 24)
Candied citrus zest
  (page 36)
dairy-free chocolate chips
  or chopped chocolate
  chunks

To make the cannoli shells, add the flour, sugar, cocoa powder and salt to the bowl of a stand mixer fitted with the paddle attachment. Begin beating on medium speed. Whisk together 120 ml (4 fl oz) of water, the oil and vinegar, then pour into the bowl. When the dough comes together, switch to the dough hook attachment. Knead the dough for another 2 minutes on medium speed.

Gather the dough into a ball, flatten slightly, then wrap in plastic wrap. Chill in the fridge for 2–12 hours. As usual, the longer the better, so either plan well in advance, or lean into forgetting you've even got a dough in the fridge.

Lightly flour a workbench. Use a dough scraper to divide the dough into six portions, weighing about 70 g (2½ oz) each, and roll into balls. Flour a rolling pin and roll each ball of dough as thinly as possible, keeping the others under a tea towel as you work. When you're done … you're not. Roll again, aiming to get the cannoli dough less than 2 mm (⅛ in) thick.

Use a 10 cm (4 in) cookie cutter to cut out circles. Place a cannoli tube in the centre of one circle, then wrap both sides of the dough around it. Use water to seal the dough, but don't wrap too tightly around the tube, as it needs room to grow. Ball together any scraps to roll out again and form another batch of cannoli.

Preheat 5–7.5 cm (2–3 in) of oil in a large heavy-based saucepan until the temperature registers above 175°C (345°F) on a kitchen thermometer, or when the handle of a wooden spoon instantly bubbles when placed in the oil. Maintain the temperature at 175°C (345°F) while frying the shells.

Working in batches, fry the shells for 1 minute on each side, flipping with a slotted spoon. Once the shells are crackly golden, transfer to paper towel or a wire rack to drain. After 10 minutes, firmly hold the shells and use a pair of tongs to slide the inner tubes out. Let the cannoli tubes cool totally, before trying to wrap another batch of dough around them and frying.

Spoon your chosen cream or curd into a piping (icing) bag with a nozzle and twist to seal. If desired, dip each tip of the cannoli tubes into melted chocolate, then let it set on a wire rack before filling. Pipe in your chosen cream or curd, adding in candied citrus or chocolate as you go. Dust the shells with icing sugar once filled. Eat fresh.

Vanilla slice

(EASY)   MAKES: 10

In the great Australian tradition of bastardising international cuisines, the vanilla slice is like a French mille-feuille that walked through a bad neighbourhood and was relieved of its valuables. Even though they left only a simple vanilla custard sandwiched between two sheets of puff pastry (with a glimmer of tangy passionfruit in the glaze), you won't feel robbed at all of deliciousness.

—

2 sheets Puff pastry
(page 48; or use
store-bought)
massive pinch of
flaky salt

VANILLA CUSTARD FILLING
165 g (6 oz) caster
(superfine) sugar
65 g (2¼ oz) vegan
custard powder
250 ml (8½ fl oz) coconut
cream or vegan cream
750 ml (25½ fl oz)
coconut milk
1½ teaspoons vanilla
bean paste

PASSIONFRUIT ICING
150 g (5½ oz) icing
(confectioners') sugar,
sifted
2 tablespoons
passionfruit pulp
2 teaspoons vegan butter
½ teaspoon vanilla bean
paste

Preheat the oven to 180°C (350°F). Line a 20 cm (8 in) square baking dish with baking paper. (If your baking dish is smaller, just trim the puff pastry sheets to fit.)

Use a fork to prick the puff pastry sheets all over. Place each sheet on a baking tray, then place another baking tray over the top to stop the pastry rising too high in the oven. (Do this in batches if needed, while preparing the custard.) Bake for 15–20 minutes, until golden, rotating the trays so both sheets brown evenly. Set aside to cool.

Meanwhile, prepare the custard filling. Thoroughly whisk the sugar, custard powder and coconut cream in a saucepan. Set over medium heat and stir until the mixture begins to thicken. Gradually whisk in the coconut milk, until the mixture is bubbling. Switch off the heat and mix in the vanilla bean paste. Leave to cool for 10 minutes before moving on.

Place one cooled baked pastry sheet in the prepared baking dish. Pour the custard mixture over, then top with the second pastry sheet. Sprinkle flaky salt over the top.

In a mixing jug, stir together all the icing ingredients until smooth, then evenly pour the icing over your vanilla slice. Allow to rest in the fridge overnight.

Using a sharp knife, carefully slice into even portions to serve, wiping the knife clean between cuts if you want to keep perfectly photographable layers. The slices will keep for 2–3 days in an airtight container in the fridge before the pastry begins to turn soggy.

MAKE IT CHOCOLATEY!
When you remove the custard from the stove, stir in 100 g (3½ oz) crumbled dark chocolate and 30 g (1 oz) Dutch (unsweetened) cocoa powder, and replace the icing with the Ganache on page 31.

Baklava

Cold syrup on hot baklava – or hot syrup on cold baklava? The main point is to have them at contrasting temperatures, so that the combination is warm and the syrup seeps through – then cool very soon afterwards, so the syrup doesn't seep away. It's generally easiest to make and cool the syrup while the baklava is being prepared, so it can go on right as the baklava comes out of the oven.

—

125 g (4½ oz) vegan butter or coconut oil, melted
375 g (13 oz) vegan filo pastry
400 ml (13½ fl oz) Citrus syrup (page 36)
dried rose petals, to serve (optional)

NUT FILLING
300 g (10½ oz) pistachios
100 g (3½ oz) walnuts
100 g (3½ oz) brown sugar
1 teaspoon ground cardamom
large pinch of sea salt

Put the nut filling ingredients in a food processor and pulse into a rough rubble. Place the butter or coconut oil in a small saucepan over low heat and gently heat until mostly melted. Set aside.

Preheat the oven to 200°C (400°F). Line a baking tray about the same size as your filo sheets with baking paper and brush a little of the butter or oil over the paper.

When working with the filo pastry, either proceed quickly or cover with a scarcely damp tea towel to stop it drying out. Place a filo sheet on the baking tray and use a pastry brush to splatter a little of the butter or oil over the top, in your best Jackson Pollock impersonation. Brush to spread it out in an even layer, then repeat with eight more sheets of filo to create your base layer.

Spread half the nut filling over the filo. As the number of sheets in a packet of filo can vary, count how many you have left. You will need ten sheets for the top layer, so use however many are remaining for your middle layer, repeating the buttering process. Top with the remaining nut filling.

Brush six sheets of filo with butter or oil and place over the final layer of nuts. Place two more sheets of filo over one half of the filling at a 90-degree angle, then brush with butter or oil and tuck the ends under the filled half of the pastry. Repeat with two more filo sheets on the other side.

Using a paring knife, and pressing down on the filo around the knife, diagonally score the baklava into diamonds, for ease of cutting later on. Delicately brush any remaining butter or oil over the top.

Transfer the tray to the oven and immediately reduce the oven temperature to 170°C (340°F). Bake for 40 minutes, or until the pastry is crisp and golden.

Remove the baklava from the oven and evenly pour the cooled citrus syrup over the top. Bake for another 5 minutes, then remove from the oven again and allow to cool to room temperature.

Use a sharp knife to separate the baklava into diamonds for serving and scatter with dried rose petals, if desired. The baklava will keep in an airtight container on the benchtop for up to 2 weeks of glorious snacking.

Galaktoboureko

Pronounced 'ga-lah-kto-BOU-re-koh', not 'Galactic Bourek-o', this slice is easier made than said – and with one bite into the buttery, flaky filo filled with sweet semolina custard, it'll be even easier to see why it's such a popular Greek treat. Go the extra effort and make fresh filo for this pie.

100 g (3½ oz) vegan butter melted but not hot
1 × quantity Filo pastry (page 44) or up to 375 g (13 oz) store-bought vegan filo

SPICED SYRUP
300 g (10½ oz) granulated white sugar
zest and juice of 1 small lemon
½ cinnamon stick
4 cloves

SEMOLINA CUSTARD
80 ml (2½ fl oz) cold aquafaba
165 g (6 oz) caster (superfine) sugar
1 litre (34 fl oz) soy or oat milk
2 tablespoons cornflour (cornstarch)
pinch of fine salt
1½ teaspoons natural vanilla extract
160 g (5½ oz) semolina (plus a little extra, if needed, to make a thick custard)
15 g (½ oz) vegan butter
a few drops of vegan yellow food colouring (optional, for aesthetics)

To make the syrup, combine the sugar and 180 ml (6 fl oz) of water in a saucepan over medium heat, stirring to dissolve the sugar. Bring to the boil, then add the other syrup ingredients. Reduce the heat and simmer for 5 minutes, without stirring. Remove from the heat and discard the cinnamon stick and cloves. Set aside to cool.

Make the semolina custard. Place the aquafaba in the bowl of a stand mixer with the whisk attached and beat on high speed until it froths and rises. Continuing to beat on high speed, slowly pour in 75 g (2¾ oz) of the caster sugar and beat for about 5 minutes, until stiff peaks form. Set aside.

Whisk together the milk, cornflour, salt and remaining caster sugar in a saucepan then bring just to the boil. Add the vanilla, then stir constantly as you add the semolina – as slowly as you can – and turn the heat to low. Continue to stir while adding the butter, and food colouring, if using, then remove from the heat. Set aside and allow to cool for at least 20 minutes.

Meanwhile, preheat the oven to 180°C (350°F). Brush a large baking tray with some of the melted butter and set aside.

Slowly fold the aquafaba mixture into the cooled semolina and mix well. (If your semolina mixture is too warm, your whipped aquafaba may deflate!)

Place two sheets of filo pastry on the buttered baking tray, splattering with butter between the layers. Top with another filo sheet, but leave half of it hanging out over one edge of the tray. Splatter with more butter, place another sheet squarely over the base filo, then splatter with more butter. Repeat this process so that there is half a pastry sheet hanging out of each of the four edges of the pan, with an alternating sheet between each that lines up with the base filo. It shouldn't surprise you by now that you should splatter the layers with melted butter each time.

Pour the custard mixture over the central filo sheets, then fold over each of the overhanging filo sheets and splatter with more butter. Add two more sheets of buttered filo on top, then use a sharp knife to score the top into 16 squares.

Transfer the tray to the oven. Reduce the oven temperature to 160°C (320°F) and bake for 50–60 minutes, until the pastry is golden.

Remove from the oven and immediately pour the cold syrup over the hot pastry, allowing it to absorb into the top. Allow to cool for at least 2 hours before slicing into portions along the pre-scored lines. Your galaktoboureko will keep in an airtight container in the fridge for up to 5 days, and can be served warm or cold.

SHE'LL BE APPLES
Add a layer of cooked apple slices over the custard filling before wrapping in filo, dust loads of icing (confectioners') sugar over the top after baking and you'll have a delightful apple and custard pie to serve instead.

Apple strudel

EASY   SERVES: 8–10

It'd be pretty rudel to not make a strudel. Ideally, use a few different varieties of apples in the filling so they can fight it out to offer the most flavour, but the strudel will still be delectable even if you just use good old granny smith apples.

—

1 × quantity Filo pastry (page 44) or up to 375 g (13 oz) store-bought vegan filo
120 g (4½ oz) vegan butter, melted
65 g (2¼ oz) brown sugar
icing (confectioners') sugar, for dusting
vegan vanilla ice cream, to serve

SPICED APPLE FILLING
100 g (3½ oz) raisins
60 ml (2 fl oz) rum or brandy
850 g (1 lb 14 oz) baking apples
zest and juice of 1 lemon
100 g (3½ oz) brown sugar
1 teaspoon ground cinnamon
½ teaspoon sea salt
¼ teaspoon ground nutmeg
pinch of ground cloves (optional)
25 g (1 oz) almond meal (or extra breadcrumbs)
25 g (1 oz) dried breadcrumbs

PASTRY POWER
This apple filling is great in a pie made with Shortcrust (page 42), Pie crust (page 43) or Rough puff (page 49). Top with a pastry lattice, following the lattice method for adorning the Fruit pies on pages 178–179.

Start by soaking the raisins for the filling. Add the raisins to a jar. Gently heat the rum in a small saucepan (or in a microwave-safe bowl) until warm but not hot, to preserve the booze content. Pour the rum over the raisins, seal the jar and set aside for a few hours – or up to a week – to soak. (If leaving for an extended time, shake the jar every day or so.) For those avoiding alcohol or effort, splash about 2 tablespoons of boiling water over the raisins for 5 minutes and drain before using instead.

Peel and core the apples, then cut into 1 cm (½ in) cubes and toss in a large bowl with the lemon zest and juice and brown sugar. Toss it all together to stop the apple browning, then toss through the cinnamon, salt, nutmeg and cloves, if using. Leave to sit for a few minutes, then stir the raisins, almond meal and breadcrumbs through to drink up the excess liquid.

Preheat the oven to 180°C (350°F). Line a large baking tray with baking paper or a silicone baking mat.

When working with the filo pastry, either proceed quickly or cover with a scarcely damp tea towel to stop it drying out.

Lay a sheet of filo on the benchtop. Using a pastry brush, splatter a little melted butter over the top, in your best Jackson Pollock impersonation, being careful to avoid over-saturating it. Similarly scatter about a teaspoon of brown sugar over. Add another filo sheet and repeat with more butter and sugar. Continue until four pastry sheets have been stacked on top of each other. (Note, you will need fewer sheets if using homemade filo pastry.)

Evenly spoon half the filling along the long edge of the pastry, smoothing the filling flat. Fold the pastry over to encase the filling, compressing slightly to pack it in. Taking care not to rip the pastry, continue to roll until a cylinder is formed. Adjust so that the filling is distributed evenly along, then tuck each end under to secure. Repeat with the remaining pastry and filling to make a second strudel.

Curve the strudels into a horseshoe shape (for a better fit) and place on the baking tray. (You can always use a second baking tray if needed!) Make sure the seam and tucked ends are under the pastry, then brush all over with more butter.

Bake for 40–45 minutes, until the pastry is golden all over. Remove from the oven and leave to cool for 20 minutes before dusting icing sugar all over the top. Slice and serve warm with ice cream.

The strudel will keep in an airtight container in the fridge for up to 5 days. Reheat in the oven or an air fryer to crisp up the pastry, as it will become soggy.

Cream horns

MEDIUM   MAKES: 6

The horn of plenty ... of time to spare! Using store-bought puff pastry can have you bringing together these miniature cream cornucopias in 30 minutes. You will need specialist cone-shaped cream horn moulds to make the signature shape of these pastries. Mini ice-cream cones clad in foil can serve as a makeshift mould if you really can't source the proper ones.

vegan butter or cooking spray, for greasing
2 sheets Puff pastry (page 48; or use store-bought)
2 tablespoons plant-based milk, for brushing
100 g (3½ oz) raspberry jam
120 ml (4 fl oz) vegan cream, chilled
1 teaspoon natural vanilla extract
30 g (1 oz) icing (confectioners') sugar, sifted
6 raspberries

Preheat the oven to 180°C (350°F). Grease the outside of six cream horn moulds with butter or cooking spray. Note that this will make getting the pastry on more difficult, but still definitely possible, so plan on persevering.

Use a sharp knife or pizza cutter to cut the pastry into 2 cm (¾ in) wide strips. Starting from the bottom of a mould, and overlapping the layers slightly as you go, wind a pastry strip around the mould and pinch the ends into the pastry.

Add a second or third piece of pastry if needed so that you continue to spiral the dough all the way up the horn mould to form a casing. Stop 1.5 cm (½ in) below the top of the mould, so there's room for the pastry to grow, and tuck the end of the strip under. Press down gently to adhere the layers. Repeat with all the moulds, then brush the pastry strips with the milk.

Bake for about 15 minutes, until your horns are golden. Remove from the oven and leave to cool for 5 minutes, before carefully slipping them off their moulds. Let them cool completely on a wire rack. (They'll keep in an airtight container on the benchtop for up to 3 days if you're making them ahead of time.)

Stir the jam to loosen it. Fit a piping (icing) bag with a nozzle and place it in a tall jug, furling the edges over the rim to hold it in place. Spoon the jam into the bag and twist the bag tightly shut.

Using a large mixing bowl and a hand-held electric mixer, or a stand mixer fitted with the whisk attachment, beat the cold cream, vanilla and 2 tablespoons of the icing sugar for 5 minutes on high speed to thicken. Fill another piping bag with the cream, but don't overfill, so you can twist the bag tightly shut.

Pipe a small amount of jam into each horn, then fill with cream. (You can also alternate the jam and cream if you have the time and desire to do so.) Toss the remaining icing sugar over the horns and push a fresh raspberry into each one to finish.

Eat within a few hours of filling so the pastry stays crisp.

Pear mille-feuille

Named after the thousand (mille) leaves (feuille) of layers in puff pastry, this version of that classic French bakery treat has honeyed hasselback pear slices to add even more thin layers of delight into each bite. This recipe is great to serve at a dinner party, as you can prep all the elements ahead of time and quickly build each stack when you're ready to serve.

2 sheets Puff pastry (page 48; or use store-bought)
2 small pears, peeled
15 g (½ oz) vegan butter, melted
2 tablespoons Vegan honey (page 39)
½ teaspoon ground cardamom
1 × quantity Crème pâtissière (page 29)

CHOCOLATE GLAZE
125 g (4½ oz) icing (confectioners') sugar
1 tablespoon plant-based milk
1 tablespoon Dutch (unsweetened) cocoa powder

Preheat the oven to 180°C (350°F). Line a wide baking tray with baking paper.

If using homemade puff pastry, roll it out to a 5 mm (¼ in) thickness. Use a pizza slicer to cut the pastry into 5 cm × 10 cm (2 in × 4 in) rectangles, to give six pieces. Use a fork to prick the puff pastry all over, then transfer to the prepared tray, cover with baking paper and place another baking tray on top, to stop the pastry rising too high. Bake for 15–20 minutes, rotating the tray halfway through cooking until the pastry is golden. Remove from the oven.

Increase the oven temperature to 200°C (400°F). Cut the pears in half and scrape out the cores. Flip a pear cut side down onto a chopping board. Place a chopstick beside each side of the pear. Use a sharp knife to make thinly spaced slices along the pear, letting the chopsticks stop the knife, so the base of the pear stays intact. Repeat with the other pear halves.

Combine the butter, 1 tablespoon of the honey and the cardamom in a small bowl, then brush the mixture over the pears. Transfer to a baking dish and bake for 40 minutes, until the pears are soft inside, with crispy edges.

Using a stand mixer fitted with the whisk attachment, beat your chilled crème pâtissière for 2 minutes on high speed to smooth it out. Spoon the crème pâtissière into a piping (icing) bag with a nozzle, but don't overfill, so you can twist the bag tightly shut.

To make the glaze, add the icing sugar to a bowl and slowly whisk in enough of the milk until you get a thick, spreadable glaze. Pour one-quarter of the mixture into another bowl and whisk in the cocoa powder until smooth.

Place a wire rack over the sink. Set two pastry rectangles on the rack, flat side up. Pour the white glaze evenly over the pastries on the wire rack, then add the chocolate glaze to a small piping bag or zip-lock bag. Snip off the very end, then pipe lines of chocolate glaze lengthways across the top of the white glaze. Now drag a toothpick across the top at a 90-degree angle to the lines, to form the signature look. Screw it up? Own it and start swirling.

Place two pastry rectangles, flat side down, on a serving plate. Cut thin groups of pear slices and splay them across the base like extra leaves growing atop your pastry ones. Use the piping bag to dollop beautiful blobs of crème pâtissière across the surface. Repeat the same steps with two more pastry rectangles, then delicately place them atop the first ones. Drizzle with the remaining honey. Pop the glazed pastry rectangles over the top so your thousand leaves look like a million bucks. Serve immediately!

Pies

Pastel de acelga

(EASY)   MAKES: 1 LARGE PIE

Make a mental note right now, so next time you come back from a farmers' market with that insanely large bunch of silverbeet you just HAD to get, you'll remember this Peruvian silverbeet pie is the recipe to come back to. (The same goes for fresh spinach, too!) The pastry crust won't take you any extra time to put together, and the filling is packed full of greens and the 'elusive' (read: abundant) plant-based calcium.

Pop slices of the pie in an air fryer for 10 minutes to reheat, and serve next to a simple salad to sort your lunches for a week.

—

2 huge bunches of silverbeet (Swiss chard)
1 large onion, diced
2 tablespoons olive oil, plus extra for greasing
sea salt and cracked black pepper
6 fat garlic cloves, crushed
large pinch of ground nutmeg
1 tablespoon dried oregano
185 g (6½ oz) grated vegan parmesan
550 ml (18½ fl oz) vegan cream
zest and juice of 1 lemon
165 g (6 oz) chickpea flour (besan)
25 g (¾ oz) nutritional yeast
lime wedges, to serve

OLIVE OIL CRUST
330 g (11½ oz) plain (all-purpose) flour
2 teaspoons fine salt
90 ml (3 fl oz) olive oil
90 ml (3 fl oz) ice-cold water

PASTRY GLAZE
2 teaspoons olive oil
1 teaspoon plant-based milk

To prepare the olive oil crust, mix the flour and salt in a large bowl using a wooden spoon. Slowly drizzle the olive oil over, stirring into the flour as you go. Add the water, 1 tablespoon at a time, and mix until you have a crumbly dough. Knead for a few seconds to form a rough dough ball, sandwich between two sheets of baking paper, and chill in the fridge for at least 30 minutes.

Clean the silverbeet well, then separate the leaves from the stalks, you will need about 600 g (1 lb 5 oz) of leaves. Roughly chop the leaves into small pieces and sit in a colander to dry. The stalks are bonus freebies that can be added to soups, stir-fries or vegetable tray bakes.

In a large saucepan or wok, fry the onion in the olive oil with a pinch of salt over medium heat for 5–6 minutes. Add the garlic, mix, then add the silverbeet leaves to begin wilting. After another 3 minutes, add the nutmeg, oregano and a hearty crack of salt and pepper. Cook, stirring, for a few minutes, until the silverbeet is wilted and any liquid has evaporated. Toss the parmesan through.

Whisk together the cream, lemon zest and juice, chickpea flour and nutritional yeast, then stir through the silverbeet mixture. Remove from the heat and let the filling cool for 30 minutes while you blind-bake the crust.

Preheat the oven to 180°C (350°F). Lightly grease a 20–23 cm (8–9 in) cake tin.

Divide the dough in half. Roll each half between the baking paper sheets with a rolling pin, into a large round. Peel off the baking paper and lay one round over the cake tin, manoeuvring it to evenly fill the tin with your fingertips. Blind-bake for 10 minutes.

Pile the filling into the crust and smooth the top. Place the other pastry round on top of the filling, and press or crimp the pastry edges together to seal. Whisk the glaze ingredients in a small bowl, then brush over the top of the pie crust using a pastry brush.

Bake the pie for 1–1¼ hours, until the crust is golden and a skewer inserted in the centre of the pie comes out clean.

Allow to cool, before serving with lime wedges to squeeze on top, and a side salad (or not … I'm not your mum). If stored in the fridge, you've got 3 days to power through leftovers before the pastry becomes irredeemable.

Kolokithopita

(EASY) **MAKES: 1 LARGE PIE**

This Greek pie is often made with pumpkin (winter squash) instead of zucchini – with the latter being my preference. The key to a great zucchini pie is taking the time to remove as much liquid from the zucchini before it's allowed anywhere near spitting distance of the filling. I recommend tangy store-bought vegan feta in the filling, but you can replace it with the same weight of tofu or cooked white rice ... for healthier but less delicious results. Your call!

Check out the step photos in the Pastilla recipe on page 171 for a visual idea of how to fold the filo pastry for this recipe.

—

1 kg (2 lb 3 oz) zucchini (courgettes)
2 red onions, finely diced
60–100 ml (2–3½ fl oz) olive oil
sea salt and cracked black pepper
200 g (7 oz) vegan feta, crumbled
30 g (1 oz) chickpea flour (besan)
4 tablespoons finely chopped parsley leaves
2 tablespoons finely chopped dill fronds
1 tablespoon finely chopped mint leaves
1 × quantity Filo pastry (page 44) or 375 g (13 oz) store-bought

Grate the zucchini, then squeeze it over a colander to remove as much liquid as possible.

In a large saucepan, fry the onion in 2 tablespoons of the olive oil with a pinch of salt over medium heat for 5–6 minutes. Add the zucchini and cook for another 5 minutes to remove more liquid. Transfer to a large bowl with the feta, chickpea flour, herbs and a hearty crack of salt and pepper. Mix well and leave to cool.

Preheat the oven to 220°C (430°F).

Either proceed quickly, or cover the filo pastry with a scarcely damp tea towel to buy time before it dries out. Use a pastry brush to cover a baking tray lightly with olive oil, then line the tray with three sheets of filo stacked on top of each other.

Brush a little oil over the pastry and place two sheets of filo next to each other on top; the ends will hang over the edges of the tray. Rotate the tray 90 degrees and repeat with another two sheets of filo. Keep going until you've used eight sheets of filo in total.

Spoon the filling onto the pastry, then spread with a spatula until flat and smooth. Fold the overhanging filo sheets over the mixture, drizzling and brushing the pastry with a little more oil as you go. Place two more sheets of filo over one half of the filling, then brush with oil and tuck the ends under the filled half of the pastry. Repeat with two more filo sheets on the other side.

With a sharp knife, score the pie into the portion sizes you'd like before baking, otherwise you'll crush the pastry trying to serve it later. For extra texture, crumple any remaining filo sheets and arrange them over each scored portion, then brush the remaining oil over the top.

Transfer to the oven and immediately reduce the temperature to 175°C (345°F). Bake for 1 hour, or until the pastry is golden and crisp. Allow to cool for 20–30 minutes before serving.

If stored in the fridge, you can ride the leftovers train for about 3 days before the pastry reaches the end of the line. Use a hot oven or air fryer to re-crisp the slices when reheating.

PIES

167

Spiral spanakopita

(EASY)   **MAKES: 1 GIANT SPIRAL INTO GLUTTONY**

Spanakopita is so wonderfully versatile. I make it as big slab pies, small triangles, rolled-up cigars – and, perhaps the most visually striking of all, as a massive spiral. An abyss of spinach and feta you'd love to fall into.

You'd be surprised at the vegan cooking tips you can get from elderly Greeks. When you cook for everyone you meet, you're bound to have encountered a few dietary requirements along the way. Greek cooking already naturally flirts with veganism through *nistisima* – food for Lent made without animal products. This filling uses a family favourite trick of throwing in a handful of cooked rice to thicken the filling in lieu of eggs.

The great aunties of my family have spent years in the trenches, bickering over what makes up the perfect filling for spanakopita – and it turns out they all do a pretty damn good job anyway. I offer this peace treaty of a recipe, with the best of all their ideas combined, then veganised.

—

1 kg (2 lb 3 oz) frozen
   spinach
1 large red onion,
   finely diced
1 large yellow onion,
   finely diced
160 ml (5½ fl oz) olive oil
   (see Tip)
sea salt and cracked
   black pepper
6 fat garlic cloves,
   crushed
4 spring onions
   (scallions), finely sliced
zest and juice of 4 lemons
2 large bunches of dill,
   roughly chopped
200 g (7 oz) cooked
   white rice
200 g (7 oz) vegan feta,
   crumbled
1 × quantity Filo pastry
   (page 44) or up 375 g
   (13 oz) store-bought

TIP
If using store-bought filo pastry, you will only need 60–100 ml (2–3½ fl oz) of olive oil.

Microwave the frozen spinach as per the packet instructions, then allow to cool. Place it in a sieve and squeeze out as much liquid as you can with your hands. If you think you're done, you're not. Keep squeezing until the spinach is just about dry, as any liquid will turn into steam and ruin the crispness of the pastry.

In a large wide saucepan or wok, fry the onion in 1 tablespoon of the olive oil with a pinch of salt over medium heat for 5–6 minutes. Add the garlic, spring onion, lemon zest and juice and cook for another 4 minutes. Toss in the spinach, dill, rice and feta and stir to combine. Transfer the mixture to a food processor, season with a hearty crack of salt and pepper and blitz to a smooth, vibrant-green paste.

Preheat the oven to 180°C (350°F). Either proceed quickly, or cover the filo pastry with a scarcely damp tea towel to buy time before it dries out. Use a pastry brush to cover your biggest baking tray lightly with olive oil.

On a benchtop, lay three sheets of filo on top of each other, long ends facing you. Generously splatter and brush oil over the top pastry sheet.

Spoon a generously heaped strip of filling along the long end of the filo sheets, aiming for an even tube around 3.5 cm (1½ in) thick. Not too tightly, roll the filling up to form a long cylinder. Coil the pastry into a spiral.

Either repeat the above step to create individual coiled portions, or place the first swirl in the centre of the baking tray and coil more filled pastry portions around the first swirl to create a large, grand spanakopita. Evenly brush the remaining oil over the top, then transfer to the oven and bake for about 1 hour or until all the pastry is totally golden and crisp. Allow to cool for 20–30 minutes, then either slice into wedges or break off sections of the swirl.

If stored in the fridge, you've got 3 days to power through leftovers before the pastry becomes irredeemable. Use a hot oven or air fryer to re-crisp the slices when reheating.

Pastilla

Here's a flavour combination that boggled me slightly when I first heard of it – but you MUST persevere. It's dead-ass simple to veganise with a quick spiced seitan and tofu filling wrapped in filo and adorned with cinnamon and icing sugar. Yes, ICING SUGAR! Get your head around it, then your lips around it next, because I'm declaring it a must-try pie. Try serving it with toasted almonds on the side or on the top, and definitely seek out ras el hanout and saffron for all the right flavours.

—

200 g (7 oz) vegan filo pastry
80 ml (2½ fl oz) olive oil, or cooled melted vegan butter
2 tablespoons icing (confectioners') sugar
2 teaspoons ground cinnamon

PASTILLA FILLING
1 tablespoon vegan butter or olive oil
1 large onion, finely sliced
400 g (14 oz) seitan, shredded
200 ml (7 fl oz) chicken-style stock
30 g (1 oz) chickpea flour (besan)
1½ tablespoons date syrup or rice malt syrup
2 teaspoons ras el hanout
½ teaspoon cayenne pepper
½ teaspoon ground ginger
cracked black pepper
large pinch of saffron threads
4 tablespoons finely chopped parsley leaves
200 g (7 oz) silken tofu

Start by preparing the filling. Add the butter to a wide saucepan over medium–high heat and cook the onion for 5 minutes, stirring occasionally. Add the seitan and cook for another 5 minutes; don't be shy to get some crispiness and browning on it before moving on – it's all extra flavour!

Bring the stock to the boil in a saucepan, then whisk in the chickpea flour, date syrup, ras el hanout, cayenne pepper, ginger, black pepper and saffron. Pour the stock into the seitan pan, stirring well to deglaze the pan, then remove from the heat once the mixture is bubbling. Stir in the parsley and tofu (which will break into small pieces), then set the filling aside to cool.

Preheat the oven to 175°C (345°F). Cover the filo pastry with a scarcely damp tea towel to buy time before it dries out. Use a pastry brush to cover the base of a 20 cm (8 in) springform cake tin with olive oil. Place three sheets of filo on top of the cake tin base. ①

Drizzle a little olive oil over the pastry and dab to spread it around evenly. Place two sheets of filo over half the cake tin base and brush the sheets with oil, then repeat to cover the other half of the tin with another two sheets of filo, brushing with oil again, to form a sturdy filo base. ②

Spoon the filling into the middle of the cake tin base, then spread with a spatula until flat and smooth. Fold each overhanging sheet of filo over the top, brushing with a little olive oil each time. ③

Place two more filo sheets squarely over the top of the filling, splashing with more oil, before tucking the overhanging filo under the pastry to create a smooth, rounded pie. ④

Brush more oil over the top, then place the springform cake ring over the pie and secure. Transfer to the oven and bake for 25–30 minutes, until golden brown all over. Pop the side off the springform tin and bake for the last 5 minutes on only the base.

Remove the pie from the oven and allow to cool for 5 minutes. Sift the icing sugar over the top of the pie, then sprinkle thin lines of ground cinnamon at about 2.5 cm (1 in) intervals to make a diamond pattern.

Serve immediately, while hot.

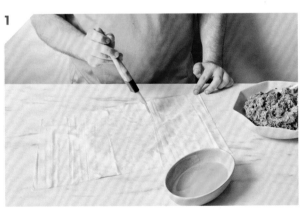

1

2

3

4

Meat pies

(EASY)　MAKES: 6

Culturally ingrained into the Aussie and Kiwi national identities, there's little fanfare in these individually sized pies filled with meat and gravy. That's part of the charm. Unceremoniously squirt some tomato sauce on at the end and you're done! You beaut.

If you want to reduce the fanfare even further, substitute the shortcrust and puff pastries for vegan store-bought equivalents.

—

Preheat the oven to 200°C (400°F).

To make the filling, scatter the mushroom, cabbage and onion in a deep-sided baking tray. Add the plant-based meat in large chunks, lightly drizzle with olive oil and toss together. Roast for about 1 hour, until the mixture is dark brown and crispy, and the moisture has been cooked out, stirring around every 15 minutes to fold in any bits browning too quickly.

Pour the beer straight into the hot tray, then deglaze by scraping up any yummy browned bits. Whisk together the gravy granules, tomato paste, sugar, pepper liquid smoke and 100 ml (3½ fl oz) of water, then stir it all through the roasted vegetable medley. Set aside to cool as you proceed, leaving the oven on.

On a lightly floured work surface, roll out the shortcrust pastry to the same thickness as the puff pastry sheets. Use a 14 cm (5½ in) cutter or bowl to cut out six circles from the shortcrust pastry. Use an 8 cm (3¼ in) cutter or bowl to cut out six circles from the puff pastry.

Lightly grease the holes of a jumbo six-hole muffin tin. Press the shortcrust pastry circles into them, then evenly spoon in the filling mixture, almost to the top. Place the puff pastry circles over the top and press the pastry edges together, crimping with a fork to seal. Use kitchen scissors to cut five or six crosses in the top of each pie. Brush the tops with milk, then sprinkle with seeds, if desired.

Bake the pies for about 15 minutes in the still-heated oven. If you're eating them straight away, carefully remove the pies from the muffin holes and place them on a baking tray, or directly on an oven rack, and bake for a further 10 minutes for a crispy outside. Or, for pies that'll reheat better later on, finish baking them in the muffin tin for another 10 minutes.

These pies are great to stash away in the freezer, sealed in plastic wrap, until you're ready to eat them, as they'll stand up to a good long-from-hibernation incineration when you want to reheat them.

STEAK & CHEESE, PLEASE?
Stir 65 g (2¼ oz) grated vegan cheese into each pie before topping with puff pastry.

CURRY UP!
Mix 3–4 tablespoons of your favourite curry powder into the filling before assembling the pies.

---

plain (all-purpose) flour, for dusting
½ × quantity Shortcrust pastry (page 42)
2 sheets Puff pastry (page 48; or use store-bought)
plant-based milk, for brushing
nigella seeds or black sesame seeds, for topping (optional)

MEAT FILLING
250 g (9 oz) mushrooms, diced into 1 cm (½ in) pieces
½ head cabbage, roughly chopped
2 large red onions, grated
450 g (1 lb) premium plant-based meat
olive oil, for drizzling and greasing
300 ml (10 fl oz) beer (non-alcoholic is fine)
2 tablespoons vegan instant gravy granules
2½ tablespoons tomato paste (concentrated puree)
1 tablespoon granulated white sugar
2 teaspoons cracked black pepper
1 teaspoon liquid smoke

Fat bastard pie

Macaroni pie in a hot water crust, filled with a cheesy honey dill sauce + BBQ pulled seitan + pickles + hot sauce? Dead sexy. Naked on top, because it's not afraid to show off.

With store-bought vegan options steadily becoming more available, substitute your preferred packet mac 'n' cheese and plant-based pulled pork to reduce effort in putting this together. Not enough for you? Add chopped vegan bacon to the macaroni mix to knock your jocks off.

—

cooking oil spray
600 g (1 lb 5 oz) seitan
2 tablespoons olive oil
2 onions, sliced
400 g (14 oz) button mushrooms, chopped
250 ml (8½ fl oz) smoky barbecue sauce
2 teaspoons hot sauce, plus extra to serve

HOT WATER CRUST
100 g (3½ oz) vegan shortening
250 g (9 oz) plain (all-purpose) flour
1 teaspoon fine salt

MAC 'N' CHEESE
2 tablespoons olive oil
25 g (¾ oz) plain (all-purpose) flour
420 ml (14 fl oz) soy milk
3 tablespoons nutritional yeast
1½ tablespoons vegan honey (page 39)
1 tablespoon dijon mustard
1 teaspoon garlic powder
130 g (4½ oz) shredded vegan cheese
4 dill pickles, diced, plus 100 ml (3½ fl oz) juice
300 g (10½ oz) cooked macaroni
2 tablespoons finely chopped dill fronds

To make the hot water crust, heat 120 ml (4 fl oz) of water and the shortening together in a saucepan. Add the flour and salt to a large bowl. Once the water hits a rolling boil, pour it over the flour and mix vigorously with a wooden spoon for 2 minutes to form a dough. While still warm, roll the dough out on a lightly floured work surface, to about 5 mm (¼ in) thick. Press the dough evenly to line the interior of a lightly greased 23 cm (9 in) cake tin. Move to the fridge while you proceed.

Preheat the oven to 200°C (400°F).

Shred the seitan using two forks. Heat the olive oil in a large saucepan or wok over medium heat and fry the seitan, onion and mushroom for 15–20 minutes, tossing around occasionally until there's browning all over the seitan shreds. Stir the barbecue sauce and hot sauce through the mixture, then remove from the heat.

For the mac and cheese, heat the olive oil in a large saucepan over medium heat. Slowly sift in the flour and stir for 1–2 minutes to make a bubbling roux. Gradually whisk in the soy milk a little at a time, then reduce the heat to low. Stir in the nutritional yeast, honey, mustard and garlic powder, followed by the cheese and pickle juice. Simmer for 3–5 minutes, until the sauce is thick and comes away from the side of the pan. Remove from the heat and stir in the macaroni, pickles and dill.

Remove the pie crust from the fridge and fill with the seitan mixture. Spoon the mac and cheese over the top, then smooth with the back of the spoon. Sprinkle some extra cheese over if you're feeling bougie!

Bake for 45–60 minutes, until the macaroni on top is lovely and crunchy. Depending on your spice capabilities, either drizzle some hot sauce over the top, or use a pastry brush to bathe the entire top layer with the stuff. This pie is best served fresh, so get it in yer belly immediately.

Curried scallop pies

(MEDIUM) MAKES: 6

The thick stems of king oyster mushrooms are marvellous scallop substitutes, with little interference from a cook. They shine in this take on a popular seafood pie from Tasmania in southern Australia.

—

60 ml (2 fl oz) vegan white wine
juice of 2 lemons
2 tablespoons vegan fish sauce
2 tablespoons curry powder
2–3 tablespoons olive oil, plus extra for greasing
2 celery stalks, finely diced
1 large carrot, finely diced
80 g (2¾ oz) frozen peas
50 g (1¾ oz) frozen green beans
½ × quantity Shortcrust pastry (page 42; or use store-bought)
500 g (1 lb 2 oz) frozen tater tots (potato gems), defrosted

KOMBU DASHI
20 g (¾ oz) kombu kelp
75 g (2¾ oz) dried shiitake mushrooms
2 litres (68 fl oz) cold water

SCALLOPS
8–10 king oyster mushrooms
750 ml (25½ fl oz) kombu dashi or water
1 tablespoon crushed garlic
2 teaspoons chicken-style stock powder
sea salt and cracked black pepper

To make the kombu dashi, use scissors to add some slits in the kombu, for more flavour release. Combine in a large bowl with the shiitake mushrooms and cold water. Cover and soak overnight in the fridge to infuse. The next day, pour the broth into a saucepan over low heat. Remove the kombu just as bubbles begin to appear; otherwise the kombu will go slimy and affect the broth. Remove from the heat and allow the stock to cool before squeezing the liquid out of the shiitake mushrooms into the broth. (You can use the rehydrated mushrooms in other recipes – bonus!) The dashi will keep in an airtight container in the fridge for up to 1 week.

For the scallops, trim the end of each mushroom stem, and reserve the mushroom caps for another recipe. Slice each mushroom stem into 2 cm (¾ in) thick rounds. Use a paring knife to score a diamond pattern into both sides of each mushroom round. Combine all the scallop ingredients in a container small enough to submerge the mushrooms. Leave to marinate for at least 30 minutes on the bench, and up to 12 hours in the fridge.

When you're ready to roll, remove the scallops from the marinade, reserving 160 ml (5½ fl oz) of the marinade in a mixing jug. Pat the scallops dry with paper towel and season one side with salt and pepper. Add the wine, lemon juice, fish sauce and curry powder to the marinade and whisk together.

Heat the olive oil in a large frying pan over high heat. Once the oil is smoking, add the scallops to the pan, seasoned side down. Season the exposed side of the scallops and cook for 2–3 minutes, until the undersides begin to char, then flip the scallops. Push the scallops to one side of the pan and add the celery, carrot, peas and green beans. Cook on high heat for a further 3–4 minutes, until both sides of the scallops are golden and beginning to blacken.

Pour the reserved marinade into the pan, stirring to deglaze the pan and mix everything together. Cook over high heat for a few more minutes, until the vegetables are just cooked and the mixture is no longer liquidy. Set aside to cool.

Preheat the oven to 200°C (400°F). Lightly grease the holes of a jumbo six-hole muffin tin.

Use a 12 cm (4¾ in) cutter to cut out six circles from the pastry. Press one into each muffin hole, then evenly spoon in the filling mixture. Press your tater tots on top to create a top crust.

Bake for 25 minutes, then remove from the oven and carefully remove the pies from the muffin holes. Transfer to a baking tray and bake for another 5–10 minutes, until the tops are golden brown. Enjoy steaming hot, right away.

PUFF PIECE
If you prefer a puff pastry topping, cut out six 8 cm (3¼ in)
pastry rounds and use these as the pie lids. Cut a few small
slits in the pastry for steam to escape during baking.

Fruit pies

See a box of fruit that's about to turn mushy and needs saving? It's going right in here. This pie recipe is a fabulous template for cycling through seasonal finds. Whatever you can find that's tasty, abundant and cheap is probably going to taste even better encased in pastry. Here are a few of my favourite fruit fillings for you to choose from, to get you started.

An American-style pie crust with a high fat content can help insulate the base from liquid that the fruit releases while baking. Cooking the fruit first and combining it with thickeners can also help combat sogginess from excess liquid. Decorating the top with your own vision of artistic direction is easy. Lovingly laying a lattice over pie fillings you've freshly made feels meditative, and you'll love the results even more!

—

vegan butter, for greasing and dotting over the pie
plain (all-purpose) flour, for dusting
1 × quantity Pie crust (page 43)
plant-based milk, for brushing
demerara sugar, for sprinkling

BLUEBERRY FILLING
1 kg (2 lb 3 oz) fresh blueberries
170 g (6 oz) granulated white sugar
2 tablespoons cornflour (cornstarch)
15 g (½ oz) vegan butter
½ teaspoon ground cinnamon
¼ teaspoon fine salt
zest and juice of 1 lemon

RHUBARB & STRAWBERRY FILLING
1 × quantity Rhubarb & strawberry filling (page 183)

First, prepare your chosen filling. For the blueberry filling, toss all the ingredients together in a large bowl.

For the blackberry, pear and sour cream filling, cook the blackberries in a large saucepan over medium heat with a splash of water for 10 minutes, stirring now and then, or until syrupy. Stir the sugar and vanilla through, then switch off the heat. Mix together the sour cream and cornflour, then stir through the blackberries.

Preheat the oven to 200°C (400°F). Lightly grease a 20–25 cm (8–10 in) pie tin with butter.

Lightly flour your benchtop and divide the dough in half. With a rolling pin, roll one half into a circle that's larger than your pie tin – about 30 cm (12 in) wide. Use a pizza cutter to evenly trim the edge, then carefully lift the dough into your pie tin and press it into place, allowing the excess to hang over the edge.

If using the blackberry, pear and sour cream filling, arrange the pear, cut side up, in the pie dish, then pour the blackberry mixture over, to fill the pie. Otherwise, just pour your chosen filling into the pie dish, smoothing out the top. If making this for loved ones, dot extra butter over the filling, for luck.

Now we'll top the pie with a lattice crust (see opposite for other decorating options). Roll the other dough half into a 25 cm (10 in) circle, then use a pizza cutter to cut the dough into thin, even strips. Remove every second pastry strip and lay it, spaced out, over the pie filling, to form the start of the lattice. Choose your strips carefully, to make sure the length runs across the whole pie to create the right effect.

Peel back every second strip on the pie, towards you. Lay one of the remaining strips at a perpendicular angle over the part of the pie closest to you. Lay the peeled-back strips back into place, to create a woven look. Peel back the strips that you didn't for the previous layer and repeat this process.

APPLE STRUDEL FILLING
1 × quantity Apple strudel filling (page 156)

BLACKBERRY, PEAR & SOUR CREAM
500 g (1 lb 2 oz) frozen blackberries

120 g (4½ oz) granulated white sugar

1 teaspoon natural vanilla extract

100 g (3½ oz) vegan sour cream

1 tablespoon cornflour (cornstarch)

4 pears, peeled and cut in half, core and seeds removed

Continue until the pie is covered in the woven top. You can turn the pie 180 degrees at the end and fix up some of the strips closer to you if needed.

Trim the excess pastry with scissors and use a fork to crimp around the edge. (You may like to cut leaves out of the leftover dough and adorn the edge of the crust to create more drama.) Brush the top with milk and sprinkle with demerara sugar.

Place your beautiful pie on the bottom shelf of the oven and turn the temperature down to 180°C (350°F). Bake for at least 1 hour (and up to 1½ hours), until the top is browned and the filling is bubbling. During baking, move the pie around the oven occasionally, for even browning. If you need to, you can blast the top under the oven grill (broiler) towards the end, for a gorgeously crisp crust.

Remove from the oven and allow to cool fully before slicing and serving. Any leftover pie will keep in an airtight container at room temperature for 2 days.

OTHER DECORATING OPTIONS

FOR A PATTERN PRINT
Roll the second dough half into a 25 cm (10 in) circle, then use a pizza cutter to evenly trim the edge. Use a cookie cutter to cut out evenly spaced areas, to create a pattern in the dough – round, scalloped, leaf or many novelty-shaped cutters work well. Alternatively, run an engraved rolling pin over the dough to indent an intricate design into it.

Carefully lift the dough and centre it over the pie. Press it into place, allowing the excess to hang over the edge.

IF YOU'VE NOT MADE A PATTERN
Just make a few slits about 4 cm (1½ in) long in the centre of the pie to allow steam to escape!

This pie has got a face like a ... er, well, dropped pie, thanks to a rogue vibrating stand mixer under the watch of a since-exiled member of *The Vegan Baker* team. You may have been robbed of seeing the gorgeous latticed crust, but no matter how you slice it, there's really no better way to show you why nothing but fresh blueberries makes for my all-time favourite pie filling.

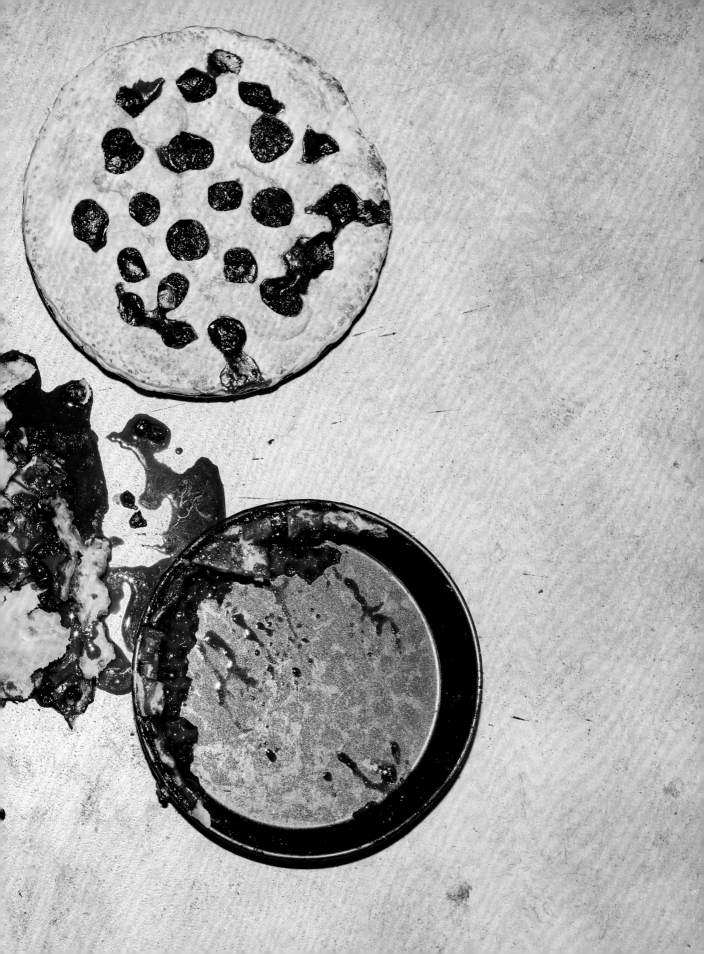

Rhubarb & strawberry handpies

(MEDIUM) **MAKES: 12**

Handpies topped with an easy 'slit lattice' will delight anyone (who doesn't suffer from trypophobia). You can swap in whichever pie filling you fancy (check out some other fillings on pages 178–179), but these rhubarb and strawberry ones are specifically a tribute to my nana, the world's biggest rhubarb lover. The tangy-sweet filling will convince you rhubarb practically goes in everything – even though, as we've learned through Nan, it definitely doesn't! Skip the savoury jelly experiments and have a go at these perfect handpies.

—

1 × quantity Rough puff
(page 49)
plain (all-purpose) flour,
for dusting
60 ml (2 fl oz) soy milk
demerara sugar, for
sprinkling

**RHUBARB &
STRAWBERRY FILLING**
300 g (10½ oz) rhubarb
stalks, finely chopped
160 g (5½ oz) strawberry
jam
55 g (2 oz) caster
(superfine) sugar
20 g (¾ oz) cornflour
(cornstarch)
30 g (1 oz) vegan butter,
softened
1 teaspoon natural
vanilla extract
big pinch of fine salt

Preheat the oven to 200°C (400°F). Line two baking trays with baking paper or silicone baking mats.

In a large bowl, mix together the rhubarb and strawberry filling ingredients until the rhubarb is coated.

Cut the rough puff in half. On a lightly floured work surface, roll each half into a 30 cm × 40 cm (12 in × 16 in) rectangle. Use a pizza slicer to trim the edges, then cut each rectangle into 12 even portions.

Transfer 12 of the dough rectangles to the prepared trays, spacing them out. Use a butter knife to make alternating slits over the remaining 12 rectangles to create a lattice effect.

Evenly spoon about 2 tablespoons of the filling into the centre of each rectangle on the prepared trays. Add the milk to a small bowl, then use a pastry brush to coat all the edges of the pastry rectangles.

Take one of the latticed rectangles, stretch it out slightly, then centre it over a filled one and press down. Use a fork to crimp the edges. Repeat to seal all the pies, then brush the tops with the remaining milk and sprinkle with a little demerara sugar.

Bake for 20–25 minutes, until the pastry is crispy and golden all around, and the filling starts trying to escape through the slits in the lattice.

Remove from the oven and allow to cool fully before serving. The handpies will keep in an airtight container at room temperature for up to 2 days.

Mini lemon meringue pies

(MEDIUM) MAKES: 10

A good lemon meringue pie doesn't come easy peasy lemon squeezy. It doesn't have to be stressed, depressed lemon zest either. The Italian-style method takes a little extra effort, but creates a sturdy, marshmallowy meringue that will stand up to a hearty scorching.

—

1 × quantity Shortcrust pastry (page 42)
plain (all-purpose) flour, for dusting
2 tablespoons aquafaba
1 × quantity Lemon curd (page 24)

ITALIAN MERINGUE
160 ml (5½ fl oz) aquafaba
white vinegar, for dabbing
½ teaspoon agar agar powder
110 g (4 oz) caster (superfine) sugar

To prepare the meringue, pour the aquafaba into a small saucepan and bring to a vigorous bubble over medium heat. Maintain the boil for about 10 minutes, until it has reduced to 85 ml (2¾ fl oz). Transfer to a heatproof bowl, then cover and chill in the fridge – ideally overnight – to get very chilly and gelatinous.

Preheat the oven to 170°C (340°F). Roll out the pastry on a floured work surface to about 5 mm (¼ in) thick. Use a 10 cm (4 in) cookie cutter to cut out 10 circles from the pastry, then transfer to a baking tray lined with baking paper. Reroll the pastry scraps, then use a sharp knife to cut thirty 1 cm (½ in) thick strips.

With a pastry brush, dab aquafaba around the outer edge of each pastry circle, then guide the strips to form an outer crust around each pie. Press down gently to adhere, then brush the entire pastry surface with more aquafaba. Repeat this step twice more to build solid castle walls that will protect their fillings.

Prick the pie cases all over with a fork. Bake for 25 minutes, rotating the tray halfway through cooking, until just the edges of the pastry have browned. Cool fully on a wire rack before proceeding.

Spoon the lemon curd into the cool pastry cases and place in the fridge while you prepare the meringue.

Use a paper towel dabbed with vinegar to wipe out the bowl of a stand mixer and over the whisk attachment. Pour the thickened aquafaba into the bowl and beat on high speed for 5 minutes or until soft peaks form.

Meanwhile, in a saucepan, mix together the agar agar powder and 180 ml (6 fl oz) of water and bring to the boil. Stir in the sugar and boil until it dissolves. Remove from the heat.

Turn the beaters to medium speed and slowly pour in the agar agar mixture in a thin stream over the course of 2 minutes until stiff peaks form. Beat on high speed for 1 minute more or until very glossy.

Set the oven grill (broiler) to high heat. While the meringue is warm but not too hot, fit a piping (icing) bag with a nozzle and spoon the meringue into the bag, but don't overfill, so you can twist it tightly shut. Pipe the meringue over the lemon curd in swirls that graduate to the centre.

Immediately place the pies about 12–13 cm (4¾–5 in) beneath the grill. Monitor closely for 3–5 minutes, until the meringue tops are browned nicely.

Eat warm if you can't wait, or cool fully to allow the meringue to set further. The pies will keep in an airtight container in the fridge for 3 days.

Black forest pie

(EASY) **MAKES: 1 LARGE PIE**

You find yourself wandering a dark, black forest, when you look up and see light glimmering through the canopy. The white chocolate ganache cream smeared atop this pie is unconventional but delightful, giving you a streak of brightness among the dense and rich flavours found on the forest floor. Here, kirsch liqueur, dark chocolate and coffee provide the necessary foliage for the beautiful cherry flavour to blossom in.

—

plain (all-purpose) flour,
   for dusting
1 × quantity Shortcrust
   pastry (page 42)
50 g (1¾ oz) vegan
   chocolate cookies
2 tablespoons icing
   (confectioners') sugar
30 g (1 oz) dairy-free dark
   chocolate, shaved
handful of fresh cherries

SOUR CHERRY FILLING
1 kg (2 lb 3 oz) frozen
   pitted cherries
100 g (3½ oz) granulated
   white sugar
60 ml (2 fl oz) lemon juice
60 ml (2 fl oz) kirsch
2 teaspoons natural
   vanilla extract
30 g (1 oz) cornflour
   (cornstarch)

COFFEE GANACHE
120 g (4½ oz) dairy-free
   dark chocolate
2½ tablespoons coconut
   cream or vegan cream
½ teaspoon instant
   coffee powder

**WHITE CHOCOLATE
GANACHE CREAM**
120 g (4½ oz) dairy-free
   white chocolate
210 ml (7 fl oz) vegan
   cream, chilled
3 tablespoons icing
   (confectioners') sugar

Preheat the oven to 150°C (300°F). Lightly grease a 25 cm (10 in) pie dish.

On a lightly floured work surface, roll the pastry out to about 5 mm (¼ in) thick. Ease the dough into the pie dish, manoeuvring it to fit evenly with your fingertips. Reroll the scraps of dough and cut a strip of pastry large enough to run around the inner edge of the pie dish to form a thicker crust. Prick the dough all over with a fork and blind-bake for about 30 minutes, until golden all over.

Meanwhile, in a saucepan, whisk together the sour cherry filling ingredients and place over medium heat. Cook, stirring occasionally, for 12–15 minutes, until the cherries have broken down and the mixture is dramatically thicker. Allow to cool for 30 minutes.

To make the coffee ganache, add the chocolate to a microwave-safe bowl and blast in a microwave, stirring at 15 second-increments, until melted. Whisk in the remaining ganache ingredients until combined, then spread all over the base of the baked pie crust. Crumble half the cookies on top. Pour the cooled sour cherry filling over the cookies, then smooth out. Let the pie sit in the fridge for a few hours to get fully cold, before proceeding with the final steps.

To make the white chocolate ganache cream, add the white chocolate and 3 tablespoons of the cream to a microwave-safe bowl and blast in a microwave, stirring at 15 second-increments, until melted. Allow to fully cool in the fridge.

Just before serving, use a large mixing bowl and hand-held electric beaters to beat the chilled white chocolate ganache cream for 2 minutes to loosen. Pour in the remaining chilled cream and the icing sugar and beat for a further 3–4 minutes on high speed to thicken. Generously scoop the white chocolate ganache cream all over the top of the pie and crumble the remaining cookies over the cream. Scatter with the shaved chocolate and throw fresh cherries on top to finish the job! Serve immediately.

Pecan cookie pie

(MEDIUM) **MAKES: 1 LARGE PIE**

Pecan pie ... but with a pie crust made from choc-chip cookie dough! The liquid from the pecan topping seeps into the crust and caramelises as the whole thing bakes. A real feast for the soul.

—

cooking spray, for greasing
1 × quantity Chocolate chip cookie dough (page 224)
20 g (¾ oz) flaxseed (linseed) meal
2½ tablespoons bourbon
250 g (9 oz) pecans
130 g (4½ oz) brown sugar
60 g (2 oz) vegan butter or vegan shortening, melted
60 ml (2 fl oz) soy milk
30 g (1 oz) cornflour (cornstarch)
75 g (2¾ oz) glucose syrup
1 teaspoon vanilla bean paste
½ teaspoon coarse salt
vegan ice cream or whipped vegan cream, to serve

Preheat the oven to 160°C (320°F). Lightly grease a 20 cm (8 in) springform cake tin. Use your hands to compress the cookie dough into the tin to form a base.

Blind-bake the cookie dough for 20 minutes, or until just beginning to set. Resist the temptation to eat the giant cookie base while it cools. Channel that energy into either a second batch of cookie dough for snacking, or proceed right on with the filling.

In a small bowl, mix the flaxseed meal with the bourbon. Set aside to thicken.

Set aside one-third of the pecans for decorating the pie. In a large bowl, break the remaining pecans into halves (you may find it easier to give them a quick pulse in a food processor). Mix in the sugar, butter, milk, cornflour, glucose syrup and vanilla bean paste, then fold the flaxseed gel through.

Spread the mixture onto the baked cookie crust. Smooth out, then jam the reserved whole pecans into the top to make the pie look generously filled.

Bake for 1 hour or until the top is golden brown and crisp. Turn the oven off and leave the pie inside to cool for a few hours.

Scatter the salt over the pie, then remove the side of the cake tin. Serve with ice cream or whipped cream piled onto each slice.

You'll eat the whole thing within 3 days if you're a smart cookie.

TOP THAT!
Want more cookie per bite of cookie pie? Make a batch of Chocolate florentine dough (page 230) and dot half the dough over the top of the pie for the last 10–15 minutes of baking. You'll get soft cookie on the base, and crunchy cookie on the top of every bite!

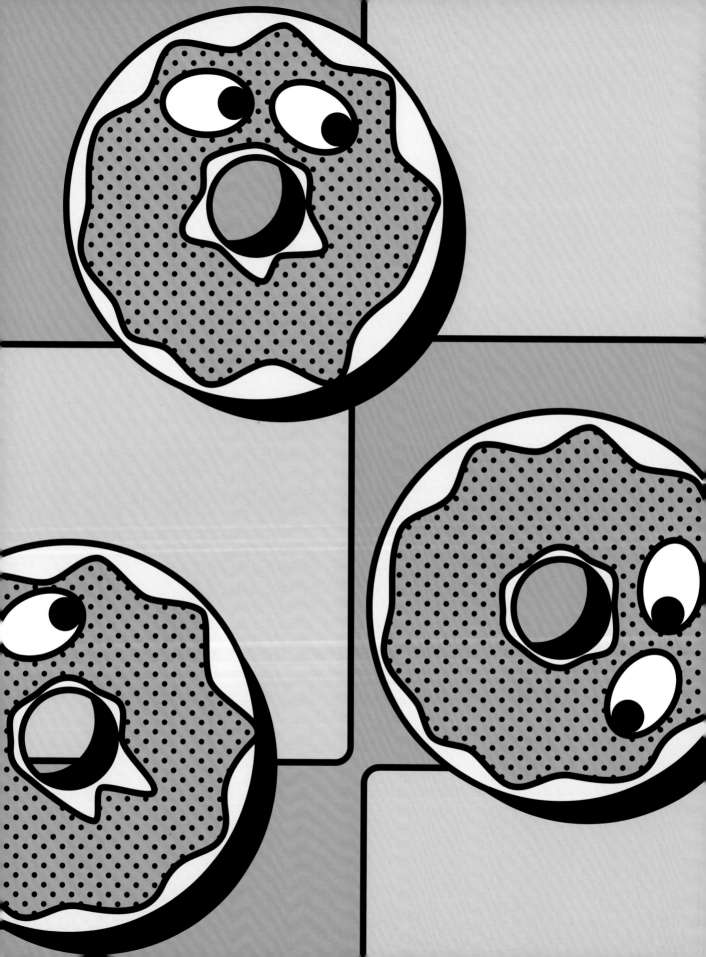

Donuts

Sweet potato beaver tails

(EASY)   MAKES: 8

These Canadian carnival classics seem like the intersection on a Venn diagram of donuts and flatbread upon first encounter. The top is scored to mimic the appearance of a beaver's tail before frying, which also helps them to hold on to flavour. I love them simply dressed with cinnamon sugar and drizzled with fresh lemon juice, but the wide surface area on these bad boys mean they'll form a dam to hold all sorts of sweet garnishes.

—

60 ml (2 fl oz) soy milk
1 teaspoon white vinegar
120 g (4½ oz) plain
    (all-purpose) flour, plus
    extra for dusting
120 g (4½ oz) wholemeal
    (whole-wheat) flour
7 g (2 teaspoons) instant
    dried yeast
25 g (1 oz) granulated
    white sugar
¼ teaspoon fine salt
45 g (1½ oz) vegan butter
125 g (4½ oz) mashed
    orange sweet potato
    (see Tip)
1 teaspoon natural
    vanilla extract
olive oil, for greasing
neutral-flavoured oil for
    deep-frying

TO SERVE
50 g (1¾ oz) Cinnamon
    sugar (page 198)
1 lemon, cut into wedges

MASH IT, SWEETIE!
To prepare the sweet potato, peel off the skin and cut the flesh into 2.5 cm (1 in) chunks. Place in a microwave-safe dish, then cover and blast on full intensity for 6 minutes, or until the sweet potato is soft. Tip into a large bowl and mash with a fork until silky smooth.

In a small bowl, combine the soy milk and vinegar. Set aside for 5 minutes to thicken and curdle into buttermilk.

In a large bowl, stir together the flours, yeast, sugar and salt.

Mash the butter into the sweet potato with a potato masher in a separate large bowl, then vigorously stir in the flour mixture to achieve a crumbly mixture. Stir in the buttermilk and vanilla until combined, then knead the dough on a benchtop for 2–3 minutes, until the dough is smooth and sexy. You won't need to flour the bench for this part, as the dough should pull away from it.

Lightly oil the first large bowl, then add the dough, cover with a tea towel and leave to rise in a warm place for 1–2 hours, until doubled in size.

Lightly flour your benchtop. Punch down the dough and divide into eight balls, each weighing about 60 g (2 oz). Roll the dough balls between your palms until smooth, then roll into flat ovals with a rolling pin. Adjust the sides so they're even, and will come out of the fryer looking camera-ready. Use a dough scraper to score a crisscross pattern into the top of each donut, to get the tell-tale look. Use the dough scraper to transfer your beaver tails to a well-floured benchtop or silicone baking mats. Cover and leave to rise for 30–60 minutes, until doubled in size.

Heat at least 5 cm (2 in) of neutral-flavoured oil in a large heavy-based saucepan until the temperature registers above 175°C (345°F) on a kitchen thermometer, or when the handle of a wooden spoon instantly bubbles when placed in the oil. Adjust the temperature slightly to keep it around 175°C (345°F) while frying the beaver tails.

Get ready to dress your beaver tails as they leave the fryer by tipping the cinnamon sugar into a shallow bowl.

Working in two batches, slide a wide spatula or dough scraper under the puffed-up beaver tails and transfer to the hot oil. Fry for about 2 minutes on each side, until golden, then remove to paper towel to drain. While still hot, quickly toss the beaver tails in the cinnamon sugar and serve right away, with lemon wedges for squeezing over.

Store any leftovers in an airtight container and demolish within a day.

Italian donut holes

(MEDIUM)   MAKES: 24

Bomboloncini – Italian donut holes – is hard to say, but easy to eat. Once they're fried, you can toss them in sugar or fill them with an endless supply of things to ooze out of the centre: créme pâtissiére, flavoured creams, jams, buttercream … just about anything that'll squeeze into a piping (icing) bag. My favourite is lime or lemon zest beaten into cream or créme pâtissiére. You can also use the method from the Cinnamon potato donuts recipe on page 198 to make these into 60 g (2 oz) classic ring-shaped donuts.

—

275 g (9½ oz) bread flour or plain (all-purpose) flour, plus extra for dusting
25 g (1 oz) granulated white sugar
3 tablespoons aquafaba
7 g (2 teaspoons) instant dried yeast
90 ml (3 fl oz) plant-based milk
1 teaspoon fine salt
20 g (¾ oz) vegan butter
zest of 1 lemon
caster (superfine) sugar, for sprinkling
neutral-flavoured oil, for deep-frying

Add the flour, sugar, aquafaba, yeast, milk and 60 ml (2 fl oz) of water to the bowl of a stand mixer fitted with the dough hook. Begin kneading on medium speed for 16–20 minutes. After the first 3 minutes of kneading, add the salt, then the butter, teaspoon by teaspoon. Dump in the lemon zest. When the dough passes the windowpane test (page 52), cover the bowl with a tea towel and let it rise in a warm spot for about 2 hours, until doubled in size.

Punch down the dough to deflate it, then divide into 20 g (¾ oz) pieces about the size of ping-pong balls. For each piece, fold the edges over the top and pinch to gather them together to create a smooth ball. Flip the ball seam side down onto a very lightly floured work surface.

Cup a hand around one side of a dough ball and push the ball from side to side, left to right and towards you, allowing the dough to balloon out as it rolls and smooth out any seams. Alternatively, use your palms to roll the dough into smooth balls. Repeat with the remaining dough balls. Allow to rest on a lightly floured surface for another 2 hours, to almost double in size again.

Heat 5–7.5 cm (2–3 in) of neutral-flavoured oil in a large heavy-based saucepan until the temperature registers above 175°C (345°F) on a kitchen thermometer, or when the handle of a wooden spoon instantly bubbles when placed in the oil. Adjust the temperature slightly to keep it around 175°C (345°F) while frying the donuts.

Place enough caster sugar to coat the donuts in a wide bowl.

Working in batches, carefully add the donuts to the hot oil and cook for 2–3 minutes, gently moving them around with a slotted spoon until evenly golden brown. Transfer to paper towel to drain, then immediately toss in the sugar until completely coated.

Eat the donuts warm, or allow to cool before proceeding to make the donut hole croquembouche on page 210. Eat within a day of making to enjoy the best and freshest results.

Berliners

A blasphemously unholy donut, or the biggest donut hole ever – depending on your perspective. Where once lay a void in this donut is now engorged with piped-in jam oozing out of the centre. How's that for efficient German design?

—

neutral-flavoured oil, for
   deep-frying
100 g (3½ oz) jam of your
   choice
60 g (2 oz) icing
   (confectioners') sugar

BERLINER DOUGH
275 g (9½ oz) bread flour
   or plain (all-purpose)
   flour, plus extra for
   dusting
25 g (1 oz) granulated
   white sugar
2 tablespoons aquafaba
7 g (2 teaspoons) instant
   dried yeast
90 ml (3 fl oz) plant-based
   milk
1 teaspoon fine salt
20 g (¾ oz) vegan butter

To make the dough, add the flour, sugar, aquafaba, yeast, milk and 60 ml (2 fl oz) of water to the bowl of a stand mixer fitted with the dough hook. Begin kneading on medium speed for 16–20 minutes. After the first 3 minutes of kneading, add the salt, then the butter, teaspoon by teaspoon. When the dough passes the windowpane test (page 52), cover the bowl with a tea towel and let it rise in a warm spot for about 2 hours, until doubled in size.

Punch down the dough to deflate it, then divide into 60 g (2 oz) pieces, about the size of a billiard ball. For each piece, fold the edges over the top and pinch to gather them together to create a smooth ball. Flip the ball seam side down onto a very lightly floured work surface.

Cup a hand around one side of a dough ball and push the ball from side to side, left to right and towards you, allowing the dough to balloon out as it rolls and smooth out any seams. Pull the ball to stretch it slightly into a fat oval shape, then repeat with the remaining dough balls. Allow to rest on a lightly floured surface for another 2 hours to almost doubled in size again.

Heat 5–7.5 cm (2–3 in) of neutral-flavoured oil in a large heavy-based saucepan until the temperature registers above 175°C (345°F) on a kitchen thermometer, or when the handle of a wooden spoon instantly bubbles when placed in the oil. Adjust the temperature slightly to keep it around 175°C (345°F) while frying the donuts.

Working in batches, carefully add the donuts to the hot oil and cook for 4–5 minutes, gently moving them around with a slotted spoon until evenly golden brown. Transfer to paper towel to drain.

Fit a piping (icing) bag with a star nozzle and place it in a tall jug, furling the edges over the rim to hold it in place. Spoon the jam into the bag, but don't overfill, so you can twist the bag tightly shut. Use a chopstick to pierce a hole in one side of each donut, then insert the nozzle and fill generously with jam. Repeat, then toss the donuts in the icing sugar to finish.

Eat within a day of making to enjoy the best and freshest results.

Cinnamon potato donuts

(EASY)   **MAKES: 12**

Yes, potato is the secret to the softest donuts ever – it's time to get with the times! Except it's no new idea: potato can be found in donut recipes for almost as long as commercial donut recipes have been around. Unseasoned leftover mashed potatoes just discovered their destiny in these vegan donuts, which taste the same as regular donuts, but with an insanely light texture, and a miraculous ability to stave off staleness longer.

60 ml (2 fl oz) plant-based milk
1 teaspoon white vinegar
50 g (1¾ oz) vegan butter
125 g (4½ oz) mashed potato (unseasoned)
270 g (9½ oz) plain (all-purpose) flour
45 g (1½ oz) applesauce
35 g (1¼ oz) granulated white sugar
5 g (1½ teaspoons) instant dried yeast
¼ teaspoon sea salt
olive oil, for greasing
neutral-flavoured oil, for deep-frying

CINNAMON SUGAR
80 g (2¾ oz) caster (superfine) sugar
1 teaspoon ground cinnamon

In a small bowl, combine the milk and vinegar. Allow to sit for 5 minutes to curdle into buttermilk.

Mash the butter into the potato with a potato masher in a large bowl, then stir in the flour, applesauce, sugar, yeast and salt, followed by the buttermilk. Bring the dough together in the bowl and knead for 2–3 minutes, until smooth. Lightly oil the bowl, then cover the dough with a tea towel and let it rise in a warm spot for 1–2 hours, until doubled in size.

Punch down the dough, then divide into 50 g (1¾ oz) balls, slighly smaller than the size of billiard balls, and roll until smooth. Working with one dough ball at a time, press down firmly on the dough to form a disc, then use an egg ring to cut out a clean round. Use the cap of a water bottle to cut a hole out of the centre … which you can bunch together with the other dough scraps to form a Frankenstein-style abomination donut to reward the baker as the others cool. Repeat with the remaining dough balls.

Transfer each donut to a square of baking paper, cover with a tea towel and leave to rise for another 2 hours in a warm place.

Heat 5–7.5 cm (2–3 in) of neutral-flavoured oil in a large heavy-based saucepan until the temperature registers above 175°C (345°F) on a kitchen thermometer, or when the handle of a wooden spoon instantly bubbles when placed in the oil. Adjust the temperature slightly to keep it around 175°C (345°F) while frying the donuts.

Combine the cinnamon sugar ingredients in a wide bowl.

Working in batches, carefully add the donuts to the hot oil and cook for about 2 minutes on each side, until golden, then transfer to paper towel to drain.

While still warm, quickly toss the donuts in the cinnamon sugar and serve hot – or not, because they'll keep for up to 3 days protected in an airtight container before these spud nuts become dud nuts.

Baked chocolate donuts

(EASY)   MAKES: 12

Dark, brooding and for adults only, these donuts skipped the carnival and found themselves at a late-night lounge bar ... and sweet tooths aren't welcome around these parts.

½ teaspoon instant
    coffee powder
40 ml (1¼ fl oz) boiling
    water
1 tablespoon flaxseed
    (linseed) meal
cooking spray, for
    greasing
190 g (6¾ oz) plain
    (all-purpose) flour
160 g (5½ oz) granulated
    white sugar
20 g (¾ oz) Dutch
    (unsweetened) cocoa
    powder
1½ teaspoons baking
    powder
¼ teaspoon sea salt
180 ml (6 fl oz) plant-
    based milk
1 teaspoon natural
    vanilla extract
50 g (1¾ oz) vegan butter,
    melted, plus 1 teaspoon
    extra
100 g (3½ oz) dairy-free
    dark chocolate, roughly
    chopped
dairy-free chocolate
    sprinkles, for
    decorating

Preheat the oven to 180°C (350°F).

Add the coffee powder to the boiling water and set aside. When cooled, whisk in the flaxseed meal and set aside to thicken. Use cooking spray to grease two six-hole donut baking trays.

In a large mixing bowl, mix together the flour, sugar, cocoa powder, baking powder and salt. Make a well in the centre.

Mix together the milk, vanilla and melted butter in a mixing jug, then pour into the dry ingredients, along with the flaxseed gel. Stir well to combine and bring the ingredients together.

Divide the mixture among the donut trays, filling each hole about three-quarters of the way up. Smooth the donuts with the back of a spoon, then transfer to the oven and bake for 14–16 minutes, until a skewer inserted in the middle of the donuts comes out clean. Cool on wire racks.

Combine the 1 teaspoon of butter and the dark chocolate in a small microwave-safe bowl. Blast in a microwave, stirring at 15-second increments, until melted and dippable. Dip the smooth side of the donuts into the glaze and return to the wire racks. Scatter chocolate sprinkles over the top and allow to set.

As always, keeping them well wrapped and in an airtight environment will buy you a few days of keeping time with these donuts.

Churros

(EASY) MAKES: 6

Churros are one of those fabulous treats that, no matter how speedy meal delivery services become, you'll always be able to make a better and faster version yourself. Using ingredients you DEFINITELY have at the back of your pantry – grab that almost-expired packet of hot chocolate mix while you're there! – you can whip together a fresh plate of hot Spanish donuts in about 30 minutes. Ándale!

120 g (4½ oz) plain (all-purpose) flour
¼ teaspoon fine salt
240 ml (8 fl oz) boiling water
½ teaspoon baking powder
2 tablespoons aquafaba
neutral-flavoured oil, for deep-frying
Cinnamon sugar (page 198), for sprinkling

TO SERVE (OPTIONAL)
Ganache (page 31)
Dulce de leche (page 33)
Caramel (page 37)

Combine the flour and salt in a small saucepan. Stir in the boiling water with a wooden spoon to make a thick batter, then cook over medium heat for 1 minute. Switch off the heat and add the baking powder, folding over the dough to mix it through. Allow to cool for 10 minutes, then stir in the aquafaba until smooth. The dough will be quite stiff.

Fit a heavy-duty piping (icing) bag with a star nozzle at least 1 cm (½ in) thick and place it in a tall jug, furling the edges over the rim to hold it in place. Spoon the churro dough into the bag, but don't overfill it, so you can twist the bag tightly shut. Leave to rest while you prepare the oil.

Heat 5–7.5 cm (2–3 in) of neutral-flavoured oil in a large heavy-based saucepan until the temperature registers above 175°C (345°F) on a kitchen thermometer, or when the handle of a wooden spoon instantly bubbles when placed in the oil. Adjust the temperature slightly to keep it around 175°C (345°F) while frying the churros.

You can pipe the churros straight into the hot oil and use scissors to snip off your ideal lengths as you go. For beginners and those who seek control of the whole process, pipe each churro onto baking paper, so you can just drop them into the oil in batches. (Popping them into the freezer for 30 minutes ahead of frying can help define the ridges in your churros.)

Fry the churros in batches for 3–4 minutes, until golden brown. Use tongs to transfer the fried churros to paper towel to drain. Toss with lots of cinnamon sugar. Serve with hot chocolate or coffee, and your choice of sweet gooey sauces for dunking into.

Churros are normally eaten for breakfast in Spain, so make them early in the day and enjoy them warm within a few hours of frying. Those who enjoy the art of an afternoon nap are welcome to count a post-siesta churro session as a traditional second breakfast for the day.

Portuguese pumpkin dreams

(EASY)   **MAKES: ABOUT 32**

Sonhos de abóbora, or Portuguese donuts, are the cool friend that I invite with me to potlucks and picnics so people think I'm more interesting by association. That friend's secret? Overcompensating with a flask in their handbag. Each of these Christmas-infused pumpkin dreams can hold a formidable volume of brandy splashed over the top, and are just what you need to turn any festivity into a *real* party.

—

2 kg (4 lb 6 oz) pumpkin (winter squash)
80 g (2¾ oz) walnuts, crumbled
14 g (5 scant teaspoons) active dried yeast
60 ml (2 fl oz) warm water
500 g (1 lb 2 oz) bread flour
150 g (5½ oz) granulated white sugar
1 tablespoon psyllium husk powder
½ teaspoon fine salt
60 ml (2 fl oz) brandy
zest and juice of 1 orange
1 teaspoon natural vanilla extract
½ teaspoon baking powder
neutral-flavoured oil, for deep-frying, plus extra for greasing

FOR COATING
brandy, for sloshing
generous pinch of sea salt or smoked salt
Cinnamon sugar (page 198)

Preheat the oven to 200°C (400°F).

Cut the pumpkin into thick slabs and bake for 45–60 minutes, until the flesh is tender when poked with a fork. Weigh out 600 g (1 lb 5 oz) of the roasted pumpkin flesh and use a food processor to blend it for a few minutes until smooth. While the oven is still on, spread the walnuts on a baking tray and bake for about 10 minutes, until toasty and fragrant.

Combine the yeast and warm water in a small bowl and leave for 5 minutes to bloom.

In a large bowl, mix together the flour, sugar, psyllium husk powder, toasted walnuts and salt. Make a well in the centre and add the pureed pumpkin, yeast mixture, brandy, orange zest and juice, vanilla and baking powder. Stir well to combine fully. Cover and rest in a warm spot to rise for 1 hour, or until doubled in size.

Heat 5–7.5 cm (2–3 in) of neutral-flavoured oil in a large heavy-based saucepan until the temperature registers above 175°C (345°F) on a kitchen thermometer, or when the handle of a wooden spoon instantly bubbles when placed in the oil. Adjust the temperature slightly to keep it around 175°C (345°F) while frying the donuts.

Pour a small amount of cold oil into a cup. Dip a dessertspoon into the oil, then scoop up a small spoonful of the risen pumpkin mixture and smooth it out with another oiled spoon (if you want truly, perfectly round donuts; otherwise just use one spoon).

Carefully slide the dough with your finger from the oiled spoon smoothly into the hot oil. Repeat until the pot is filled – but not so much that the donuts don't have their own personal space.

Fry for about 2 minutes on each side, until dark golden, then transfer to paper towel to drain. Repeat in batches to use all the pumpkin mixture.

While still warm, slosh some brandy over the donuts, then toss with the salt, followed by the cinnamon sugar. Allow to cool before entering pumpkin dreamland.

Store the donuts spread out in an airtight container to travel with you to picnics and potlucks within 2 days of frying.

Loukoumades

My grandmother always says that loukoumades are best enjoyed on a cold, rainy day. Given that her hometown boasts the annual rainfall record for the country, I take this to mean Greek-style donuts are an everyday treat. Some emerge from the fryer wonderfully round, others with their own tails, but what really makes these is the post-fry drenching in something syrupy.

—

7 g (2 teaspoons) active
    dried yeast
125 ml (4 fl oz) warm
    water, plus an extra
    185 ml (6 fl oz)
300 g (10½ oz) plain
    (all-purpose) flour
½ teaspoon sea salt
neutral-flavoured oil, for
    deep-frying, plus extra
    for greasing

FOR COATING
Vegan honey (page 39),
    for drizzling
crushed pistachios, for
    sprinkling

OPTIONAL TOPPINGS
Dulce de leche (page 33)
Chocolate hazelnut
    spread (page 105)
    and nuts
ground cinnamon
icing (confectioners')
    sugar
maple syrup

Combine the yeast and the 125 ml (4 fl oz) of warm water in a small jug and set aside for 5 minutes to bloom.

Combine the flour and salt in a large bowl. Make a well in the centre and add the yeast mixture and the remaining 185 ml (6 fl oz) of warm water. Using a wooden spoon, bring the mixture together until you have a sticky and relatively runny dough. Cover with plastic wrap and set aside in a warm spot for at least 1 hour, until doubled in size.

Heat 5–7.5 cm (2–3 in) of neutral-flavoured oil in a large heavy-based saucepan until the temperature registers above 175°C (345°F) on a kitchen thermometer, or when the handle of a wooden spoon instantly bubbles when placed in the oil. Adjust the temperature slightly to keep it around 175°C (345°F) while frying the donuts.

Pour a small amount of cold oil into a cup. Dip a dessertspoon into the oil, then scoop up a small spoonful of the risen dough and smooth it out with another oiled spoon (if you want truly, perfectly round donuts; otherwise just use one spoon).

Carefully slide the dough with your finger from the oiled spoon smoothly into the hot oil. Repeat until the pot is filled – but not so much that the donuts don't have their own personal space.

Fry for 1–2 minutes, gently turning the donuts in the oil until evenly golden, then transfer to paper towel to drain. Repeat in batches to use all the dough.

While still warm, transfer the loukoumades to a serving dish, drizzle with honey and sprinkle with crushed pistachios. Add any other toppings of your choice and serve warm, with little forks or toothpicks to snag the donuts with.

TO MAKE A SPICED SYRUP
Bring a few generous globs of vegan honey to a simmer with a dash of water, and an equal dash of sugar. Add a cinnamon stick, the zest of a lemon or orange, a few cloves or a pinch of ground cardamom – or add a little of everything! Allow to simmer for about 5 minutes without stirring, and the syrup will be good to go. Store any leftover syrup in a clean jar in the fridge.

Koeksisters

(EASY)   **MAKES: 8**

These aren't yeasted donuts, which means they do all their rising in the hot oil at the end, just like a true procrastinator. The trick is to dip them in ice-cold syrup right after deep-frying for a crunchy exterior and syrup-soaked middle. The second trick is that the dough is braided before frying, which means the crunchy exterior AND syrup-soaked middle is everywhere, all at once.

If you have some leftover spiced syrup in the fridge from the loukoumades recipe on page 206, add a fresh splash of lemon juice and use it here as the syrup instead!

—

190 g (6¾ oz) plain (all-purpose) flour, plus extra for dusting
20 g (¾ oz) granulated white sugar
4 teaspoons baking powder
5 teaspoons cornflour (cornstarch)
½ teaspoon fine salt
20 g (¾ oz) vegan butter
125 ml (4 fl oz) plant-based milk
neutral-flavoured oil, for deep-frying

DUNKING SYRUP
500 g (1 lb 2 oz) granulated white sugar
2 teaspoons lemon juice

To make the syrup, place the sugar in a saucepan, add 300 ml (10 fl oz) of water and stir to dissolve over medium heat. Boil for 10 minutes, then switch off the heat and add the lemon juice. Very carefully pour the syrup into a heatproof container and allow to cool fully in the fridge, moving to the freezer 20 minutes before frying the koeksisters.

In a large bowl, sift together the flour, sugar, baking powder, cornflour and salt. Use your fingertips to rub the butter into the flour mixture, until it is in fine crumbs. Slowly knead in the milk by hand to bring the dough together, then knead for a minute or so. Wrap in plastic wrap and chill in the fridge for at least 2 hours.

Lightly flour a work surface and use a rolling pin to roll the dough into a large rectangle, about 5 mm (¼ in) thick. Use a pizza cutter to trim the dough into a 10 cm × 40 cm (4 in × 16 in) rectangle, then cut into eight 5 cm (2 in) thick strips.

Place a strip in front of you. Leaving a 5 mm (½ in) edge intact at the top of the strip (to hold the strands of your plait together), cut two long slits down the length of the dough, to give you three even strips (still attached at the top) for braiding. Tightly braid the strips into a plait, then pinch the ends together to seal. Now pinch the top to complete the look. Repeat with the remaining dough.

Heat 5–7.5 cm (2–3 in) of neutral-flavoured oil in a large heavy-based saucepan until the temperature registers above 175°C (345°F) on a kitchen thermometer, or when the handle of a wooden spoon instantly bubbles when placed in the oil. Adjust the temperature to keep it around 175°C (345°F) while frying the koeksisters.

Divide your syrup between two shallow bowls, and keep one in the freezer to keep the syrup cold, until you have used all the syrup in the first bowl.

Fry the koeksisters in two batches for about 1½ minutes on each side. Remove with a slotted spoon, drain well on paper towel, then plunge immediately into the cold syrup.

Allow to set on a wire rack and serve once cooled, to be eaten the same day.

Donut hole croquembouche

(HARD)   MAKES: 1 DAZZLING TOWER

The donut holes might be mini, but each one is stuffed with a creamy custard filling and attached to one another with caramel to form a saccharine tower that tastes a bit like crème brûlée and teeters like a Christmas tree. It lights up like one, too, thanks to the spun caramel strands glimmering around the whole thing. A grand 'doughverload' that my roommate and in-house taste tester Stef says you should put on hair and makeup to eat.

—

1 × quantity Italian donut holes (page 194)
½ × quantity Custard (page 23)
icing (confectioners') sugar, for dusting

CARAMEL
300 g (10½ oz) granulated white sugar
2 tablespoons glucose syrup or corn syrup

Prepare the Italian donut holes as directed, but don't coat the donuts in sugar; instead, let them cool to lukewarm to prepare them for getting stuffed. Make sure the custard is fully cooled, too, and have it ready in a piping (icing) bag fitted with a thin nozzle.

Use a chopstick to pierce a hole in each donut hole, insert the piping nozzle, then fill generously with custard. Repeat until they are all done, then toss all the donuts in icing sugar to finish.

In a saucepan, whisk together the caramel ingredients and 120 ml (4 fl oz) of water over high heat. Cover the pan, then bring to the boil until the sugar has dissolved. Remove the lid and maintain a boil for 5–10 minutes, until the caramel just starts to change colour.

For a dense donut pyramid, simply stack the donuts as directed, filling the middle with donuts for structure. For a sweet skyscraper, make a sturdy, thin and tall pyramid out of foil to form the croquembouche base. Use another sheet of foil to cover the outside to make a clean appearance, should anything peek through the final tower. Use a little caramel to secure the makeshift croquembouche mould to the centre of a serving plate or cake platter.

Dip the bottom of each donut into the caramel to arrange as the croquembouche, using the caramel to secure them to the base of the plate, and then the following donuts onto the layer above them. (Leave the caramel on low heat if you need to buy yourself time to finish your tower before the caramel sets.)

Dip the prongs of two forks into the remaining caramel, hold them in one hand and swirl the caramel around the croquembouche to form strands encasing the whole pyramid. Tidy up any strands to form a sugary whirlwind.

Serve soon after, expect applause.

Cookies

Shortbread cookies

EASY   **MAKES: ABOUT 72 × 5 CM (2 IN) COOKIES**

Shortbread is a simple ratio of 1 part sugar to 2 parts butter to 3 parts flour. The dough can also be used as a base in some sweet pie recipes, especially the kind where the pie base is cooked separately ahead of time, for a 'no-bake' filling to be added before serving – such as the mini lemon meringue pies on page 184.

200 g (7 oz) vegan butter or shortening
100 g (3½ oz) icing (confectioners') sugar
300 g (10½ oz) plain (all-purpose) flour or 00 flour, plus extra for dusting
1 teaspoon fine salt

Using a large mixing bowl and a hand-held electric mixer, or a stand mixer fitted with the paddle attachment, cream together the butter and icing sugar for 2 minutes or until well beaten. Sift in the flour and salt and continue to beat together until a dough forms.

Turn the dough out onto a workbench and briefly knead with your hands to bring the dough into a ball. Cover with plastic wrap and refrigerate for 2 hours.

Preheat the oven to 160°C (320°F) and line two baking trays with baking paper or silicone baking mats.

On a floured benchtop, roll the dough out to a 1 cm (½ in) thick circle and use a 5 cm (2 in) wide cookie cutter of your choice to cut out cookies. Space the cookies on the baking tray and bake for 12–15 minutes, until lightly golden. Once cooled, the cookies will keep in an airtight container for up to 1 week.

Jam drops

These jam-drop cookies are one of the first things I made when I was young. They're simple enough that an inexperienced baker – or, literally, a child! – can put them together, but delicious enough that even the most experienced palates won't turn them down, fresh from the oven. Don't you dare use a fancy jam, either – just strawberry or raspberry. Anything more is trying too hard.

—

120 g (4½ oz) vegan butter
100 g (3½ oz) caster (superfine) sugar
200 g (7 oz) plain (all-purpose) flour
25 g (1 oz) cornflour (cornstarch)
2½ teaspoons baking powder
generous pinch of fine salt
4 teaspoons plant-based milk
160 g (5½ oz) jam of your choice

Preheat the oven to 200°C (400°F). Line a baking tray with baking paper or a silicone baking mat.

Using a large mixing bowl and a hand-held electric mixer, or a stand mixer fitted with the paddle attachment, cream together the butter and sugar for 2 minutes or until well beaten.

Sift in the flour, cornflour, baking powder and salt, then stir the dry ingredients through the creamed butter. Pour in the milk and use your hands to briefly knead together – you may need slightly more or less milk to achieve the nice stiff dough we're aiming for.

Tear off 30 g (1 oz) of the dough and use your hands to roll it into a smooth ball. Flatten the ball slightly, then use your thumbprint to indent the centre of the ball; alternatively, the end of a thick wooden spoon will do the trick. Use a teaspoon to fill the indentation with your chosen jam, then transfer to the prepared tray and repeat until all the dough is used up.

Bake the jam drops for 10–13 minutes, until beginning to brown around the edges. Cool fully on a wire rack, then store in an airtight container in the pantry. They'll keep for up to 1 week, ready for loved ones to drop in for a cup of tea and a cookie – until someone nicks them all!

Kourambiethes

Stolen straight out of my Aunt Honey's Christmas playbook, everybody clamours for a bite of these Greek Christmas cookies. Booze, cloves and a splash of rosewater are what make these buttery bites so popular during the holidays.

—

250 g (9 oz) vegan butter
75 g (2¾ oz) caster (superfine) sugar
1 tablespoon aquafaba
2 teaspoons brandy, ouzo or metaxa
330 g (11½ oz) plain (all-purpose) flour
60 g (2 oz) slivered almonds
about 25 whole cloves (optional)
60 g (2 oz) icing (confectioners') sugar, plus extra to serve
1 tablespoon rosewater

Ensure all the ingredients are cold for this recipe! (This will help stop the cookies spreading when the oven heat hits them.)

Lightly grease two large baking trays.

Using a large mixing bowl and a hand-held electric mixer, or a stand mixer fitted with the paddle attachment, cream together the butter, sugar, aquafaba and booze for 2 minutes, or until well beaten.

Sift the flour, then stir one-third of it through the creamed butter mixture, followed by half the slivered almonds. Add another one-third of the flour and the remaining almonds. Mix well before folding in the remaining flour.

Tear off 30 g (1 oz) of the dough and use your hands to roll it into a smooth ball. Evenly spread the balls across the baking trays, then place a whole clove in the centre of each. Press down lightly as you do so to create a dimple in the centre of each cookie for even baking.

Alternatively, to make half moon–shaped kourambiethes, shape each cookie into a log. Use your hands to curve the log around and press into a crescent. Lightly flatten each cookie to complete the half moon shape.

Move the cookies to the fridge for 1 hour to get fully chilly again before baking.

Preheat the oven to 150°C (300°F).

Bake the cookies for 25–30 minutes, watching closely and removing them from the oven when you start to see signs of browning on the edges.

Sift the icing sugar and spread half over a tray. Pour the rosewater into a shallow bowl.

Carefully place the warm cookies in the icing sugar – they will still be soft! – then use your fingers to sprinkle the rosewater over them. Toss the remaining icing sugar over the top to fully coat the cookies.

Allow the cookies to cool completely in the sugar, then serve with additional icing sugar on a plate, so guests can pluck a festive cookie from a sugary snowfield. They'll keep in an airtight container in the pantry for up to a week.

Palmiers

You'll find these swirly cookies around the world, known variously as butterfly cookies, pig's ears, elephant ears and more – oh my! They're the perfect way to use up leftover strips of puff pastry, or simply to run a quick quality check of your own homemade puff pastry. For me, the magic comes when you scale this recipe down and take out your day's bake from the oven – alongside just a few low-waste palmiers as a baker's reward.

—

50 g (1¾ oz) demerara or Cinnamon sugar (page 198)
2 sheets frozen vegan puff pastry, just thawed

OPTIONAL ACCESSORIES
75 g (2¾ oz) dairy-free dark chocolate, crumbled
2 teaspoons vegan butter
3 tablespoons crushed toasted nuts of your choice

Preheat the oven to 180°C (350°F). Line a large baking tray with baking paper or a silicone baking mat.

Sprinkle 1 tablespoon of the sugar over a work surface to serve as a sweet version of flouring a benchtop. Place one puff pastry sheet on top of the sugar and sprinkle with another tablespoon of sugar. Top with the remaining pastry sheet, then perform a 'book' fold by folding over the top quarter of the dough into the middle, then the bottom quarter so the ends meet. Fold over once more where the ends meet in the middle of the dough. Press lightly together. Use a sharp knife to cut the roll into 1 cm (½ in) thick slices.

Gently prise apart the puff layers, then stretch out slightly. Roll the ends inwards towards each other to create a swirled love-heart shape. (If using puff pastry scraps, approximate this process with whatever leftover pastry strips you have to make a thin swirl of layered puff pastry. Their hearts might be broken, but they'll still taste good.)

Transfer to the prepared tray, leaving a little space between each palmier. Bake for 16–20 minutes, flipping the palmiers over halfway through cooking and sprinkling with a little of the remaining sugar, until golden and fully baked.

Add the remaining sugar to a wide bowl, then toss the warm palmiers in the sugar to coat, before cooling on a wire rack.

If glamming them up, combine the chocolate and butter in a microwave-safe dish and blast in a microwave, stirring at 15-second increments, until melted and dippable. Dip a corner of each palmier into the chocolate, then into the nuts. Allow to rest on baking paper or a silicone baking mat until the chocolate has set.

Keep the palmiers sealed from the elements in an airtight container in the pantry, and devour within 3 days.

Anzac cookies

EASY **MAKES: 14**

Born of a time in Australia when eggs were scarce and food needed to keep for a long time, these golden biscuits were bound with golden syrup, hence their colour. Golden syrup is absolutely authentic, but a begrudging compromise could be to use rice malt or corn syrup if these ingredients are easier to find.

Easy and inexpensive to make, Anzac bikkies are still king of the cookie game Down Under.

—

100 g (3½ oz) vegan
   butter
200 g (7 oz) brown sugar
70 g (2½ oz) golden syrup
½ teaspoon baking soda
2 tablespoons boiling
   water
140 g (5 oz) plain
   (all-purpose) flour,
   plus extra for dusting
110 g (4 oz) rolled
   (porridge) oats
90 g (3 oz) desiccated
   coconut
¼ teaspoon fine salt

In a tall saucepan (as the mixture will bubble up), melt the butter over medium heat. Add the sugar and golden syrup and stir until the sugar has dissolved. Combine the baking soda and boiling water in a cup, then pour into the saucepan and mix. Switch the heat off and let the mixture cool.

Preheat the oven to 180°C (350°F). Line a large baking tray with baking paper or a silicone baking mat.

In a large bowl, mix together the flour, oats, coconut and salt. Add the golden syrup mixture and mix together.

Lightly flour your hands to make the next step easier, then roll the dough into 50 g (1¾ oz) balls. Space them out on the prepared tray with plenty of room to spread, and bake for 12–15 minutes, until golden brown.

These sturdy cookies, when kept in an airtight environment, can keep their crisp for at least 1 week.

Chocolate chip cookies

(EASY) **MAKES: 8**

It seems obvious now, but when the idea of adding chunks of whole chocolate to cookies served to inn guests first popped into Ruth Wakefield's mind back in 1938, it was a revelation. Chocolate chips, albeit perfectly shaped, aren't worth the extra cost in my opinion. And when quality vegan chocolate can still be a slog to source at times, I'd much rather go with the original method employed by Ruth at the advent of the choccy-chip cookie. Simply chop up a tried-and-tested favourite chocolate bar, rather than use those perfectly shaped chocolate melts, that deliver barely half the flavour – at double the cost.

This is the kind of simple but significant recipe you could pass off as an old family heirloom – withholding the truth that these are new cookies on the block because they are totally vegan!

—

160 g (5½ oz) plain
(all-purpose) flour
70 g (2½ oz) brown sugar
70 g (2½ oz) caster
(superfine) sugar
½ teaspoon baking
powder
¼ teaspoon baking soda
large pinch of sea salt
80 g (2¾ oz) vegan butter
40 ml (1¼ fl oz) plant-
based milk
1 tablespoon almond,
cashew or peanut
butter
1 teaspoon vanilla
bean paste
80 g (2¾ oz) dairy-free
chocolate, roughly
chopped

Preheat the oven to 160°C (320°F). Line a baking tray with baking paper or a silicone baking mat.

In a large bowl, mix together the flour, brown sugar, caster sugar, baking powder, baking soda and salt.

Melt the butter to soften it, then whisk it with the milk, nut butter and vanilla bean paste. Pour into the dry ingredients and mix to combine. Toss in the chocolate chunks and stir through.

Divide the mixture into eight portions, about 60 g (2 oz) each, and roll into smooth balls with the palms of your hands. Space the cookie balls out evenly on the prepared tray.

Bake the cookies for 16–18 minutes (or up to an extra 5 minutes for chewier cookies), until the edges are beginning to brown. Remove the baking tray from the oven and gently drop it onto your benchtop to flatten and 'drop' the cookies slightly.

Cool on a wire rack … yadda yadda … we both know you're going to scoff these while hot! They're best enjoyed the same day – or pop them in the freezer to nail your long-term baked-bikkie backup strategy.

Maple pecan cookies

(MEDIUM) **MAKES: 20–22**

Maple butter is a one-ingredient wonder made through heating the sugars in maple syrup to right around the thread stage of candy making, then whipping until it becomes creamy and spreadable. Keep it stored in a jar in the pantry for on-demand smearing, and see how it takes these cookies to gourmet heights.

You can read more about how cooking sugar to different temperatures produces sweet treats, from gooey to shatter-ya-teeth solid, on page 35.

—

125 g (4½ oz) pecans
120 g (4½ oz) rolled
  (porridge) oats
200 g (7 oz) plain
  (all-purpose) flour
1 tablespoon psyllium
  husk powder
1 teaspoon baking
  powder
¼ teaspoon sea salt
170 g (6 oz) vegan butter
115 ml (4 oz) rice malt
  syrup
75 ml (2½ fl oz) maple
  syrup

MAPLE BUTTER
cooking spray
500 ml (17 fl oz) maple
  syrup

TOPPING
40–44 pecan halves
flaky sea salt

Begin with the maple butter. Fill your sink with cold water and have a stand mixer bowl handy. Coat the base of a deep saucepan with cooking spray, add the maple syrup and place over medium–high heat. Using a kitchen thermometer and careful monitoring, bring the mixture to just below 112°C (234°F). Pour the maple syrup into the stand mixer bowl and place it in the sink to cool – making sure no water gets into the bowl. Once the bowl has cooled to below room temperature, dry the outside of the bowl and set up the mixer with the whisk attachment. Whisk the maple syrup on medium speed for 20–30 minutes, until thick, opaque and buttery.

Preheat the oven to 180°C (350°F). Spread all the pecans (including those for the topping) over a baking tray and toast for 10 minutes, or until golden brown. Remove from the oven, and reduce the oven temperature to 160°C (320°F). Reserve 40–44 of the pecans for topping.

In a food processor, pulverise the oats until no visible pieces remain. Add the pecans and whiz again until everything is finely processed. Mix in the flour, psyllium husk powder, baking powder and salt.

Using either a stand mixer or a large bowl and a hand-held electric mixer, cream the butter for 3 minutes. Leave the mixer running and pour in the rice malt syrup and maple syrup and mix to combine.

Add the oat mixture to the mixing bowl and use a spatula to combine the wet and dry ingredients. Move the mixture to the fridge until fully cooled.

Line two baking trays with baking paper or silicone baking mats. Scoop 1½ tablespoon portions of the mixture onto the trays, leaving plenty of room between each cookie. Slightly squash the cookies in the middle with a teaspoon.

Bake the cookies for 20–22 minutes, until lightly golden all over, then cool on a wire rack. Spoon a little maple butter onto each cooled cookie, then press two toasted pecan halves on top with a sprinkle of flaky salt. Note that the butter will set harder when it is fully cooled.

Keep the cookies in an airtight environment for up to 5 days of maple pecan perfection. Do the same for maple butter in a jar for up to 6 months.

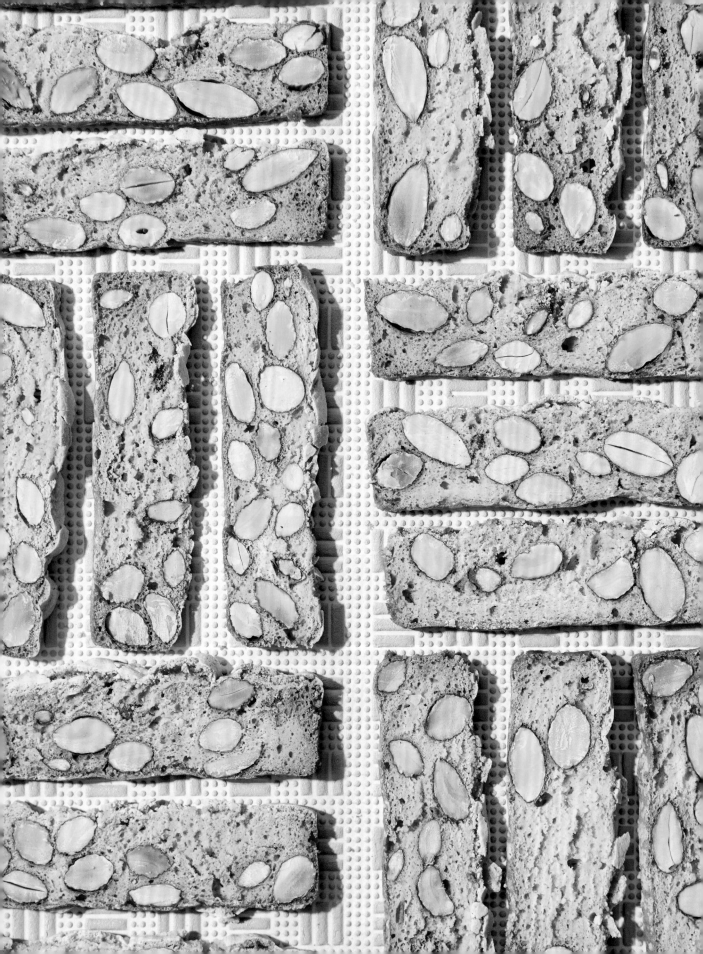

Biscotti

With their dry, crunchy texture, these twice-baked cookies from Italy beg to be paired with coffee. Aquafaba does a fabulous job veganising my family's version, which comes courtesy of a hand-written recipe slipped to me from Aunty Rene, like a back-alley drug deal, one evening over dinner. We enjoy these cut wafer-thin before the second bake, but you might like to slice them thicker to mirror the more traditional biscotti style.

—

90 ml (3 fl oz) chilled aquafaba
100 g (3½ oz) caster (superfine) sugar
120 g (4½ oz) whole almonds
120 g (4½ oz) plain (all-purpose) flour
pinch of sea salt
cooking spray, for greasing
icing (confectioners') sugar, for dusting (optional)

Preheat the oven to 175°C (345°F).

Using either a large bowl and a hand-held electric mixer, or a stand mixer with the whisk attachment, beat the cold aquafaba for 10 minutes, or until you achieve soft peaks. Leave the mixer running and slowly add the sugar, 1 tablespoon at a time.

Add the almonds, flour and salt to a fine-meshed sieve. Sift the flour into the aquafaba, which will coat the almonds in flour, too. Gently fold in both the flour and almonds until mixed through, along with any additional flavourings if using (see options below).

Lightly grease a 10 × 20 cm (4 × 8 in) bread tin with cooking spray, then add the biscotti mixture and smooth out. Bake for about 40 minutes, then allow to cool on a wire rack. When at room temperature, wrap the biscotti block in foil and allow to rest for a day or two to fully dry out.

When you're ready for the second baking, preheat the oven to 160°C (320°F). Use a sharp knife to cut the biscotti block into wafer-thin slices. Spread them out on baking trays (no need to line these ones). Bake for 20–25 minutes, flipping halfway through cooking, until golden on both sides.

Allow the biscotti to cool fully on a wire rack, before adding a light dusting of icing sugar, if desired. Store in an airtight container; thanks to the double baking steps, these cookies will stay good for up to 2 weeks at room temperature.

GLAM IT UP
Add a small splash of natural almond, orange or vanilla extract for extra flair.

Chocolate florentines

(EASY)   MAKES: 12

Also known as lace cookies, these look like a terrible mistake for most of the baking process until – ta-dah! – they're suddenly gorgeous. They're versatile, too! With a gloved hand, you can even shape large florentines, while still very warm from the oven, around the handle of a wooden spoon to create cigars that can be filled like a cannoli tube, or mould them into edible cookie bowls to hold a delightful dollop of whipped cream.

—

150 g (5½ oz) whole almonds
70 g (2½ oz) pecans
100 g (3½ oz) brown sugar
35 g (1¼ oz) plain (all-purpose) flour
large pinch of fine salt
60 g (2 oz) vegan butter
3 tablespoons plant-based milk
60 g (2 oz) corn syrup or golden syrup
½ teaspoon vanilla bean paste
80 g (2¾ oz) dairy-free white or dark chocolate

Preheat the oven to 170°C (340°F). Line two large baking trays with baking paper or silicone baking mats.

Pulse the almonds and pecans in a food processor until finely chopped. Add the sugar, flour and salt for the last pulse to blend through.

In a saucepan, combine the butter, milk, corn syrup and vanilla bean paste over medium heat and boil for 30 seconds. Dump in the nut mixture and mix enthusiastically in the saucepan. Remove from the heat and sit for 5 minutes to cool slightly.

Use a teaspoon to scoop one rounded teaspoon of dough per cookie onto the prepared trays, to make 24 cookies, with lots of clearance for them to spread out. Use your fingertips to round out the cookies and avoid any jagged edges, then bake for 10 minutes. Remove from the oven and allow to cool completely – they will harden further into delicate lacy cookies. .

Add the chocolate to a microwave-safe bowl and blast in a microwave, stirring at 15-second increments, until melted. Using a pastry brush, thinly smear the melted chocolate onto the underside of one cookie, then sandwich the chocolate with another florentine of a similar shape to complete. Repeat to make 12 florentines.

Wrap the florentines up as is convenient for you and whack them in the fridge for up to 1 month.

Wagon wheels

(MEDIUM/HARD) **MAKES: 24**

You wouldn't drive a car with a flat tyre – and in the same way, treating your kitchen like a spick and span mechanic's workshop will yield the best fine-tuned cookies for this recipe. Change the oil (to vegan butter, for a divine shortbread cookie base), pump up the wheels (with marshmallow filling and jam), then give it all a fresh coat of chocolate paint.

—

1 × quantity Shortbread cookie dough (page 214)
300 g (10½ oz) raspberry jam
250–275 g (9–9½ oz) dairy-free dark chocolate

MARSHMALLOW FILLING
60 ml (2 fl oz) chilled aquafaba
pinch of cream of tartar
115 g (4 oz) caster (superfine) sugar
1¼ teaspoons agar agar powder
40 ml (1¼ fl oz) glucose syrup
¼ teaspoon xanthan gum
1 teaspoon natural vanilla extract

Wrap the shortbread cookie dough in plastic wrap, then flatten into a rough square. Leave the dough in the fridge for at least 2 hours to cool and firm up.

Preheat the oven to 160°C (320°F). Line two large baking trays with baking paper.

Sandwich the cooled dough between two large sheets of baking paper. Roll the dough out to an even 5 mm (¼ in) thickness. Use a 5 cm (2 in) round cookie cutter to press out cookies, then place them on the baking trays. Re-roll any scraps of dough and cut out more cookies until you have 72 small cookies.

Bake the cookies for 12–15 minutes, until beginning to brown around the edges. Allow to cool in the freezer as you proceed.

To make the marshmallow filling, beat the aquafaba and cream of tartar in a stand mixer with the whisk attachment for about 5 minutes, until you achieve soft peaks. Combine the sugar and agar agar powder in a saucepan, then place over medium–low heat and stir in the glucose syrup and 80 ml (2½ fl oz) of water. Using a kitchen thermometer, and without stirring, bring the mixture to 110°C (230°F). Between 100°C (212°F) and 110°C (230°F), the mixture will rise quickly, so be vigilant. Give it a stir once done.

Slowly pour the sugar mixture into the whipped aquafaba, beating to incorporate as you go. Once done, beat in the xanthan gum and vanilla. Allow to cool for 10 minutes before proceeding.

While the marshmallow is still warm, smear a heaped teaspoon over two-thirds of the cookies. Let them sit for 15 minutes for the marshmallow to set further.

Smear 1 teaspoon of jam over one side of an untopped cookie, then press it into a marshmallow-topped cookie, jam side down. Add another teaspoon of jam on top, then sandwich with another marshmallow-topped cookie, marshmallow side down and press down lightly. Repeat with the remaining cookies, then transfer to the freezer for 1 hour.

Scrape away any filling that has oozed out of the sandwiched cookies. Crumble the chocolate into a large microwave-safe bowl, then microwave in 30-second increments until melted. Use two forks to dip each wagon wheel into the chocolate, turning to coat fully.

Place the wagon wheels on a sheet of baking paper and allow to set fully, then keep any spare wheels sealed from any road hazards in the fridge, to keep them set and safe for up to a week.

Alfajores

These crumbly, pale, lightly flavoured cookies are a fabulous flavour vehicle for rich dulce de leche (think milky caramel) and coconut flavours. I find many quick-vegan methods don't yield a dulce de leche thick enough to spread comfortably between delicate cookies, so I recommend using the 'from scratch' stovetop method on page 33 for alpha-grade vegan alfajores!

—

1 × quantity Dulce de leche (page 33)
25 g (1 oz) desiccated coconut
icing (confectioners') sugar, for dusting

COOKIES
125 g (4½ oz) coconut oil or vegan butter
90 g (3 oz) icing (confectioners') sugar
2 tablespoons aquafaba
2 teaspoons brandy, cognac or pisco
zest of 1 lemon
½ teaspoon natural vanilla extract
170 g (6 oz) cornflour (cornstarch)
100 g (3½ oz) plain (all-purpose) flour
1 teaspoon baking powder
¼ teaspoon sea salt

To make the cookies, place the coconut oil or butter, icing sugar, aquafaba, booze, lemon zest and vanilla in a large bowl and cream together using a hand-held electric mixer for 2 minutes.

In a separate bowl, mix together the cornflour, flour, baking powder and salt. Tip this over the creamed mixture and use a spatula to mix until fully combined.

Move the dough to the fridge to chill out for at least 1 hour.

Preheat the oven to 180°C (350°F).

Remove the dough from the fridge and sandwich it between two sheets of baking paper, then roll out until 5–8 mm (¼–⅓ in) thick. Use a 5 cm (2 in) round cookie cutter to press out cookies, placing them on baking trays as you go; you can reuse the baking paper to bake on. Ball up the excess dough, roll it out again and continue the process until the dough is all used up, or you have 36 cookies.

Bake the cookies for 18–20 minutes, removing the cookies just before the edges brown; the signature colour of alfajores is a pale cream.

Place a generous tablespoon of dulce de leche on the underside of one cookie, then use your fingertips to gently spread it around for better coverage. Sandwich the base of another cookie onto the dulce de leche. Wriggle the cookie back and forth to squish it on – don't press down, or you'll risk crumbling your alfajores prematurely. Roll the side of the cookies in the coconut, pressing it onto the dulce de leche if needed to make it attach. Dust the coconut edge with icing sugar and repeat with the remaining cookies to make 18 alfajores.

Keep the alfajores in an airtight container to grab whenever you're feeling a bit dulce de lecherous. They'll go alright for a week in the fridge, or 2 months if frozen.

Caramel slice

It's not a misprint to find this recipe here in the Cookies chapter, as the shortbread base makes a caramel slice technically a cookie bar. It may seem like there's only a thin layer of caramel, but don't be deluded. The rich caramel is prepared on the stovetop, but finished in the oven, so it sets at the perfect chew while seeping into the shortbread base. Every bite will excite – and borderline exhaust – your taste buds.

—

cooking spray, for greasing
¾ × quantity Shortbread cookie dough (page 214)
flaky salt, for scattering
250 g (9 oz) dairy-free chocolate
40 ml (1¼ fl oz) vegan cream

OVEN CARAMEL
180 g (6 oz) vegan butter
150 g (5½ oz) brown sugar
80 g (2¾ oz) soy or coconut milk powder
2 tablespoons glucose, maple, golden or rice malt syrup
1 teaspoon natural vanilla extract

Preheat the oven to 150°C (300°F). Lightly grease the base of a 20 cm (8 in) square cake tin or brownie tin.

Don't bother chilling the shortbread dough once prepared, just press it into the base of the tin. Make sure it's smooth, then prick all over with a fork. Bake for 30 minutes, then remove from the oven and set aside to cool. Increase the oven temperature to 160°C (320°F).

To prepare the oven caramel, fit a kitchen thermometer to a tall saucepan with room for the caramel to rise freely. Melt the butter in the pan over medium heat. Add the sugar and whisk until dissolved, then mix in the remaining caramel ingredients and 80 ml (2½ fl oz) of water. Allow to bubble away over medium heat for about 10 minutes, increasing the temperature gradually as needed, until the mixture reaches 120°C (248°F) on the thermometer.

Remove the caramel from the heat and give it a quick whisk to deflate. Pour the caramel evenly over the shortbread and bake for another 10 minutes.

Rest the caramel slice on the benchtop for 1 hour to finish setting, then scatter a little salt over the top.

Add the chocolate and cream to a microwave-safe bowl and blast in a microwave, stirring at 15-second increments, until melted and smooth. Pour over the caramel and use a spatula to smooth the top.

Wait for another 30 minutes, then cut the caramel slice with a sharp knife into 5 cm (2 in) squares. They will keep in an airtight container in the fridge for up to a week.

GO NUTTY!
Spread crunchy peanut butter over the shortbread base before pouring the caramel over.

Macarons

(HARD) **MAKES: 12**

If a baker asks you for feet pics, this is what they want. The art of the perfect macaron is measured by the 'feet' or ruffles that form on the bottom of the shell as it bakes, pushing the dome up. French almond-meringue cookie sandwiches have become bakery staples worldwide, but the omnipotence of vegan versions is only an emerging phenomenon.

—

200 ml (7 oz) aquafaba
white vinegar, for dabbing
90 g (3 oz) caster (superfine) sugar
1/16 teaspoon vegan food colour gel
delicate drop of your chosen flavour extract
1/2 teaspoon vanilla bean paste
120 g (4 1/2 oz) fine almond meal
pinch of fine salt
100 g (3 1/2 oz) icing (confectioners') sugar

FOR FILLING
Ganache (page 31) or Buttercream (page 30)

Pour the aquafaba into a small saucepan and bring to a vigorous bubble over medium heat. Maintain the boil for about 10 minutes, until it has reduced to 85 ml (2¾ fl oz). Cover the aquafaba and move to the fridge for 2 hours – ideally overnight – to get very chilly and gelatinous.

Use a paper towel dabbed with vinegar to wipe out a large metal bowl and over the attachments on your electric beaters, or the bowl of a stand mixer and the whisk attachment. Pour the thickened aquafaba into the bowl. Beat on high speed for 5 minutes. It will bubble, froth and foam, then turn into soft peaks.

Turn the beaters to medium speed and add the caster sugar, 1 tablespoon at a time and incorporating each tablespoon before adding the next, until stiff peaks form. Add your chosen food colour gel, flavour extract and the vanilla bean paste and beat on high speed for 1 minute longer. The meringue is ready when it doesn't budge when you flip the bowl upside down.

Line two baking trays with baking paper or silicone baking mats.

Add the almond flour, salt and icing sugar to a food processor and churn for a minute. Sift the mixture to make sure that it's completely fine. Use a spatula to fold half the almond mixture into the meringue, then fold in the remainder for about a minute until well combined.

Fit a piping (icing) bag with a thick nozzle and spoon the meringue mixture into the bag, but don't overfill it, so you can twist it tightly shut. Pipe the meringue onto the baking trays, into even 5 cm (2 in) rounds. Tap the trays on the bench a few times to knock out air bubbles. For those with sloppy piping skills, use a skewer to smooth the tops of the macarons. Rest, uncovered, on the bench for 1 hour, or until a skin has formed over each macaron.

Preheat the oven to 110°C (230°F). You'll need to bake the macarons one tray at a time on the middle rack of the oven, keeping the door shut until you check from 20 minutes onwards. Bake for about 25 minutes, until the tops feel crisp.

Switch off the oven and let both trays of macarons cool fully in the oven before moving to an airtight container ahead of filling.

Use a piping bag to pipe chocolate ganache or buttercream onto the underside of a macaron shell and sandwich with the underside of another to complete.

The macarons will keep in an airtight container for 1 week in the pantry, and up to 1 month in the fridge.

Cakes & Puddings

Victoria sponge

All rise! The Victoria sponge's reign began around the same time as the invention of baking powder, celebrating the new heights cakes had risen to. Its two tiers are clad simply in jam, cream and icing sugar. Adding fresh berries that match your choice of jam will make this extra posh.

200 g (7 oz) vegan butter, plus extra for greasing
440 ml (15 fl oz) plant-based milk
20 ml (¾ fl oz) white vinegar
250 g (9 oz) caster (superfine) sugar
2 teaspoons vanilla bean paste
400 g (14 oz) plain (all-purpose) flour
4 teaspoons baking powder
1 teaspoon baking soda
2 large pinches of fine salt
150 g (5½ oz) raspberry or strawberry jam
1 × quantity Buttercream (page 30)
fresh berries, for extra flair (optional)
icing (confectioners') sugar, for dusting

Preheat the oven to 160°C (320°F). Lightly grease and line two 20 cm (8 in) cake tins with baking paper.

Whisk together the milk and vinegar in a small bowl, then set aside for 5 minutes to make a quick buttermilk.

Using a large mixing bowl and a hand-held electric mixer, or a stand mixer fitted with the paddle attachment, beat the sugar, butter and vanilla bean paste for 3 minutes on medium speed until combined, light and fluffy.

Sift the flour, baking powder, baking soda and salt into a large mixing bowl. Running the mixer on low speed, spoon in the flour mixture and buttermilk until everything just comes together.

Divide the cake batter evenly between the prepared tins. Tap the tins on the bench a few times to release any large air bubbles, then smooth the top with a spatula. Bake for about 30 minutes, until a skewer inserted in the middle comes out clean.

Allow the cakes to cool in the tins for 20 minutes, before gently up-ending them onto a wire rack. You may need to trim the tops of the cakes to make them level.

Place one of the cakes on a serving plate or cake stand. Stir the jam vigorously with a spoon to loosen it, then lavishly spread the jam over the top of the cake. Cover the jam with half the buttercream and dot fresh berries all over the top, if you're using them. Carefully spoon the remaining buttercream over the berries and position the second cake on top. Finish with a few more berries and a dusting of icing sugar.

The untopped cake will keep in an airtight container on the benchtop for up to 3 days, but should be eaten within a day of being built.

Basbousa

(MEDIUM)   SERVES: 8–12

When you find a recipe that several cultures lay claim to, it's either a sign that it's a particularly good recipe, or perhaps that those cultures have a history of not seeing eye to eye. The beautiful scoring on top makes this cake feel like an event, but also allows the delicious rosewater or orange blossom water to seep into every bite.

—

tahini, for coating
    (or use vegetable oil)
350 g (12½ oz) coarse
    semolina
75 g (2¾ oz) desiccated
    coconut
100 g (3½ oz) caster
    (superfine) sugar
2 teaspoons baking
    powder
1 teaspoon ground
    cardamom
100 g (3½ oz) vegan
    butter
250 g (9 oz) coconut
    yoghurt
2 tablespoons applesauce
24 almonds

SPICED SYRUP
300 g (10½ oz) granulated
    white sugar
1½ tablespoons orange
    blossom water or
    rosewater
zest of 1 lemon, plus
    1 tablespoon juice

Combine the syrup ingredients and 250 ml (8½ fl oz) of water in a small saucepan, stirring well. Simmer and stir over low heat for 10 minutes, stopping stirring once the sugar has dissolved. Allow to cool before using.

Preheat the oven to 180°C (350°F). Using just the top part of your tahini (the separated oil), dip a pastry brush in, then coat the base of a 20 cm (8 in) round cake tin (preferably springform) or baking dish.

In a large bowl, stir together the semolina, coconut, sugar, baking powder and cardamom.

Microwave the butter in a microwave-safe dish until softened, then stir in the yoghurt and applesauce. Add to the semolina mixture and stir until combined. Spoon the batter into the prepared tin and use the back of a spoon to evenly smooth it out.

Using a knife, gently score the top of the cake before baking. First, cut across the diameter of the cake, rotate 90 degrees, then repeat to create four wedges. Make two more similar cuts across the diameter to give you eight even wedges. From halfway down one of the sides of a wedge, score a line to the centre of the edge of the wedge, then repeat on the other side. Repeat until the basbousa has half-diamond shapes running all around the edge. (Just refer to the photo opposite if your brain fails you halfway through!)

Stud an almond into the centre of each of the scored pieces, like a medallion, to celebrate you getting through the scoring.

Bake on the centre rack of the oven for 30–35 minutes, until the cake is fully bronzed on top. Moving the cake to the top rack and turning on the oven grill (broiler) for the last few minutes will help if that's not happening in time.

Remove the cake from the oven, switch the oven off and place the cake on a tray. Use a knife to cut fully through the pre-scored lines. Pour the syrup over the top, then return the basbousa to the switched-off oven for 10 minutes, to allow the syrup to fully penetrate the crumb.

Allow the cake to fully cool in the tin (popping off the outer edge if yours is springform), before serving at room temperature. The cake will keep in an airtight container in the pantry for up to 3 days, or up to a week in the fridge.

Galette de rois

A 'king's cake' is usually baked with a trinket hidden inside, for one lucky eater to claim the title of royalty for a day. By hiding a dried bean somewhere in your filling, you can carry on this tradition, while also exciting the sorts of vegans who would see a dried bean as a prize! Anyone could assume this was a pie or a pastry – but who's going to argue with the king if he deems it a cake?

—

4 sheets Puff pastry
   (page 48; or use
   store-bought)
60 ml (2 fl oz) aquafaba
icing (confectioners')
   sugar, for dusting

CRÈME D'AMANDE
80 g (2¾ oz) vegan butter
pinch of fine salt
zest of 1 lemon
100 g (3½ oz) icing
   (confectioners') sugar
20 g (¾ oz) cornflour
   (cornstarch)
200 g (7 oz) fine
   almond meal
1 tablespoon rum
40 g (1½ oz) applesauce
1 teaspoon vanilla bean
   paste

Start with the crème d'amande. Begin beating the butter, salt and lemon zest in a large bowl using a hand-held electric mixer, or a stand mixer fitted with the whisk attachment. Sift together the icing sugar and cornflour and fold the mixture through the butter mixture, followed by the almond meal, then the rum, applesauce and vanilla bean paste.

Fit a piping (icing) bag with a star nozzle at least 1 cm (½ in) thick and place it in a tall jug, furling the edges over the rim to hold it in place. Spoon the crème d'amande into the bag, but don't overfill, so you can twist the bag tightly shut. Refrigerate for several hours until fully chilled out, or whack it in the freezer for a shorter duration if preparing this dish for an impatient royal.

Preheat the oven to 200°C (400°F). Line a baking tray with baking paper or a silicone baking mat.

Cut out four 20 cm (8 in) circles from the puff pastry and place one circle on top of another to create a double layer. Place on a baking tray, then repeat with the other two puff pastry circles. Use the excess pastry to cut 2.5 cm (1 in) thick strips.

Use a pastry brush to dab aquafaba around the edge of the pastry circle on the baking tray as a form of glue, then lay the strips around to fashion a border ring; imagine you're making fort walls, to keep the filling secure. Repeat this step to make the border three to four layers thick. Evenly pipe the cold crème d'amande in the middle of the pastry, spiralling from the centre outwards.

Without fully piercing the pastry anywhere, use the side of a fork to score a pattern on top of the second pastry circle. First, make five or six evenly spaced lines towards you, across the diameter of the pastry, like you're making columns. Fill each of the columns with ladder-like scoring, perpendicular to your first lines. If you slant the direction of your ladder markings in alternating directions, you'll get the zig-zag effect in the image.

Place your decorated puff pastry circle, dabbing with more aquafaba to connect it to the border wall, on top of the créme d'amande and very gently use a fork to crimp the pastry edges and secure the puff sheets together.

Brush the top with more aquafaba, then bake for 20 minutes. Dust icing sugar all over the top of the pie and bake for another 10–15 minutes, until the pastry is puffed and golden. Cool completely on the baking tray before slicing and serving. Your king's cake will keep in an airtight container in the fridge for up to 3 days.

Rum baba

Proper rum baba moulds can be a hassle to find and store, so try using donut baking tins here to make mini bundt-style babas – which, accommodatingly, have a small built-in centre hole for you to spoon rum-whipped cream into. The dough is based on the infinitely soft brioche on page 100, so you can easily make a batch of these in the same time it'll take to make a half-batch of brioche dinner rolls. That's dinner and dessert sorted!

The rum-whipped cream uses a jar hack to quickly aerate cream. You can swap in any of the flavoured syrups from this book to make speedy whipped cream that can be used wherever whipped cream is asked for.

½ × quantity Brioche
   dough (page 100)
cooking spray, for
   greasing

QUICK RUM-WHIPPED
CREAM
200 ml (7 fl oz) vegan
   cream, chilled
2 tablespoons Rum syrup
   (see below)
1 teaspoon natural
   vanilla extract

RUM SYRUP
80 g (2¾ oz) granulated
   white sugar
50 ml (1¾ fl oz) dark
   spiced rum

Leave the brioche dough in a warm place to rise for 1 hour before beginning the rum babas.

Grease a six-hole donut baking tin with cooking spray. Punch down the dough, then use a dough scraper to divide it into six pieces, about 60 g (2 oz) each. Roll the dough into smooth balls. Press a finger in the centre of each ball until you break through to the other side. Fit a second finger in and gently stretch out the gap until you make an even ring. Nestle each baba in a donut mould, cover with a tea towel and rise for 1 hour in a warm place.

Preheat the oven to 160°C (320°F). Bake the babas for 20–25 minutes, until golden brown on the outside.

Meanwhile, make the rum syrup. Bring the sugar and 80 ml (2½ fl oz) of water to the boil in a saucepan over medium heat, then simmer over very low heat for 3 minutes, adding the rum for the last minute. Remove from the heat.

As you remove the babas from the oven, generously ladle the syrup over them. Allow to cool for 10 minutes, then flip them over in the tin and drench them again. (Sprinkle extra rum on top now if you want a potent flavour and nobody's driving.)

To make the rum-whipped cream, add the ingredients to a jar, seal well and shake vigorously for 30–60 seconds.

When the babas have largely cooled, fit a piping (icing) bag with a star nozzle and place it in a tall jug, furling the edges over the rim to hold it in place. Spoon the rum-whipped cream into the bag, but don't overfill, so you can twist the bag tightly shut.

Place each baba on a serving plate, drizzle on more rum syrup if desired, then pipe in the rum-whipped cream to fill the entire centre hole. The babas are best eaten within a day.

Iced vovo jelly cakes

(MEDIUM) **MAKES: 6**

Two of my Australian childhood favourites – jelly cakes and iced vovo biscuits – smashed into a beautiful ball. Jelly cakes (a.k.a. 'peach blossoms') are creamy, jelly-wrapped pink versions of lamingtons baked lovingly by the grandmothers of Australia. My version doesn't require a specialist baking tin, and opts to make them bigger, with double the cream layers to preserve the traditional cream-to-sponge ratio. In the middle is a strip of raspberry jam, like an iced vovo biscuit – because this isn't just a vegan version, it's a *better* version, too.

cooking spray, for greasing
1 × quantity Victoria sponge batter (page 243)
120 g (4½ oz) desiccated coconut
½ × quantity Buttercream (page 30)
2 tablespoons raspberry jam

JELLY
85 g (3 oz) vegan strawberry or raspberry jelly crystals
150 ml (5 fl oz) boiling water
100 ml (3½ fl oz) cold water

Preheat the oven to 160°C (320°F).

Lightly grease a 12-hole muffin tin. Evenly distribute the cake batter among the holes, then bake for 16–18 minutes, until a skewer inserted in the middle of a cake comes out clean. Cool the cakes in the tin for a few minutes, before cooling on a wire rack. Set aside in the fridge for 30 minutes to get completely cold.

Meanwhile, make the jelly. In a heatproof bowl, whisk together the jelly crystals and the boiling water until dissolved, then pour in the cold water. Set aside to partly set for 20–45 minutes, keeping an eye on it so that you use it in the sweet spot where it'll cling to the cakes.

Spread the coconut in a wide bowl.

Trim the cakes to get a flat surface, if necessary, and use a sharp knife to slice each cake horizontally into two even rounds. With a teaspoon, spread a thin layer of buttercream on the cut sides of the sponge pieces and sandwich the two halves back together. Now spread the jam on top of the cakes and sandwich two cakes together, jam side down, to make six jumbo cakes. Move to the fridge to firm up.

The jelly is ready for dipping when it is gloopy and half-set, but not liquidy enough to soak into the cake. Use a spatula to lower an assembled cake into the gloopy jelly, and use a spoon to thinly coat it all over in the jelly. Move the cake into the coconut and use another spoon to coat all over. Lightly pack the whole thing in with your hands so that everything adheres, remoulding the cake gently to make an even round. Finish with a light sprinkling of coconut to give a dusted appearance. Repeat with the remaining cakes.

Let the cakes sit in the fridge for 1 hour to set fully. They'll keep on the benchtop in an airtight container for up to 3 days.

10-minute chickpea brownies

(EASY) **SERVES: 8**

Using up a whole tin of chickpeas, this recipe is a godsend for avid aquafaba aficionados struggling with a chickpea surplus. For the uninitiated, chickpeas are the edible little packaging pellets that come in a tin of heavenly aquafaba. It takes just 10 minutes to make these vegan brownies in a microwave. You'll use up your chickpeas, increase your protein intake – and, by saving the aquafaba in the tin, you have a liquid-gold egg replacer! When using instant coffee powder to boost the taste of chocolate, feel free to use decaf for all the flavour nuance without the caffeine.

400 g (14 oz) tin of chickpeas (garbanzo beans)
cooking spray, for greasing
200 g (7 oz) dairy-free dark chocolate
150 g (5½ oz) brown sugar
100 g (3½ oz) vegan butter
1 teaspoon natural vanilla extract
½ teaspoon instant coffee powder
110 g (4 oz) plain (all-purpose) flour
30 g (1 oz) Dutch (unsweetened) cocoa powder
1 teaspoon baking powder
¼ teaspoon fine salt

FOR TOPPING
1 × quantity Ganache (page 31)
50 g (1¾ oz) walnuts, hazelnuts, pistachios or macadamias, finely chopped

Drain the chickpeas, reserving all the incredible aquafaba (which freezes fantastically well) to serve as a future egg substitute. Use a food processor to grind the chickpeas into a fairly smooth puree. Set aside.

Cut out two squares of baking paper and use cooking spray to adhere them to the base of two 14 cm (5½ in) square Tupperware containers, spraying the tops as well.

Break half the chocolate into small chunks and set aside. Place the remaining chocolate in a microwave-safe dish, along with the sugar and butter. Blast in the microwave, stirring at 15-second increments, until pourable but not too hot. Stir the chickpea puree, vanilla and coffee powder through the melted chocolate.

Sift together the flour, cocoa powder, baking powder and salt, then whisk this through the chocolate mixture as well. Finally, stir in the reserved chocolate.

Divide the batter between the Tupperware containers, then smooth the tops with the back of a spoon. Tap the containers on the bench to knock out the air bubbles. One at a time, microwave the containers on full blast for 3–5 minutes, checking from 3 minutes if a skewer inserted in the brownie comes out almost clean, but a little fudgy. Microwave ovens vary, so check frequently for your first crack at this recipe to find the sweet spot. Be careful not to overcook your brownies, noting that the batter will continue to cook after the microwave stops, and you want to retain moisture. Carefully up-end the brownies onto a wire rack to cool.

Once cooled, spread the ganache evenly over the top of each brownie slab and sprinkle with the chopped nuts.

Cut each slab into four generous pieces and serve with something cold and creamy to cut through the deep chocolate richness.

It's best to make the brownies fresh in batches as desired. Freeze leftovers for emergency late-night snacking. Report to the panic station (the back of your freezer) as required, popping the brownies straight into the microwave for reheating, with a scoop of ice cream waiting in a bowl to go alongside.

Red velvet cupcakes

(EASY) **MAKES: 12**

In a society plagued by the same tired pastel cupcakes filled with animal products again and again, these vivid vegan cupcakes are a sight you can't miss, with a flavour you can't pin down. Instead of a frosting that's doing *too much*, these death-free restylings of a red velvet are topped with a simple but effective cream cheese frosting (or use the buttercream on page 30) and contain a hidden pocket of fresh raspberry jam inside. Be aware that red food colouring can often use colour 120, made from crushed beetles, so give any colours with cochineal or carmine in the ingredients list a wide berth.

Nature has chosen the colour red to assert dominance, so submit to these cupcakes that those other cupcakes call Daddy.

300 ml (10 fl oz) soy milk
1 tablespoon white
   vinegar
80 g (2¾ oz) vegan butter
180 g (6½ oz) caster
   (superfine) sugar
1 teaspoon natural
   vanilla extract
½ teaspoon vegan red
   food colouring
220 g (8 oz) plain
   (all-purpose) flour
40 g (1½ oz) cornflour
   (cornstarch)
2 tablespoons Dutch
   (unsweetened) cocoa
   powder
2 teaspoons baking
   powder
large pinch of fine salt
3 tablespoons raspberry
   jam

CREAM CHEESE FROSTING

180 g (6½ oz) vegan
   butter
200 g (7 oz) vegan cream
   cheese
400 g (14 oz) icing
   (confectioners') sugar
½ teaspoon natural
   vanilla extract

To make the frosting, use a hand-held electric mixer to cream the butter and cream cheese for 3 minutes. With the mixer running, slowly beat in the icing sugar until a smooth, pipeable consistency is formed.

Place a piping (icing) bag fitted with a round nozzle in a tall jug, furling the edges over the rim to hold it in place. Load it up with the frosting, but don't overfill, so you can twist the bag tightly shut. Refrigerate for at least 30 minutes.

Preheat the oven to 175°C (345°F).

Whisk together the milk and vinegar in a small bowl, then set aside for 5 minutes to make a quick buttermilk.

Using a large mixing bowl and a hand-held electric mixer, or a stand mixer fitted with the paddle attachment, beat the butter, sugar, vanilla and food colouring for 3 minutes on medium speed until combined, light and fluffy.

Sift the flour, cornflour, cocoa powder, baking powder and salt into a large mixing bowl. Running the mixer on low speed, spoon in the flour mixture and buttermilk until everything just comes together. Make sure you're happy with the colour, noting it will fade a little during baking.

Line a 12-hole muffin tin with paper cases and evenly distribute the batter among them. Make a smooth move with the back of a spoon to level the tops. Bake for 20–24 minutes, until a skewer inserted in the middle comes out clean. Leave to cool in the tin for a few minutes, before turning out onto a wire rack to cool completely.

Use a small paring knife to cut a small hole in the top of each cupcake, and use a teaspoon to scoop out a small void in the top of each cupcake. Alternatively, use the narrow end of a wooden spoon to squash out the space you need. Fill the void with raspberry jam (this tip does not apply to other parts of your life).

Swirl the frosting over each cupcake. The cupcakes will keep in an airtight container in the fridge for up to 3 days.

30-minute lamingtons

For those short on time and shits to give, a whole cake can be cooked in as little as 5 minutes in the microwave. Take advantage of this hack to speed through the preparation of this Australian classic in a mere half hour.

—

1 × quantity Victoria
   sponge batter
   (page 243)
250 g (9 oz) desiccated
   coconut

CHOCOLATE ICING
350 g (12½ oz) icing
   (confectioners') sugar
30 g (1 oz) Dutch
   (unsweetened) cocoa
   powder
15 g (½ oz) vegan butter
120 ml (4 fl oz) boiling
   water

Find yourself a 25 cm (10 in) square microwave-safe baking dish – either glass, plastic or silicone. Place paper towels on the bottom so that they cover the base and come up the edges a little. Pour the cake batter evenly into the dish. Tap the base on the bench a few times to release any large air bubbles, then smooth the top. Microwave for about 5 minutes at full power, until the cake is set and a skewer inserted in the middle comes out clean.

Gently up-end the sponge cake onto a wire rack to cool for 10 minutes (near a fan if you're racing the clock!). If the cake has domed slightly, use a bread knife to trim the top flush, for a perfectly level cake. Use a sharp knife to divide the cake into nine even pieces (or 12 smaller ones). If you don't have time to spare, place them in the freezer, or let them fully cool on the benchtop, so they have no residual warmth left.

To make the chocolate icing, sift the icing sugar and cocoa powder into a large bowl. Melt the butter, stir it into the boiling water, then slowly whisk this mixture into the icing sugar and cocoa powder until thick and smooth.

Spread the coconut in a wide bowl.

Dip, drip and then go coconuts: place a sponge square in the chocolate icing, and use a fork to gently flip it around to coat each side, then carefully lift into the coconut. Use a spoon to toss the coconut over to evenly coat all sides of the lamington. Lightly pack in with your hands so that everything adheres. Repeat with the remaining cakes.

Let the lamingtons sit in the fridge for 30 minutes to set fully. They will keep on the benchtop in an airtight container for up to 3 days.

LAMING-TONNE:
Increase the quantity and use the instructions in the Victoria sponge (page 243) to prepare one giant, full-sized 'laming-tonne' cake with two choc-coconut–coated cakes sandwiching jam and cream. On a smaller scale, sandwiching two small lamingtons with jam and cream between is a winning combination for your smoko break (afternoon tea).

Sticky date pudding

Oh my god, Becky, look at that bundt – it's so big! Get this round thing in your face for juicy flavour and a crumb that's as delightful to slide your fork through as it is to eat. You can use a traditional bundt tin or a deep baking tray to bake this pudding, but purchasing a decorative novelty bundt tin is a simple way to serve up a wildly extravagant eye-catcher, with no extra preparation steps on your end. By adding teabags to your initial date soak, you'll introduce a bitterness that plays well with the heavy sweetness from a date-loaded pudding. Need an excuse for seconds? Using date syrup in place of the caramel can make this entire dessert refined-sugar free.

cooking spray, for greasing
3 black tea, English breakfast or chai teabags
375 ml (12½ fl oz) boiling water
250 g (9 oz) medjool dates
1 teaspoon baking soda
150 g (5½ oz) date syrup or golden syrup
125 g (4½ oz) cold vegan butter, chopped
1 teaspoon natural vanilla extract
250 g (9 oz) plain (all-purpose) flour
3 teaspoons baking powder
3 teaspoons psyllium husk powder
large pinch of fine salt
1 × quantity hot Caramel (page 37)

Preheat the oven to 160°C (320°F). Lightly grease a classic bundt (ring tin) or novelty bundt tin that's about 22 cm (8¾ in) in diameter. Alternatively, use a classic cake tin or deep baking tray.

Dangle the teabags in a heatproof measuring jug and pour the boiling water in. Allow it to brew while you pit the dates and toss into a separate container. Once the tea is dark and bitter, remove the teabags, stir in the baking soda, then pour the tea over the dates to submerge them. Set aside for 10 minutes to let the dates begin having a breakdown, then use a stick blender to puree the mixture.

Use an electric hand-held mixer or a stand mixer fitted with the paddle attachment to beat the date syrup, cold butter and vanilla on medium speed for 3 minutes or until combined, light and fluffy.

With the mixer running on low speed, slowly pour the pureed dates into the butter mixture until combined. Stir together the flour, baking powder, psyllium husk powder and salt, then dump it into the stand mixer bowl and run on low speed until just folded through – avoid overmixing.

Pour the batter evenly into the bundt tin and tap it on the bench to spread the batter out. Smooth the top with the back of a spoon.

Get your hot date into the oven and bake for about 40 minutes, until a skewer inserted in the middle and a few spots around the pudding comes out clean. Allow the pudding to cool in the tin for 10 minutes, then up-end onto a wire rack.

Use the skewer to prod access points all over the pudding. Transfer to a plate, then pour half the hot caramel sauce over the top to glaze the pudding.

Cut pudding slices out of the bundt tin and serve warm, with the remaining caramel sauce drizzled over everyone's serving. If your date isn't ready to go home at the end of the night, the pudding will last for up to 1 week in the fridge.

Om ali

SERVES: 6

Bread and butter pudding, fit for royalty. We take the elements of this peasant food and replace the bread with puff pastry–based palmiers, swap the custard with cream, then soak the fruit in booze. Every layer is embellished with the most exquisite flavours – pistachio, vanilla, cardamom, cinnamon – and garnished with rose petals. Blind-baked chunks of puff pastry can be used in place of the palmiers.

30 g (1 oz) sultanas
  (golden raisins)
2 tablespoons rum
  or other liquor (or
  2 tablespoons boiling
  water)
400 ml (13½ fl oz) vegan
  cream
300 ml (10½ fl oz) soy milk
55 g (2 oz) caster
  (superfine) sugar
½ teaspoon natural
  vanilla extract
½ teaspoon ground
  cardamom
¼ teaspoon ground
  cinnamon
250 g (9 oz) Palmiers
  (page 220; or use store-
  bought), left out for
  a day to dry out
25 g (1 oz) desiccated
  coconut
35 g (1¼ oz) pistachios,
  lightly crushed
30 g (1 oz) slivered
  almonds
semi-dried rose petals,
  to serve (optional)

TO SERVE ... YOU CHOOSE!
vegan ice cream
halva
vegan Greek-style yoghurt
vegan pouring cream
vegan labneh

Add the sultanas to a jar. Gently heat the rum in a small saucepan (or in a microwave-safe bowl) until warm but not hot. Pour the rum over the sultanas, seal the jar and set aside for a few hours – or up to a week – to soak. (If leaving for an extended time, shake the jar every day or so.) If using boiling water instead of rum, simply pour it over the sultanas, leave for 5 minutes and drain before using.

Preheat the oven to 175°C (345°F).

Gently warm the cream, milk, sugar, vanilla, cardamom and cinnamon in a saucepan, stirring until the sugar has dissolved.

Distribute half the palmiers in a 1 litre (34 fl oz) baking dish or brownie tin, breaking up where needed to evenly spread them out. Sprinkle with half the soaked sultanas along with half the coconut, pistachios and almonds. Repeat with the remaining palmiers, sultanas, coconut and nuts, to make a second layer. Evenly pour the cream mixture over the top and bake for 15–20 minutes, until the top is nicely golden. Once it's out of the oven, sprinkle with rose petals, if desired.

This pudding is best eaten freshly baked. Scoop into bowls and serve with ice cream, halva, yoghurt or cream … or luxuriously dollop vegan labneh all over your portion!

Gran's rice pudding

(EASY) **SERVES: 6**

This simple pudding is the top dessert request I make of my grandmother every time I visit, and I once considered it her ultimate culinary achievement – until she confessed it originated from the back of a rice packet. Gran subtly lets you know that you're her favourite grandchild by being insanely generous during the final step of melting pure vanilla ice cream into the pudding. It's what makes it extra special, so it'd be disrespectful to not carry on that tradition in your home, too. She has lovingly helped me veganise the family recipe for your pleasure, and now rates this egg- and dairy-free version as being just as good as the one I grew up eating.

360 g (12½ oz) cooked white rice
500 ml (17 fl oz) soy milk
pinch of fine salt
2 tablespoons Condensed milk (page 32), made with coconut milk or oat milk
1⅓ tablespoons vegan custard powder
½ teaspoon natural vanilla extract
60–80 ml (2–2¾ fl oz) vegan vanilla ice cream
60 ml (2 fl oz) coconut cream
ground cinnamon

TO SERVE
vegan vanilla ice cream
fresh fruit salad

Add the rice, milk and salt to a saucepan over low heat. Break up the rice with a wooden spoon. Simmer for 10 minutes, stirring constantly to make sure the rice keeps swimming.

In a mixing jug, whisk together the condensed milk, custard powder and vanilla. Ladle 60 ml (2 fl oz) of the hot rice mixture from the saucepan into the jug, whisk well, then pour it all back into the saucepan. Simmer for another 2 minutes, stirring, or until thick.

Turn the heat off. Stir the ice cream and coconut cream through the rice pudding. Transfer to a dish that'll live in the fridge, and straight away sprinkle cinnamon over the top, so it sets into the pudding.

The rice pudding will keep for up to a week in the fridge, and is best served cold with a scoop of ice cream. My gran pairs it with a fresh fruit salad using whatever is in season, and I can't imagine a better way to eat it.

Peach cobbler for one

EASY   **SERVES: 1**

Life can be a real peach sometimes ... especially when you find yourself having a solo night in. Luckily, this easy treat and total dreamboat of a dessert is sweet, warm and more than willing to curl up on the couch with you instead. It pairs beautifully with the scrapings from the bottom of an ice-cream tub, and absolutely not texting your exes. Drop the booty calls and reach for a peach instead. Of course, you can always scale the recipe up whenever you have company.

vegan butter, for greasing
2 peaches
1 teaspoon lemon juice
¾ teaspoon natural
   vanilla extract
45 g (1½ oz) brown sugar
1 teaspoon cornflour
   (cornstarch)
⅓ teaspoon ground
   cinnamon
vegan ice cream, to serve

COBBLER TOPPING
65 g (2¼ oz) plain
   (all-purpose) flour
½ teaspoon baking
   powder
pinch of fine salt
35 g (1¼ oz) brown sugar,
   plus 1 teaspoon extra,
   for sprinkling
35 g (1¼ oz) vegan butter
2 tablespoons vegan
   cream
1 tablespoon flaked
   almonds

Preheat the oven to 180°C (350°F). Use butter to grease the base of a 200–300 ml (7–10 fl oz) ramekin.

Slice the peaches into thin wedges and add to a bowl. Gently toss the lemon juice, vanilla, sugar, cornflour and cinnamon through. Pile the mixture into the ramekin, then bake for 10 minutes.

Meanwhile, prepare the cobbler topping. Add the flour, baking powder, salt and sugar to a food processor. Pulse to combine. Cut the butter into small chunks, then pulse them through to create fine crumbs. (Alternatively, use your fingertips to rub the butter into the flour mixture to create a similar effect.) Use your hands to form the mixture into a dough, adding small splashes of the cream, if needed.

Squash the dough into several thick rounds and place atop the peach mixture. Brush the top with the remaining cream, then scatter the almonds and extra sugar over the top.

Bake for another 20 minutes or until the top is beginning to brown. Leave to cool slightly for safety's sake, then serve with a scoop of ice cream on top.

To Share

Fennel seeded dinner rolls

(MEDIUM) **MAKES: 10**

Fresh dill and fennel fronds are long lost identical twins that heart-warmingly reunite in stuffed dinner rolls that are trying their best to inch from the side plate right into the spotlight. Built to be breezy, split these herb-infused, seed-topped dinner rolls in half and serve warm with vegan cream cheese inside for a roll–bagel cross-bred bread. Mix and match the cooked vegetables to use up those veggies that have spent a bit too long in the crisper – and make a double batch of any of the suggested doughs below to bake a bonus loaf while you're at it.

—

1 fennel bulb, cut into
    2.5 cm (1 in) thick
    wedges, fronds
    reserved
1 large onion, cut into
    thin wedges
1 tablespoon olive oil,
    plus extra for greasing
sea salt and cracked
    black pepper
zest and juice of 1 lemon
plain (all-purpose) flour,
    for dusting
small bunch of dill
2 tablespoons aquafaba
    or water
2 tablespoons
    Everything bagel
    seasoning (page 88)

FOR THE DOUGH
1 × quantity Basic
    sourdough (page 58),
    refrigerated overnight,
    then brought to room
    temperature
OR 1 × quantity Shokupan
    dough (page 80)
OR 1½ × quantities
    Brioche dough
    (page 100)

Prepare the dough, then place in a bowl, cover with a tea towel and leave to rise in a warm spot for 1–2 hours, until doubled in size.

Preheat the oven to 180°C (350°F). Toss the fennel and onion in the olive oil in a baking dish. Bake for 45–60 minutes, until browning. Set aside to cool, but keep the oven on for the dough.

Using a pastry brush, grease a wide cake tin, or a pie tin with tall sides. (Both options are good, and springform tins are ideal – but don't stress too much. Your rolls will just end up slightly fatter or taller, depending on how much room they're given to rise.) Punch down the dough, then use a dough scraper to divide it into 10 even pieces.

Flatten each piece into a disc with your palms. Scoop about 1½ tablespoons of the baked fennel and onion mixture into the centre. Crack salt and pepper over the top and sprinkle with a little of the lemon zest and juice. Fold the bottom edge of the dough over the filling and pinch to seal. Flip the ball seam side down onto a very lightly floured work surface. Slightly cup a hand against the base of the ball to push it to the side, from left to right. Using the same process, drag the ball towards you to create tension, then roll between your palms to round the ball out and smooth out any seams. Repeat with the other pieces of dough.

Evenly space the rolls in the cake tin so they aren't personal space hogs. Insert sprigs of dill and fennel fronds between the gaps of the rolls, so they get trapped by the rising dough and look like moss growing around bready cobblestones. Cover with a tea towel and allow to rise for another 1 hour, basking in warmth.

Use a pastry brush to coat the rolls with the aquafaba, then sprinkle the seasoning mix over the top of each. Insert more fresh dill and fennel if desired. Bake for about 30 minutes, until the tops are golden brown. If using a springform tin, remove the sides to allow extra crisping for another 5–10 minutes in the oven.

Allow to cool in the tin for 10 minutes before tearing off a bun and enjoying warm. I recommend splitting them in half and adding vegan cream cheese and other fillings for perfect packed lunches.

The buns will keep in an airtight container on the bench for up to 3 days. You can return any leftover buns to the oven (or an air fryer) for 5–10 minutes to make them lovely and warm again for serving.

Vegemite & cheese scrolls

(**EASY**) **MAKES: 12**

These insanely savoury swirls have vegan sour cream poured over them just before baking, making them extra soft and flavoursome. They'll turn anyone into a scroll troll under the oven door as they come out, trying to cajole a scroll toll from any scroll that dares try to pass.

7 g (2 teaspoons) instant dried yeast
100 ml (3½ fl oz) warm water
500 g (1 lb 2 oz) plain (all-purpose) flour, plus extra for dusting and kneading
300 ml (10 fl oz) warm soy milk
1 tablespoon white vinegar
80 g (2¾ oz) vegan butter or margarine, softened
40 g (1½ oz) granulated white sugar
2 tablespoons nutritional yeast
1 teaspoon baking soda
1 teaspoon fine salt
cooking spray, for greasing

VEGEMITE & CHEESE FILLING
150 g (5½ oz) Vegemite
80 g (2¾ oz) vegan sour cream or vegan cream
300 g (10½ oz) shredded vegan cheese

In a bowl, combine the yeast, warm water and a pinch of flour and leave for a few minutes to bloom until frothy. In a separate bowl, mix together the milk and vinegar and leave to thicken into a quick buttermilk. Pour this into the yeast mixture, along with the softened butter.

In a large bowl, stir together the flour, sugar, nutritional yeast, baking soda and salt. Pour in the yeast mixture and use a spoon to mix until combined.

Scatter another 50 g (1¾ oz) of flour on a clean work surface. Knead the dough for 5–7 minutes, keeping in mind it will be very sticky. If needed, lightly spray the bench with cooking spray after the flour is used up to prevent sticking. Resist the urge to add more flour, as it will only make the dough less gorgeously moist once baked.

Spray the inside of the bowl, put the dough back in, then cover with a tea towel and leave somewhere warm for 1 hour or until doubled in size.

Lightly grease and line a 29 cm × 32 cm (11½ in × 12½ in) deep-edged baking tray. Flour your work surface once more, then plop the dough onto it, flouring the top as well. Roll the dough out into a 35 cm × 45 cm (14 in × 18 in) rectangle, with the long end towards you. To make the filling, whisk the Vegemite with 2 tablespoons of the sour cream to loosen it. Spread the mixture evenly over the dough rectangle, leaving a 1 cm (½ in) border, then sprinkle with the cheese.

From the edge closest to you, tightly roll the dough into a long tube. Use floss or a sharp knife to cut the dough into 12 even pieces, about 7.5 cm (3 in) thick, then space them out on the baking tray. Cover and allow to rise in a warm spot for 1½–2 hours, until considerably risen and fighting for real estate on the tray. Leave the remaining sour cream on the bench, to come to room temperature during this time.

Preheat the oven to 180°C (350°F). Majestically pour the remaining sour cream evenly over the top of the scrolls. Bake for 25–30 minutes, until lovely and brown on the outside.

Remove from the oven and leave to cool. The scrolls will keep in an airtight container on the bench for up to 2 days.

ON A ROLL?
Swap the Vegemite and cheese filling for a mix of pizza sauce and vegan cheese, or the artichoke pesto on page 280, or a layer of the spanakopita filling on page 168.

Langos

(EASY)   SERVES: 4–6

If you're lucky you'll have stumbled upon this food-truck staple of Hungarian flatbread (lan-gosh), bathed in hot oil and deep-conditioned in garlic. They often use a potato-based dough and are pretty reliably vegan – until you get to the toppings. Vegan offerings I've found in the wild often end up looking like a vegetable-laden pizza, whereas I can't go past the simple luxury of vegan sour cream topped with shredded vegan cheese, chives and spring onions. The sharp, shredded cheese over the protective sour cream layer on langos often doesn't really melt – which is, coincidentally, vegan cheese's favourite state of being. Perfect!

It's not officially traditional, but I like to make Lebanese garlic sauce (toum: literally 'garlic') to brush the bread with post-frying. It's the most potent way to add fresh garlic flavour to anything, so use the rest of the highly flavoured sauce for cooking, basting, marinating vegetables and in vinaigrettes.

olive oil, for greasing
neutral-flavoured oil,
    for deep-frying

TOUM
1 very fat garlic bulb,
    peeled
large pinch of flaky salt
80 ml (2½ fl oz) lemon
    juice
120 ml (4 fl oz) light
    olive oil
240 ml (8 fl oz) neutral-
    flavoured oil

DOUGH
120 ml (4 fl oz) warm
    water
7 g (2 teaspoons) active
    dried yeast
15 g (½ oz) granulated
    white sugar
300 g (10½ oz) plain
    (all-purpose) flour,
    plus extra for dusting
1 teaspoon fine salt
1 potato, cooked and
    mashed

To make the toum, toss the garlic in a food processor with the salt. Whiz to a paste, then drizzle in a tablespoon of the lemon juice. Leave the processor running and slowly pour in 60 ml (2 fl oz) of the olive oil, then 1 teaspoon of lemon juice, followed by the remaining olive oil. Alternate drizzling in tablespoons of the neutral-flavoured oil, followed by a splash of the lemon juice, pouring slowly to maintain the emulsion. When you're done, it should be thick and fluffy. Taste and adjust to make sure the primary flavour is getting slapped with a bulb of garlic. The toum will keep in a sealed jar in the fridge for up to 1 month, but the fresh garlic flavour will lose intensity over time.

To make the dough, mix together the warm water, yeast and sugar in a small bowl, then sprinkle in a small pinch of the flour and set aside to bloom until frothy.

In a large bowl, mix together the flour and salt. Make a well in the middle, then pour in the yeast mixture. Stir until combined, then slowly knead in the potato until combined. Knead on an unfloured work surface for another 3 minutes. Lightly oil the bowl, put the dough back in, then cover with plastic wrap. Leave the dough to rise in a warm spot for 1 hour.

Very lightly flour a work surface. Use a dough scraper to divide the dough into two balls. Slather some of the toum onto your hands, then press each piece of dough between your palms to make a 20 cm (8 in) round. It doesn't need to be beautiful – in fact, the more bumps and ridges there are, the more garlicky oil can fit atop.

On the benchtop, press your palms into the dough rounds, to form a slightly thicker edge. Cover with a tea towel and leave to rise for another 1 hour on the benchtop or a silicone baking mat.

1 teaspoon flaky salt
160 g (5½ oz) vegan sour
   cream
150 g (5½ oz) vegan
   parmesan or other
   sharp vegan cheese,
   shredded
2 spring onions
   (scallions), finely sliced
1 tablespoon finely
   chopped chives

Heat 5–7.5 cm (2–3 in) of neutral-flavourd oil in a large heavy-based saucepan until the temperature registers above 180°C (350°F) on a kitchen thermometer, or when the handle of a wooden spoon instantly bubbles when placed in the oil. Aim to keep the oil temperature between 175°C and 190°C (345°F and 375°F) while frying the langos.

Slide a wide spatula or dough scraper under the puffed-up langos and transfer to the oil. Fry for about 3 minutes on each side, until completely golden, using tongs and the spatula to guide the langos over as you flip them. Transfer to a paper towel or wire rack, blotting away any excess oil with paper towel.

Time to get topping. Transfer the langos to a plate and use a pastry brush to generously coat both sides with more toum. Go in with a sprinkle of flaky salt.

Mix another tablespoon of toum into the sour cream, then smear over the entire surface, except the very edge. Evenly sprinkle the cheese over. Ideally, microwave each langos for about 30 seconds to meld the toppings together. Scatter with a pretty aggressive amount of spring onion and chives. Use a pizza slicer to cut into wedges and serve while hot.

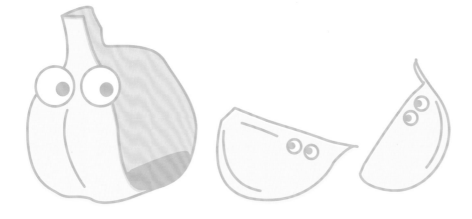

Langos

Khachapuri

(HARD)   MAKES: 6

This is a fairly easy recipe, listed as difficult only due to the inconvenient advance notice needed to source the special vegan egg yolk ingredients. The extra effort to make the vegan yolks with their runny centres – to fully replicate the egg traditionally cracked on the khachapuri at the end of baking – is well worth the gasps they elicit. Feel free to leave this step out, though. As cheese is the real star, below-average cheeses have nowhere to hide here. You'll need to fork out for the extra good stuff, but you'll be glad you did. Use a combination of vegan melty cheeses (like mozzarella) and tangy cheeses (like feta) to make a Georgian cheesy bread that's engorgin' and tastes absolutely gorge!-ian.

500 g (1 lb 2 oz) fancy
    vegan cheeses,
    crumbled or grated
1 lemon, cut in half
cracked black pepper,
    for sprinkling
3 tablespoons aquafaba,
    for brushing
chives, to serve
black salt (kala namak),
    for sprinkling

DOUGH
7 g (2 teaspoons) active
    dried yeast
125 ml (4 fl oz) warm
    water
125 ml (4 fl oz) warm
    plant-based milk
320 g (11½ oz) plain
    (all-purpose) flour, plus
    extra for dusting
2 teaspoons garlic
    powder
2 teaspoons granulated
    white sugar
¾ teaspoon fine salt
1 tablespoon olive oil,
    plus extra for greasing

To make the dough, combine the yeast in a small bowl with the warm water and milk, and a pinch of the flour. Leave to bloom for a few minutes until frothy.

In a large bowl, mix together the flour, garlic powder, sugar and salt. Make a well in the centre, then pour in the yeast mixture. Stir until combined, then press into a loose dough. Transfer to a lightly floured work surface and knead for 10 minutes, or use a stand mixer fitted with the dough hook on medium speed for 5 minutes. Gradually add the oil during the last few minutes of kneading. Lightly oil the bowl, add the dough ball, then cover with plastic wrap. Leave to rise in a warm spot for 1–1½ hours.

Meanwhile, get cracking on those egg yolks. Put the carrot in a microwave-safe dish, pour in 80 ml (2½ fl oz) of water, then cover and microwave for 5 minutes or until tender. Drain, then allow to cool for 10 minutes. Add to a blender with the remaining egg yolk ingredients and whiz until smooth.

To make the setting solution, dissolve the calcium chloride by whisking it into 750 ml (25½ fl oz) of water in a large bowl. Dip a dessertspoon into the calcium chloride solution, then use a teaspoon to heap some egg yolk mixture on top, until it forms a rounded egg yolk shape. Slowly lower the spoon back into the calcium chloride solution until the egg yolk floats. Carefully spoon more calcium water over the top, then repeat five more times to make six yolks. Leave the yolks in the solution until needed – but don't prepare these more than a few hours ahead of serving, or the yolks may set completely hard.

Flour a work surface generously, and keep it floured as you work. Punch down the dough, then divide into six pieces and roll each into a smooth ball. Working gently, pull and stretch each ball with your hands, into a 20 cm (8 in) round. Crumble the cheeses over one, squeeze on some lemon juice, then crack some pepper over. Roll in the edge to create a crust, with the cheese filling trapped inside. Grab an edge of the round and pinch it firmly together, curving slightly up to create a tapered end, like the bow of a boat. Repeat on the other end, curving in the opposite direction to create a large boat-shaped rim around the filling. Continue until you've made all the boats. Place each boat on its own square of baking paper, then cover with a tea towel and leave to rise for another 30 minutes.

EGG YOLKS
80 g (2¾ oz) carrot,
  chopped
1½ teaspoons olive oil
1 teaspoon nutritional
  yeast
¼ teaspoon mustard
  powder
⅓ teaspoon sodium
  alginate
⅛ teaspoon black salt
  (kala namak)

SETTING SOLUTION
1 teaspoon calcium
  chloride

Remove the oven racks from your oven, then place one rack about 20 cm (8 in) below the oven grill (broiler). Select an appropriate pizza tray that will conduct very high heat – pizza stones, baking steel sheets or dark-coloured metal perforated pizza baking trays are ideal; a large baking tray will work, too. Place the pizza tray in the oven, preheat the oven to its highest setting – 250°C (480°F) or higher – and turn the oven grill on.

Using a pastry brush, glaze the pastry edges of each khachapuri with aquafaba. Carefully remove the hot tray from the oven, load it up with the khachapuris, then bake for 2–3 minutes. Switch off the grill, then continue to bake for another 10–15 minutes, until the toppings are sizzling. (If your vegan cheese is being too resilient, brush water or oil over the top of it while in the oven to encourage melting.)

Remove from the oven and cool the khachapuris on a wire rack for 5 minutes.

Carefully rinse the egg yolks in a bowl of fresh water and lay one in the centre of each bread boat. Finely snip chives all over the top. Finally, sprinkle black salt directly on top of the egg yolk and the area around it.

These dreamboats are best served fresh and warm, so you can marvel in the ooze of the yolk as you crack in.

Korean sausage buns

When I first encountered savoury–sweet Asian breads, they seemed almost otherworldly. Super-enriched doughs with lots of kneading fill bakeries with breads that are softer, sweeter and shinier than any Western counterpart. You'll find familiar concepts like a sausage roll that instead looks closer to the biblical description of an angel. Sausage ppang (Korean sausage buns) are topped with a delicious signature mix and are just as fun to make as they are to eat. The brioche-like dough can be used in place of the Shokupan dough on page 80 for recipes in this book.

10 vegan sausages

PPANG DOUGH

250 ml (8½ fl oz) warm plant-based milk
50 g (1¾ oz) granulated white sugar
10 g (3 teaspoons) active dried yeast
420 g (15 oz) bread flour
2 teaspoons psyllium husk powder
1 teaspoon sea salt
60 g (2 oz) cold vegan butter

TOPPING

150 g (5½ oz) vegan mozzarella, chopped
100 g (3½ oz) finely chopped green bell pepper (capsicum)
100 g (3½ oz) chopped onion
100 g (3½ oz) tinned corn kernels, drained well
80 g (2¾ oz) vegan mayonnaise

FINISHING TOUCHES

2 tablespoons plant-based milk, for glazing
20 g (¾ oz) vegan butter, at room temperature
2 tablespoons finely chopped parsley
tomato ketchup

To make the dough, combine the warm milk in a bowl with the sugar and yeast. Leave to bloom for several minutes, until frothy and excited to go to work.

Add the yeast mixture, flour and psyllium husk powder to the bowl of a stand mixer fitted with the dough hook and knead on medium speed for about 15 minutes. After the first 3 minutes of kneading, add the salt, then the cold butter, teaspoon by teaspoon, until the dough passes the windowpane test (page 52). Cover with a tea towel and allow to rise in a warm spot for 1–2 hours, until doubled in size.

Divide the dough into 10 pieces, about 80 g (2¾ oz) each. On a lightly floured work surface, roll each piece into a ball and then into a cylinder of even thickness, just longer than your sausages. Place a sausage on top, then bring the dough around the sausage to enclose and roll to hide it inside the dough. With kitchen scissors, snip most of the way through the cylinder and sausage at 1.5 cm (½ in) increments, leaving the base intact. Carefully rotate each freshly snipped piece in alternating directions to lay them flat on the bench with the sausage facing up. Tuck the doughy ends under.

Cover with a tea towel and leave to rise for up to 1 hour on the benchtop (or on a silicone baking mat, using a dough scraper to transfer), until doubled in size.

Preheat the oven to 175°C (345°F). Mix the topping ingredients together in a bowl.

Transfer the buns to a baking tray lined with baking paper or a silicone baking mat. To finish them off, brush the tops with the milk, then spoon the topping over the middle of each. Bake for about 15 minutes or until golden on top. During the last 2 minutes, brush the tops all over with the butter, to help the unamenable vegan cheese to melt; you can turn on the oven grill (broiler) at the very end if you must.

Just before eating, sprinkle parsley on top and drizzle with tomato ketchup. The buns will keep in an airtight container on the bench for up to 3 days.

Artichoke pesto filo tart

(EASY) SERVES: 6–8

You can draw on the wide landscape of store-bought filo pastry and vegan egg replacements (either the bottled egg mixes designed for pan scrambling, or the trusty powdered versions made for baking, prepared as per the packet instructions) to bring this tart together in minutes.

A crispy terrain of filo pastry gets flooded with artichoke pesto, then blistered tomatoes dot the balmy basin like islands. The more variety in your tomatoes, the more beautiful the view from the top. Serve with a rocket salad on the side to take this meal to the moon.

—

80 ml (2½ fl oz) Confit garlic oil (page 76) or olive oil
12 sheets filo pastry
320 g (11½ oz) mixed cherry tomatoes, sliced into thirds
6 garlic cloves, finely chopped
sea salt and cracked black pepper
100 g (3½ oz) prepared vegan egg replacer
100 g (3½ oz) shredded vegan cheese
100 g (3½ oz) vegan feta (optional)
lemon wedges, to serve
rocket (arugula) leaves, to serve

ARTICHOKE PESTO
150 g (5½ oz) marinated artichoke hearts
25 g (¾ oz) chopped parsley
handful of basil leaves
35 g (1¼ oz) pistachios
2 garlic cloves, peeled
2 tablespoons lemon juice
2 tablespoons nutritional yeast
sea salt and cracked black pepper
80 ml (2½ fl oz) olive oil

Prepare the artichoke pesto by adding all the ingredients except the olive oil to a food processor. With the motor running, slowly pour in the oil, scraping down the side of the bowl as needed. Adjust the seasoning to taste, then store in the fridge until ready to use.

Preheat the oven to 180°C (350°F).

Using a pastry brush, coat the base of a 25 cm (10 in) quiche dish with some of the confit garlic oil. Lay a sheet of filo pastry over the centre. Rotate the dish 45 degrees, brush the pastry with oil and lay another sheet on top. Repeat, rotating the dish, to cover the entire base. Crumple the remaining pastry in the dish to create lots of weird textures: think hills, peaks, valleys, a few mountain ranges; the goal is to create lots of crispy areas throughout the base for the filling to fit into. Fold in the sticking-out edges of the filo pastry to form a rim, then generously drizzle the whole lot with more of the oil. Blind-bake for 15–20 minutes, until the pastry is golden.

In a bowl, toss the sliced tomatoes with the garlic, salt and pepper.

Mix the prepared egg replacer and shredded cheese through the pesto, then spoon the pesto mixture into the baked pastry shell, into all those nooks and crannies you created earlier. Lay the tomato mixture over the top, covering the entire surface, and pushing down slightly. Brush any excess tomato liquid and remaining oil over the top.

Bake for 25–30 minutes, until the filling has set and the tomato begins to blister. As soon as the tart comes out of the oven, crumble the feta over the top, if using.

Serve warm, with lemon wedges and rocket. The tart will keep in the fridge for 2 days as you finish it off.

Cornish pasties

Originally designed with the pie pastry being inedible packaging to protect the hearty filling from grubby hands after a hard morning working in the coal mines of Cornwall, we thankfully can now eat the pastry *and* filling while comfortably not down a mineshaft. Using an easy shortcrust pastry and store-bought plant-based meat makes these pasties super simple to prepare ahead of time for lunches on busy days – just as they were always intended to be eaten. You can also make these half-sized for snacking.

plain (all-purpose) flour,
   for dusting
1 × quantity Shortcrust
   pastry (page 42)
sea salt and cracked
   black pepper
2½ tablespoons plant-
   based milk
tomato ketchup, to serve
   (optional)

FILLING
15 g (½ oz) vegan butter
340 g (12 oz) plant-based
   mince
200 g (7 oz) potatoes,
   finely diced
100 g (3½ oz) swede
   (rutabaga), finely diced
2 tablespoons vegan
   worcestershire sauce
1 tablespoon finely
   chopped thyme leaves

To make the filling, melt the butter in a large saucepan over medium–high heat until bubbling. Add the mince, without breaking it up out of the condensed shape it is packed in. Leave it alone for 3–4 minutes, until nicely browned underneath, then flip it over and repeat on the other side; this will help create chunks of meat the right size for a pasty filling. Now use a wooden spoon to break up the meat, then toss in the potato, swede, worcestershire sauce and thyme. Cook for 2 minutes, then remove from the heat.

Preheat the oven to 160°C (320°F). Line two baking trays with baking paper or silicone baking mats.

Lightly flour a workbench and rolling pin. Use a dough scraper to divide your prepared shortcrust pastry into six pieces, weighing about 95 g (3¼ oz) each. Roll one dough piece into a ball, then allow to rest for a few minutes while you roll the others, so the gluten can relax and stretch without tearing.

Now roll each dough ball into a 20 cm (8 in) round (about the width of a cake tin). They don't need to be perfectly round, as you'll use a pizza slicer to trim the wonky edges.

Spoon the filling onto one side of the pastry rounds, cracking salt and pepper over the top, and leaving a 2.5 cm (1 in) border around the edge. Brush some of the milk around the edge using a pastry brush. Fold the other pastry half over and press the edges together to adhere. From one side of the seal, with your thumb and index finger, twist the edge of the pastry over to form a crimp. Continue along the edge of the pastry, then tuck the ends in to finish. Repeat with all the pasties, then brush milk over the tops.

Transfer to the baking trays and bake for up to 1 hour. Remove the pasties from the oven when they're completely crispy all over, but not so much that they'd survive a trip down a mineshaft (here's looking at you, traditionalists and oven-timer ignorers alike) – so check to see if they're done from 45 minutes onwards.

If you're not eating them straight away, they'll keep in an airtight container in the fridge for up to 3 days. You can serve them warm, although traditionally they're eaten well after any heat has left the pastry, with a splodge of tomato ketchup on top, if desired.

Sausage rolls

(EASY) **MAKES: 4 JUMBO PORTIONS, OR A PLATTER OF SNACKS**

Construction workers and children's party attendees alike, rejoice! Your traditional meal has been veganised. Pick whatever mushrooms are cheap this week as they get blended up anyway. Now, let me show you how I roll.

2 sheets Puff pastry
    (page 48; or use
    store-bought)
4 teaspoons olive oil
2 teaspoons soy milk
sesame seeds and/
    or poppy seeds, for
    sprinkling
tomato ketchup, to serve

FILLING
1 large onion, finely
    chopped
olive oil, for pan-frying
500 g (1 lb 2 oz) mixed
    mushrooms, finely
    chopped
½ teaspoon sea salt
large pinch of cracked
    black pepper
4 garlic cloves, finely
    chopped
1½ tablespoons flaxseed
    (linseed) meal
1 tablespoon vegan
    worcestershire sauce
75 g (2¾ oz) rolled
    (porridge) oats
90 g (3 oz) dried
    breadcrumbs
2 tablespoons nutritional
    yeast
3 tablespoons chopped
    parsley leaves
1½ teaspoons chopped
    rosemary leaves
1½ teaspoons chopped
    thyme leaves
½ teaspoon dried
    oregano
½ teaspoon liquid smoke

Start by making the filling. In a large saucepan, cook the onion with a light-handed drizzle of olive oil over medium heat for 5 minutes. Add the mushroom, salt and pepper. Cook, stirring, over medium–high heat for 10–15 minutes, until the mushroom gives up its moisture and the liquid evaporates. Remove the pan from the heat and toss in the garlic to bask in the residual heat.

Combine the flaxseed meal and worcestershire sauce to form a gel egg. Transfer the mushroom mixture to a food processor, then add the gel egg and remaining filling ingredients. Blitz for 1 minute or until the texture is uniform. (If adding some plant-based meat, as per the tip at the end of the recipe, break it up and fold it through at this point.) Set aside.

Preheat the oven to 200°C (400°F).

Divide the mushroom mixture into quarters (or into six portions if you've added some plant-based mince). Cut the pastry sheets in half and place them in front of you. Evenly spoon a thick strip of filling along the long edge of each pastry sheet. Smooth the filling out, then fold the pastry sheets over to enclose the filling, using a teaspoon to press down and seal the edges. Press the sausage rolls down on this crease to seal them shut. Cut them in half and stuff any filling that's fallen out back into the open ends. Use a sharp knife to make slits along the side of the pastry, to let the steam escape in the oven, alternating on each side.

Whisk the olive oil and soy milk together in a small bowl and brush over the top of each sausage roll. Sprinkle with sesame seeds and/or poppy seeds. Cut the rolls in half or thirds for individual serves, or quarters for party snacks.

Bake for 25–35 minutes, then scoff warm with tomato ketchup as they leave the oven. Any that survive the first wave can be reheated in an air fryer or a hot oven for 5–10 minutes.

The rolls will keep in an airtight container in the fridge for up to 3 days.

DON'T SLOW YOUR ROLL YET
You can stretch out this recipe and add more meatiness by folding up to 300 g (10½ oz) plant-based meat (or crumbled burger patties) into the mushroom mixture. Add another sheet of puff pastry to accommodate the extra filling and you'll get a few extra rolls for your efforts.

Jalapeno cornbread

Horny cornbread that's gotten a little flustered under the collar! It's spicy from jalapeno chillies both pickled and fresh, some would say a little too cheesy – and so corny that there's literally fresh corn in every bite. A square is a whole meal, perfect for serving on the side of a whole other meal. Try it with Vegan honey (page 39) or Maple butter (page 226) drizzled on top.

—

cooking spray, for greasing
235 ml (8 fl oz) soy milk
1 tablespoon white vinegar
2 tablespoons flaxseed (linseed) meal
220 g (8 oz) polenta (cornmeal)
150 g (5½ oz) plain (all-purpose) flour
2 tablespoons caster (superfine) sugar
3 teaspoons baking powder
1 teaspoon baking soda
1 teaspoon sea salt
100 ml (3½ fl oz) pickled jalapeno brine from the jar
200 g (7 oz) tinned corn kernels, drained well
100 g (3½ oz) vegan cheese, grated
50 g (1¾ oz) pickled jalapeno chillies, roughly chopped
20 g (¾ oz) nutritional yeast
2–3 fresh jalapeno chillies, finely sliced into rounds

Preheat the oven to 180°C (350°F). Lightly grease a 20 cm (8 in) square baking tin.

In a bowl, mix together the milk and vinegar and leave for about 5 minutes to thicken into a quick buttermilk. Stir in the flaxseed meal.

In a large bowl, combine the polenta, flour, sugar, baking powder, baking soda and salt. Add the buttermilk, jalapeno brine, corn, cheese, pickled jalapenos and nutritional yeast. Stir to combine, but don't overmix. Spoon the batter into the prepared tin and use the back of a spoon to smooth the top. Scatter the fresh jalapeno chilli over the top.

Bake for 25–35 minutes, until the crust is brown and a skewer inserted in the middle comes out clean. Cut into 16 squares and serve warm.

The cornbread slices freeze well to pop in the microwave whenever a fresh chilli number comes off the stovetop.

CHILL OUT, MAN
Serving with a spicy soup, or not into spicy food at all? Replace the jalapeno brine with water in the batter, and either don't add jalapenos, or replace them with sun-dried tomatoes or roasted bell peppers (capsicums).

Toad in the hole

(MEDIUM)   SERVES: 4–6

Designed to stretch out meat in poor households, toad in the hole is made by pouring a Yorkshire pudding batter over meat (most popularly sausages) and baking it all together in sizzling hot oil. We're tossing in some fresh herbs here to help excuse cheap vegan sausages that might need a little flavour boost – or, find small chipolata-style vegan sausages with big flavour to get closer to the real deal. Bulk out your plate with green beans, peas, mashed potatoes and other leftovers from a Sunday roast and you'll find yourself with a good square meal. Just make sure to slather on a good vegan gravy to give the toads a good drink.

2½ tablespoons canola oil
8 vegan sausages
1 × quantity Yorkshire pudding batter (page 290)
2 teaspoons chopped rosemary leaves
2 teaspoons chopped thyme leaves
vegan gravy, to serve

Preheat the oven to 230°C (445°F). Pour the canola oil into a 25 cm (10 in) round baking dish, then place in the oven for 10 minutes until sizzling hot, so that the batter rises high enough for the toads to nestle comfortably inside.

In a wide saucepan, fry the sausages as per the packet instructions. Switch off the heat and toss the herbs over them.

When the baking dish is smoking hot, you'll want to work quickly to retain the oven heat. Open the oven door, slide the rack with the baking dish out a bit, then deftly ladle the pudding batter into the baking dish. Use tongs to space out the sausages and herbs on top. Push the rack back in and promptly close the oven door.

Bake for 20 minutes or until the pudding batter is dark gold on top. Remove from the oven and cool slightly before slicing up into portions. Flood the gloriously golden swamp with your favourite gravy: the toads peeking up out of the batter will love it – and so will you!

FILL THE POND
This batter will hold more than just sausages! In the spirit of toad in the hole, use up your pre-cooked vegan meat leftovers and offcuts. Alternatively, add in the confit shallots or garlic on pages 68 and 76, the baked fennel and onion on page 268, the roasted mushrooms on page 298, or other pre-cooked vegetables to clear out your fridge.

Yorkshire puddings

(MEDIUM) MAKES: 6

Here's cheers to the edible gravy boats of the Sunday roast world. Heat your oiled-up muffin tin in the oven until searing hot, and then batter up! These savoury chalices can happily sizzle away next to a veggie tray bake or your favourite vegan roast.

60 ml (2 fl oz) canola oil
vegan gravy, to serve

YORKSHIRE PUDDING
BATTER
200 ml (7 fl oz) soy milk
35 ml (1¼ fl oz) aquafaba
½ teaspoon white
    vinegar
½ teaspoon dijon
    mustard
40 g (1½ oz) chickpea
    flour (besan)
90 g (3 oz) plain
    (all-purpose) flour
2 teaspoons baking
    powder
pinch of sea salt

Preheat the oven to 230°C (445°F). Pour 2 teaspoons of the canola oil into each hole of a six-hole muffin tin or Yorkshire pudding pan. Place in the oven for 10 minutes to get sizzling hot, much like you, dear reader.

Meanwhile, you big hunk-a-spunk, you should whisk together the milk, aquafaba, vinegar and mustard in a bowl. In a large bowl, mix together the flours, baking powder and salt. Pour in the wet ingredients and mix everything together.

When your pudding tin is smoking hot – and not before, or your puddings won't rise properly! – you'll want to work quickly to retain the oven heat. Open the oven door, slide the shelf with the muffin tin out a bit, then deftly ladle the batter into the moulds. Push the muffin tin back in and promptly close the oven door.

Bake for 20–25 minutes, until the puddings are dark gold on top. Remove them from the moulds as soon as they come out of the oven and allow to cool slightly.

Serve hot and fresh on the side of a vegan Sunday roast and it's all gravy, baby.

Korean cream cheese buns

(MEDIUM) **MAKES: 8**

These are Asian savoury–sweet breads at their drool-worthy peak – buns with sweet cream cheese piped into the very middle, and garlic butter poured over. The top of each bun is deeply scored into eight wedges for the garlic butter to better seep into, and for your convenience as you tear off pieces like a mandarin. This recipe is made using wholemeal brioche dough so you can delude yourself into thinking these could be healthy.

WHOLEMEAL BRIOCHE DOUGH
260 ml (9 fl oz) warm plant-based milk, plus extra for brushing
60 g (2 oz) granulated white sugar
10 g (3 teaspoons) active dried yeast
220 g (8 oz) bread flour, plus extra for dusting
200 g (7 oz) wholemeal (whole-wheat) flour
1 teaspoon sea salt
60 g (2 oz) cold vegan butter

CREAM CHEESE FILLING
300 g (10½ oz) vegan cream cheese
30 g (1 oz) icing (confectioners') sugar
½ teaspoon sea salt
45 g (1½ oz) vegan Japanese mayonnaise

To make the dough, combine the warm milk in a bowl with the sugar and yeast. Leave to bloom for several minutes, until frothy and excited to go to work.

Add the yeast mixture and flours to the bowl of a stand mixer fitted with the dough hook and knead on medium speed for 16–18 minutes. After the first 3 minutes of kneading, add the salt, then the cold butter, teaspoon by teaspoon. The dough hook will cut the butter through the dough for a while before it begins to clump together, form a ball and then resist the dough hook. Stop when the dough passes the windowpane test (page 52). Cover with a tea towel and allow to rise in a warm spot for 1–2 hours, until doubled in size.

Line two baking trays with baking paper or silicone baking mats. Punch down the dough, then roll into an even cylinder. Cut into eight pieces weighing about 95 g (3¼ oz) each.

Lightly flour a work surface and rolling pin, then roll out each piece of dough into a disc. For each piece, fold the edge over the top and pinch to gather it together to create a smooth ball. Flip the ball, seam side down, onto a very lightly floured benchtop. Slightly cup a hand against the base of the ball to push it to the side, from left to right. Using the same process, drag the ball towards you to create tension, round the ball out and smooth out any seams. Repeat with the other pieces of dough.

Evenly space the buns on the baking trays, with room to balloon out and up as they rise. Cover with a tea towel and allow to rise and double in size for another 1–1½ hours, while basking in warmth.

Preheat the oven to 180°C (350°F).

Brush the top of the buns with extra milk, then bake for about 25 minutes, until the tops are beginning to turn golden brown. Remove from the oven and leave to cool for 20 minutes. Leaving the bottom of the buns intact, use a bread knife to cut eight deep wedges into the top of each bun, across the middle.

Reduce the oven temperature to 150°C (300°F).

GARLIC BUTTER SAUCE
120 g (4½ oz) vegan
    butter
2 tablespoons nutritional
    yeast or finely grated
    vegan parmesan
1½–2 tablespoons very
    finely chopped garlic
2 tablespoons very finely
    chopped parsley leaves,
    plus extra to serve
2 teaspoons dijon
    mustard
½ teaspoon flaky salt

To make the filling, use a large mixing bowl and a hand-held electric mixer, or a stand mixer fitted with a paddle attachment, to beat the cream cheese for 1 minute. With the mixer running, sift in the icing sugar and toss in the salt. Fit a piping (icing) bag with a small nozzle and place it in a tall jug, furling the edges over the rim to hold it in place. Spoon the cream cheese mixture into the bag, but don't overfill, so you can twist the bag tightly shut.

To make the garlic butter sauce, add the butter to a microwave-safe bowl and blast, stirring at 15-second increments, until melted but not too hot. Whisk in the remaining sauce ingredients.

Prise a wedge of one of the buns open, insert the piping nozzle and pipe a strip of cream cheese filling inside the bun. Repeat to fill all the crevices, then pipe some more filling directly into the centre. Further fill the crevices with a squeeze of the mayo towards the top of the bun. Painstakingly repeat this process with all the buns, trusting in the knowledge that it will be completely worth it.

Dip each bun, top down, into the garlic butter sauce to fully coat the entire thing. The sauce should be thick enough to cling generously to the outside.

Bake the buns for another 12–15 minutes, to crisp up on the outside. Sprinkle with extra parsley and serve warm.

If you're eating the buns over a few sessions, skip the garlic butter dunk on any potential leftover buns, then continue from that step when you're ready to reheat them. The buns will keep in an airtight container on the bench for up to 3 days, and a few days longer if refrigerated.

Korean cream cheese buns

Margherita pizzas

Margherita pizzas

(HARD) MAKES: 3

As a (reformed!) vegetarian who would (and could) only cook cheesy pizzas covered in chilli, I openly wept when I ate my first real Neapolitan-style vegan margherita in a restaurant. Here's my best shot at recreating this simple but incredible classic pizza at home. The trick is less in the dough, and more in pulling out all the stops to apply high heat to all parts of the dough, in and out of the oven. I prefer to use two kinds of vegan cheese – one to focus on adding flavour, and the other tasked with melting. Chilli isn't traditional, and neither is the dairy-free cheese – but I think they both make it better anyway.

olive oil and cooking
  spray, for greasing
plain (all-purpose) flour,
  for dusting
semolina, for sprinkling

PIZZA DOUGH
2½ teaspoons fine salt
260 ml (9 fl oz) warm
  water
350 g (12½ oz) bread flour
  or pizza flour
3 g (1 teaspoon) instant
  dried yeast

One full day before you'd like to pull the pizzas out of the oven, make the dough. Dissolve the salt in the warm water in the bowl of a stand mixer fitted with the dough hook. Dump the flour and yeast on top and knead on medium speed for 15 minutes to create a marshmallowy dough. Place in a lightly oiled bowl, cover with plastic wrap and rest in the fridge for 24 hours.

The next day, remove the dough from the fridge and leave for 2 hours at room temperature.

Use a dough scraper to split the dough into three pieces, about 200 g (7 oz) each. Lightly flour a work surface. Working with one dough portion at a time, fold the edge over the top and pinch to gather together to create a smooth ball. Flip the ball, seam side down, onto the benchtop. Slightly cup a hand against the base of the ball to push it to the side, from left to right. Using the same process, drag the ball towards you to create tension, round the ball out and smooth out any seams.

Cover with a tea towel and allow to rise on the floured bench for another 1–1½ hours, until doubled in size. (During this time, preheating your oven to its maximum temperature should help give the dough the temperature boost it needs to spring to action.)

Prepare a pizza-making station, so you can move quickly when the time comes. Remove the oven racks from your oven, then place one rack about 10–15 cm (4–6 in) below the oven grill (broiler). Select an appropriate pizza tray that will conduct very high heat – pizza stones, baking steel sheets or dark-coloured metal perforated pizza baking trays are ideal; a large baking tray will work, too. Place the pizza tray in the oven. Now preheat the oven to its highest setting – 250°C (480°F) or higher – and turn the oven grill on.

400 g (14 oz) tin fire-
roasted tomatoes or
san marzano tomatoes,
drained and crushed
with your hands
100 g (3½ oz) vegan
parmesan, grated
2 tablespoons olive oil
flaky salt and cracked
black pepper
100 g (3½ oz) melty
vegan bocconcini or
mozzarella, sliced
into rounds
80 g (2¾ oz) tiny cherry
tomatoes (optional)
1 long red chilli, sliced on
the diagonal (optional)
1 long green chilli, sliced
on the diagonal
(optional)
basil leaves, to serve

Lightly flour the bench again and place one of the dough balls on top. Hold the fingers on each hand together (like you're about to give an emphatic chef's kiss after eating an exquisite pizza) and use them to peck the centre of the dough ball, flattening the centre. Use your hands to stretch the dough from the centre outwards, avoiding touching the edge as you go, to preserve the air pockets in the eventual crust. Rotate the dough as you pull it to enlarge the round. Flip the dough upside down, with your knuckles now under the centre of the dough round. Use them to gently stretch out then twirl the dough to further elongate it into a thin, even base surrounded by a risen border around the edge.

Give the dough one last adjusting to make sure everywhere except the crust is as thin as possible, then place it on a large square of baking paper. Pull the edge out to form a rounded shape, then spoon on one-third of the crushed tomato. Scatter with one-third of the parmesan, drizzle with a little of the olive oil, sprinkle with salt and pepper, then haphazardly throw on the bocconcini, and cherry tomatoes and chilli, if using.

It's go time! Place a very wide frying pan – one large enough to comfortably fit your pizza – over low heat and very lightly spray with cooking oil. Wearing oven mitts, open the oven door, slide the rack with the pizza tray out a bit, then deftly transfer the pizza and the baking paper onto the tray. Crank the stovetop up high. Bake the pizza for 4–5 minutes, under careful supervision, rotating two or three times until the toppings are sizzling and the crust has risen and is beginning to char all over. Slide the pizza off the baking paper (very carefully, as the base has not set yet) into the frying pan. Cook for another 4–5 minutes, until the base is fully charred.

Repeat in quick succession with the other pizzas. With a properly preheated oven and pizza tray – and quick hands! – a stream of hot pizzas can be coming out of your oven with little wait time between each.

Just before serving, scatter fresh basil over and slice with a pizza cutter, or kitchen scissors. The pizzas are best cooked and eaten straight out of the oven, but any leftovers can be refrigerated for up to 3 days, and reheated in the oven or an air fryer as desired.

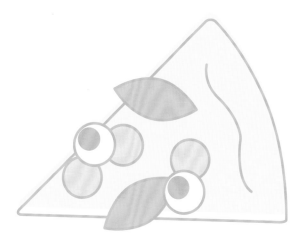

Roasted mushroom pide

(EASY) SERVES: 6

Whole roasted mushrooms are marvellous in this Turkish pizza flatbread, which is popularly filled with lamb. The trick is to water-fry the mushrooms first, so their liquid evaporates well before stuffing them into the dough. Like pizza, pide can play host to most delegations of topping ingredients – pre-cooked fillings like plant-based meat, vegetables, your favourite cheeses and anything else you might expect to find on a pizza. You can also try adding the vegan egg yolks from pages 276–77 atop the filling after baking, to form a vegan pide you can truly take pride in.

olive oil, for greasing
    and brushing
flaky salt, for scattering
3 tablespoons finely
    chopped parsley leaves
lemon wedges, to serve

PIDE DOUGH
7 g (2 teaspoons) instant
    dried yeast
100 ml (3½ fl oz) warm
    water
300 g (10½ oz) plain
    (all-purpose) flour
1 tablespoon nigella seeds
1 teaspoon sugar
1 teaspoon fine salt
150 g (5½ oz) coconut
    yoghurt, plus extra
    for brushing

FILLING
600 g (1 lb 5 oz) whole
    button mushrooms
3 garlic cloves, grated
cracked black pepper
3 tablespoons tomato
    paste (concentrated
    puree)
1 red onion, finely diced
2 long green chillies,
    chopped
10 pitted black olives,
    sliced
100 g (3½ oz) tangy
    vegan cheese, grated

To make the dough, combine the yeast in a small bowl with the warm water and a pinch of the flour. Leave to bloom for a few minutes until frothy.

In a large bowl, mix together the flour, nigella seeds, sugar and salt. Make a well in the centre, then pour in the yeast mixture and yoghurt. Stir until combined, then press into a loose dough. Transfer to a lightly floured work surface and knead for 10 minutes, or use a stand mixer fitted with the dough hook on medium speed for 5 minutes. Lightly oil the bowl, add the dough ball, then cover with plastic wrap. Leave to rise in a warm spot for 1–1½ hours.

Get started on the filling. Add the whole mushrooms to a wok over high heat, and have a cup of water on standby. Add a tablespoon of the water and fry, stirring, until the water evaporates. Continue adding small splashes of water until the mushrooms begin to release their own liquid. Shallow water-fry for 10–15 minutes, until the liquid from the mushrooms has evaporated. Turn off the heat, add the garlic and pepper and toss to coat. Set aside to cool completely.

Preheat the oven to 200°C (400°F). Line your largest baking tray with baking paper or silicone baking mats.

Punch down the dough on a lightly floured work surface, then roll into a smooth ball. Working gently, pull and stretch the ball with your hands into a long, fat oval measuring about 20 cm × 60 cm (8 in × 24 in). Adjust as needed so that it is evenly flattened all the way around and transfer to the prepared tray.

Spread the tomato paste across the centre, then cover in the garlicky mushrooms. Scatter the onion, chilli and olives around. Grab one short end of the oval and pinch it firmly together, curving slightly to one side to create a tapered but tucked-in end, like the bow of a boat. Repeat on the other end, curving in the opposite direction to create a large boat-shaped rim around the fillings. Roll in the edges to create a sturdy crust, then scatter with the cheese and brush the pastry edges with extra yoghurt.

Bake for 25–30 minutes, until the dough is lovely and brown. Brush olive oil over the crust as it comes out of the oven, then scatter flaky salt and the parsley over the top. Serve hot, slicing or scissoring off portions like a pizza! A wedge of lemon on the side, for manual squeezing, will go down a treat.

Any leftovers can be refrigerated for up to 3 days, and reheated in the oven.

MORE IS MORE
Make six individual pide
boats instead, following the
directions for the Khachapuri
on pages 276–77.

Pampushky

These plump and soft Ukrainian rolls, doused in a garlicky and herby oil, are traditionally served next to something like a borscht. They look absolutely beautiful plated up next to just about anything you could put on your table – and the taste is divine, like nothing else. Well, they taste overwhelmingly like garlic. That's why they're so good.

—

80 ml (2½ fl oz) aquafaba, for glazing

PAMPUSHKY DOUGH
7 g (2 teaspoons) active dried yeast
250 ml (8½ fl oz) warm soy milk
420 g (15 oz) bread flour, plus extra for dusting
3 tablespoons olive oil, plus extra for greasing
1 tablespoon rice malt syrup or granulated white sugar
2 teaspoons garlic powder
2 teaspoons fine salt

TOPPING
60 ml (2 fl oz) olive oil or sunflower oil
1 large garlic bulb, cloves minced
2 tablespoons finely chopped parsley leaves
2 tablespoons finely chopped dill fronds
1 tablespoon flaky salt

To make the dough, combine the yeast in a small bowl with the warm milk and a pinch of the flour. Leave to bloom for a few minutes until frothy. Whisk in 2 tablespoons of the oil and the syrup or sugar.

In a large bowl, mix together the flour, garlic powder and salt. Make a well in the centre, then pour in the yeast mixture. Stir until combined, then press into a loose dough. Transfer to a lightly floured work surface and knead for 10 minutes, or use a stand mixer fitted with the dough hook on medium speed for 5 minutes. Lightly oil the bowl, add the dough ball, then cover with a tea towel. Allow to rise in a warm spot for at least 1 hour, until doubled in size.

Brush the remaining 1 tablespoon of oil around the interior of a 20 cm (8 in) round cake tin. On a clean work surface, punch down the dough, then roll into an even cylinder; flouring shouldn't be required. Cut into eight pieces weighing about 90 g (3 oz) each. Roll each piece into a long tube, grab the ends with each hand, then twist the dough until the strand is taut. From one end, coil the still tightly twisted strand, tucking the last bit under to make a twisted dough ball. Repeat with the other pieces of dough, then evenly space them out in the cake tin. Cover with a tea towel and allow to rise for 30 minutes.

Preheat the oven to 180°C (350°F). Liberally spread half the aquafaba over the buns. Bake for 25 minutes, basting with the remaining aquafaba and rotating in the oven halfway through cooking.

Combine the topping ingredients in a small bowl. Pour the topping over the rolls and bake for another 5 minutes to warm through.

Remove from the oven and leave to cool for 20 minutes while you brace yourself for a near lethal dose of garlic, then enjoy warm. Any leftover rolls will keep in an airtight container for up to 5 days at room temperature, ready for reheating in the oven or an air fryer as desired.

SHAPE SHIFTER
You can also shape the rolls into smooth balls following the instructions for the Korean cream cheese buns on page 292.

French onion cob loaf

You can't have a decent shindig without a cob loaf, I reckon. The filling perfectly fits a day-old sourdough boule or most large round loaves. Bread as a bowl filled with dip becomes an ornament, the meal, the serving dish and the plate – all at once.

—

½ head of cauliflower
olive oil, for drizzling
   and massaging
20 g (¾ oz) French onion
   soup mix
6 Confit shallots (page 68)
200 ml (7 fl oz) vegetable
   stock
3 tablespoons tahini
2 teaspoons cornflour
   (cornstarch)
juice of ½ lemon
100 g (3½ oz) shredded
   vegan cheese
1 day-old Boule (pages
   58–61) or cob loaf
snipped chives, for
   sprinkling
crudites, to serve

Preheat the oven to 180°C (350°F). Break the cauliflower into small bite-sized chunks and scatter across a baking tray. Use a light-handed drizzle of olive oil and your fingertips to coat the cauliflower chunks, then bake for about 25 minutes, until the edges are charring. Keep the oven on.

Add the soup mix, shallots, stock, tahini and cornflour to a blender and whiz until smooth. Transfer the mixture to a bowl and stir through the cauliflower pieces, lemon juice and cheese.

Use a bread knife to cut about 2.5 cm (1 in) off the very top of the boule, to use as a lid. Using your hands, scoop out the bread to create a cavity inside. Tear the torn-out bread into large, bite-sized chunks and reserve. Ladle or pour the filling into the bread cavity, slip the lid on and place the loaf on a baking tray. (You can refrigerate the loaf in advance for a few days at this point.)

Bake the loaf for 15 minutes, then reduce the oven temperature to 160°C (320°F).

Massage some olive oil into the reserved bread chunks to make makeshift croutons. Scatter them around the loaf and bake everything for another 15 minutes.

Remove the bread lid and sprinkle chives over the hot dip. Serve the loaf immediately! Start with dipping the croutons and crudites in, then tear the loaf apart, from the top down. Finish every last bite and the clean-up is done, too.

Pesto-stuffed sourdough pull-apart

(**EASY**) **SERVES: A SMALL GROUP**

Like a flower crafted by mother nature to attract the bee, this bread has been made by a brother baker to invite sharing and tearing from the moment you lay eyes on it. Sometimes called 'crack bread' or 'blooming onion bread' when made with a boule loaf, this style of bread is cut into the perfect bite-sized grid portions that beg to be plucked hard. Flavour-wise, petals of fresh basil peek out of a bready canopy stuffed with those perennial crowd favourites: butter, garlic, cheese and herbs.

200 g (7 oz) vegan cheese, grated
1 Batard (pages 58–61), or crusty oval or oblong-shaped loaf
60 g (2 oz) vegan butter, softened
flaky salt, for sprinkling
handful of basil leaves

PESTO
30 g (1 oz) basil leaves
2 tablespoons nutritional yeast
1½ tablespoons finely grated garlic
pinch of fine salt
2 tablespoons olive oil

Preheat the oven to 180°C (350°F).

To make the pesto, use a mortar and pestle or food processor to grind or blend the basil, nutritional yeast, garlic and salt into a paste, then pour in the olive oil and stir until combined. Set aside about one-quarter of the pesto. Scoop the remaining pesto into a bowl and stir the cheese through.

Use a bread knife to slice the loaf, securing the bread with your other hand as you go. Create cuts about 2.5 cm (1 in) apart across the long side of the loaf, leaving the bottom attached by about 1–1.5 cm (½ in). Rotate the loaf 90 degrees and slice a series of cuts about 2.5 cm (1 in) apart across the other direction, to form a grid all over the top.

Use your fingers or a teaspoon to evenly fill the slits with the cheesy pesto mixture, pushing it down into the crevices. Brush the outside with the butter. Place the loaf on a baking tray and bake for 15 minutes.

Remove the loaf from the oven, brush all over with the reserved pesto, sprinkle with flaky salt and bake for another 5 minutes. Push basil leaves into the cracks of the bread while still warm and serve straight away.

I can't imagine leftovers are possible with this bread, but if there were, I'd recommend keeping them in an airtight container in the fridge and consuming within 3 days.

Thanks

Thank you to Gran, Nanna, Megan, Rene and Honey, the smart cookies who have shared their tested and treasured recipes.

Thank you to sweetie pies Stef, Nigel (sourdough starter), Nigel (human father), Kerry, Josh, Charlotte, Ava, Sophie, Britt, Murphy, Tim, Amy, Rowan and Sven for taking on eating, critiquing and dish-washing duties.

Thank you to Lucy, Katri, Paul, Andy, Emily, Deb and Caroline from Smith Street Books who put all the cherries on top, as well as Mel from VeGood and Sara Kidd.

About the author

Zacchary Bird is the vegan butcher, the vegan baker and, above all, the vegan rule breaker. He's vegan, BTW. No matter which hat he's wearing, the job is the same: to perfect the plant-based version of absolutely every menu item known to humankind, and then some.

With a background in commercial plant-based meat development and teaching cooking classes (that go heavy on the deep-frying), Zac and his recipes alike are known for being extra AF. Flipping through his cookbooks will reveal a bounty of bold flavours, vibrant eye candy and (at times) bewildering creativity. Scrolling through his social media, you'll find Zacchary teaching recipes as well as performing as a global dance icon (live from his living room), to kill time between tours of a croissant dough.

Zacchary's first book, *Vegan Junk Food* was published in 2020 and was once used as a political prop by Jacinda Ardern. *The Vegan Butcher* won the PETA Australia Vegan Cookbook of the Year 2021, which Zacchary claims makes him the world's number one vegan butcher/baker hybrid who can also do a backbend.

Index

THE VEGAN BAKER

Smith Street Books

Published in 2023 by Smith Street Books
Naarm (Melbourne) | Australia
smithstreetbooks.com

ISBN: 978-1-9227-5455-4

Smith Street Books respectfully acknowledges the Wurundjeri People of the Kulin Nation, who are the Traditional Owners of the land on which we work, and we pay our respects to their Elders past and present.

Publisher: Paul McNally
Project editor: Lucy Heaver, Tusk Studio
Editor: Katri Hilden
Design and illustrations: Andy Warren
Design layout: Megan Ellis
Photographer: Emily Weaving
Food stylist: Deborah Kaloper
Home economists: Zacchary Bird and Caroline Griffiths
Proofreader: Pamela Dunne
Indexer: Helena Holmgren

Printed & bound in China by C&C Offset Printing Co., Ltd.

Book 282
10 9 8 7 6 5 4 3 2 1

MIX
Paper | Supporting responsible forestry
FSC® C008047

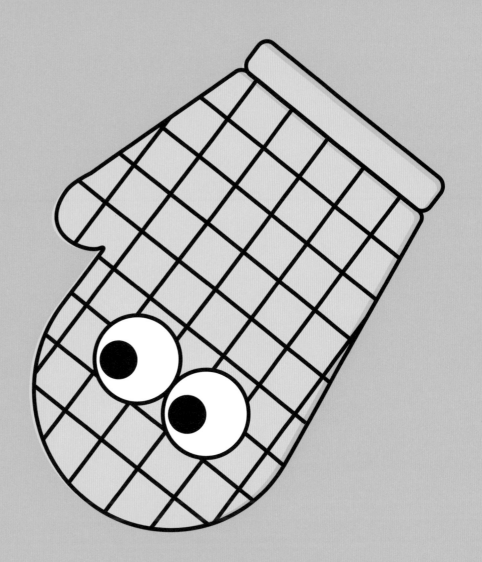